Stacking the Chips

To our children

Stacking the Chips
Information Technology and the
Distribution of Income

John Bessant and Sam Cole

Frances Pinter (Publishers), London
Rowman & Allanheld, Publishers

338.06
B464s

First published in Great Britain in 1985 by
Frances Pinter (Publisher) Limited
25 Floral Street, London WC2E 9DS

Published in the United States of America in 1985 by
Rowman & Allanheld, Publishers
(A Division of Littlefield, Adams and Company)
81 Adams Drive, Totowa, New Jersey 07512

British Library Cataloguing in Publication Data
Bessant, John
    Stacking the chips: information technology
    and the distribution of income
    1. Technology—Social aspects 2. Information
    storage and retrieval systems—Social aspects
    I. Title   II. Cole, Sam
    303.4'83   T14.5
ISBN 0-86187-359-9 (UK)

Library of Congress Cataloging in Publication Data
Bessant, J. R.
    Stacking the Chips.
    Bibliography: p.
    Includes index.
    1. Technological innovations—Economic aspects.
2. Job vacancies—Effect of technological innovations on.
3. Labor supply—Effect of technological innovations on.
I. Cole, Sam.   II. Title.
HC79.T4B47   1985   338'.06   85-11883
ISBN 0-8476-7461-4

Typeset by Joshua Associates Ltd, Oxford
Printed in Great Britain by SRP Ltd, Exeter

Contents

Acknowledgements

The present study grew out of a project on Technology and North-South Relations funded by the United Nations Institute for Training and Research. We are most grateful to the United Nations and to Philippe de Seynes, former director of the UNITAR Project on the Future and Under-Secretary General for Social and Economic Affairs, for their support. When that project began, the topic of a 'Microprocessor Revolution' was still little discussed. Now it is almost inescapable. Our understanding of the subject and the way in which it is addressed in this book has been influenced by many people. We are especially grateful to colleagues at the University of Sussex in the Science Policy Research Unit and the Institute for Development Studies and at Brighton Polytechnic. Among these we would mention Professors Christopher Freeman and Raphael Kaplinsky. We are also grateful for discussions with working groups of the United Nations Advisory Committee on Science and Technology for Development. With respect to the economic modelling undertaken we recognise Professor Graciella Chichilnisky, now of Columbia University, whose ideas were one starting point for the model, Tony Meagher of Monash University and John Clark at Sussex University whose efforts contributed to the initial development of the present model. While we are grateful to these colleagues and organisations, they cannot be held responsible for any oversights. In the writing of this book there was inevitably a 'division of labour': the empirical reviews of information technology were conducted by John Bessant and the modelling and analysis were carried out by Sam Cole. Both are grateful to their respective highly incompatible microcomputers!

1   Technological revolutions: past, present and future

'Revolutionary' is a term extensively applied to information technology as even a cursory glance at the news media soon confirms. Whilst this reflects in part the dramatic and rapid change and convergence which have taken place in fields such as computing, telecommunications and micro-electronics (and more recently opto-electronics and artificial intelligence), it also extends to the many social and economic implications. The parallel with the first industrial revolution is hard to escape; certainly all the characteristics are there: rapid technological change (often accompanied by the growth of totally new industries), major investment in expectation of rapid growth in established and new markets, and the emergence of 'leader' countries dominant in particular industrial sectors and/or techno-logical fields. Above all there is the increasing importance of innovation as the determinant of international competitiveness and economic growth.

One other aspect which the information technology revolution shares with its predecessor, is the potential for radical change in the structure of society: the pattern of employment, education, power and wealth. The first industrial revolution led to a polarisation of society and many com-mentators fear that the second, ushered in by information technology, will follow a similar pattern. In this respect it is clear that it will not only be wealth which divides countries, but also possession of the neces-sary skills with which to come to terms with advanced technology, and to participate in the benefits of new economic growth.

Whilst information technology has many implications for society, there are perhaps two major concerns which have been expressed: its impact on unemployment and on the 'pecking order of nations'. The OECD representing the advanced countries, who arguably are best equipped to adapt and intervene in their economies to cope with unemployment, consider that 'It is necessary to create several thousand jobs per *day* even to return to 1975 employment levels.' The United Nations through UNIDO (1983) consider that

> The advances (in technology) are expected to alter the rate and pattern of industrial production in the present and coming decades and thus have particular relevance to the efforts of the developing countries to achieve the Lima target (25 percent of world industrial production by

the year 2000), to widen the technological gap between developed and developing countries and accentuate the technological dependence of the latter, and to change the life style of their people.

Whereas the first revolution involved a small number of producer economies and large, passive and often highly dependent markets, the present picture is characterised by world-wide competition and a rapidly industrialising Third World. Although world trade and technology continues to be dominated by the developed countries of the North, it is clear that this position is increasingly threatened by many of the advancing economies of the South, which not only feel they have a right of access to world markets but increasingly have the capability to enter them. Thus, the developed world sees itself as fighting a defensive action using the twin weapons of short-term protectionism and long-term technological change. This results in a pattern of continuing acceleration in the pace of technological change and rapidly spiralling investment costs for R & D and new production facilities. But both between and within these groups of countries, there is equally fierce competition.

It is perhaps the employment question more than any other which has aroused fears of a repeat of the pattern of the past century. With unemployment in most developed countries running at near-record levels, and with even bleaker prospects for less-developed economies, this concern is clearly well-founded. It is, of course, easy to exaggerate the role of technological change in this. Certainly there is some effect both in a quantitative and qualitative sense, and has been almost since the first use of tools by our Stone Age ancestors. But, it is impossible to isolate technological factors from their wider economic context; the most we can do is examine trends within a more general macro-economic framework. Employment levels are related to competitiveness, to structures and market behaviour in different industrial sectors, to international trade policies and patterns, to local labour markets and educational systems, and so on. And if the prospect of rising unemployment raises fears from the past, the loss of status of the old industrial countries and the frustration of expectations of the developing world is perceived as a denial of the future.

Specifically, technology affects employment in several ways. Directly, its adoption might lead to labour displacement as machines are substituted for labour in industrial process and service sector activities. Indirectly the failure to adopt new technology might adversely affect a firm's competitive position to the point where falling demand leads to layoffs or even plant closure. (This second pattern repeated over a number of key sectors is often given as an explanation of the severe job losses in European manufacturing over the last five years.) At the qualitative level, the introduction of machines with 'intelligent' control functions might well eventually lead to a reduction in the human skills and judgement required for many tasks and encourage the breaking down of production operations into small, simple steps suitable for automation. Such changes would undoubtedly reduce the 'quality' of working life: but, by contrast, new technology offers scope for its improvement as well. With the potential of advanced and intelligent tools the opportunity also exists for increasing the level of control and responsibility which the operator has over the tasks in hand. Much here depends on the way the technology is actually used, rather than on the nature of the equipment itself.

While technology is not, in our view, the *cause* of the present crisis, it is an important contributor to the pattern of change in the world economy and its increasing use will undoubtedly affect the employment picture on a global scale. Our intention in this book is to explore some of its implications for the distribution of employment and income in various sub-groups of the world economy.

To focus on the twin issues of employment and income is hardly contentious. To assert that both are social 'goods' which should be better distributed requires some justification. There have been many suggestions, past and present, as to how work in society may be distributed as humans become liberated from repetitive toil through the advances of science and technology. But so long as employment serves as the primary means of gaining identity and respect which some have and others do not, and no alternatives are provided, the provision of fulfilling jobs must be a primary goal of the economic system. In the industrial world typically some 10 per cent of workers are unemployed, in some developing countries half the workforce may be under- or unemployed. The distribution of income is even less equal. Between the richest and the poorest in the world the gap is many hundred fold. Such income gaps are difficult to countenance; certainly it seems immoral to adopt a technology route which widens the gap further if others can provide both improved standards of living and more equitable distribution.

The global race to new technology

Advances in new technology may herald a new era of material wellbeing, though, as with the technological revolutions of the past, the route to this prosperity may be difficult. The first industrial revolution, and the agricultural revolution before it ultimately led to very great improvements in the living standards of people in the now industrialised countries. But, the process of change typically was associated with great trauma; the break-up of traditional communities, the displacement of labour, massive migration to new parts of the world, and a revolution in social as well as economic structures.

For the developing countries which in this century and especially since the Second World War also have accelerated their rate of industrialisation, the process has been equally hard. In some respects little appears to have been learned from earlier experiences with industrialisation. While developing countries have often benefited from the technological advances of the industrial countries, the application and the benefits have been uneven. Furthermore, developing countries generally have not had the safety valve of exporting their surplus or displaced labour to overseas colonies, or obliging others to accept their surplus production.

What of the new revolution? What will be its impact on the international division of labour, patterns of employment and economic distribution? Above all, can it deliver the benefits of economic prosperity without the social hardships of the past? These questions are especially relevant to information technology, since it is this breakthrough which has so far raised the greatest hopes for 'high' technology and the greatest fears for job destruction. Despite the importance of these questions, to answer them may well defy present understanding. Too little is known about the possibilities for the technology itself, while the very complexity of the modern world economy makes an evaluation of all the direct and indirect effects impossible to enumerate, let alone evaluate. We believe, nevertheless, that sufficient is known for a research agenda to be established and some tentative appraisal attempted. In order to clarify the agenda and indicate the appropriate framework for analysis in the remainder of this book, we make a brief preliminary review here.

In the past, changing technology has had a very great impact on the distribution of income and employment within as well as between the world's economies. Information technology promises to be especially labour displacing. Thus, there is the likelihood that unless output can be sufficiently expanded, for some time unemployment may result. Certainly this has been the concern of many commentators. Further, the new technology requires a different and typically more skilled labour force than the old. Thus the distribution of employment and wage income among workers with different skills must be expected to change. Other commentators consider that information technology may also increase capital productivity and efficiency in the use of raw materials to the extent that, with increased investment, jobs could be gained rather than lost. The magnitude of the resulting employment and income changes depends in part on just how great the productivity shifts are likely to be. Some estimation of this can come from a review of experiences so far with the new technologies. Whatever the actual shifts, it is reasonable to expect that, in the future, the share of national income going to different socio-economic groups—capital and labour or investors and households—will change.

The new technological revolution will also shift the international distribution of income. More than any other, the industrial 'revolution' of the modern age is based on the cumulative advances in scientific knowledge. And, because most research and development is carried out in the already industrialised countries, this has led to concern by some commentators that developing countries will be increasingly disadvantaged by the technology gap between them and the advanced industrial economies. Some authors argue that for the foreseeable future only the most advanced industrial countries with their highly developed infrastructure will be able to realise the full potential of the new technologies. Despite this assessment, there are many conflicting views as to how, where and indeed by whom the new technologies will be implemented. Others argue that through their own scientific or technological endeavours and the practices of international firms (who generally are able to appropriate the technology), some newly industrial developing countries will maintain their advancing position in the world economy. Yet, others consider that an increasing international division of labour motivated by the search for ever decreasing labour costs will continue to push industrialisation towards the poorest regions of the world.

Given the acknowledged importance of technical change to long term economic growth it is obvious that such conflicting hypotheses foretell contrasting profiles for the future world economy and raise more detailed questions. For example, can new technology stem the tide of de-industrialisation in the old industrial world? If the industrial countries are the principal beneficiaries of the new technology, will the economic situation of developing countries then worsen and their expectations for the future be defeated? Or, even if new technologies are introduced more rapidly into the less industrialised economies, would their acute problems of unemployment and poverty be relieved?

All actors appear to have legitimate fears. Industrial countries are concerned that they will not be able to match the advances of other industrial countries or that they will not be able to compete with the low wages of some developing countries. Firms in these countries are concerned that their competitors will take advantage of new opportunities if they do not. Employees are concerned that their jobs will be lost abroad or to new technology. The newly industrialised developing countries are concerned that their industries will be snatched back to the industrial countries with their more advanced technology or lost to poorer developing countries. The poorest countries fear that the process of global industrialisation will take yet longer to reach them.

Industrial countries especially see the adoption of new technologies as an absolute necessity if they are to defend their wealth and jobs against encroachment from the industrialising developing nations. Major sectors such as steel and shipbuilding are already becoming the prerogative of these countries. In any case industrial countries are in competition with each other, just as are domestic and multinational firms, economic regions within countries, trade unions, cities and so on. Thus the emphasis is on competitiveness. The overriding belief is that only by improving technology so as to cut production costs and to bring new products to the global market place can these agents hope to compete and so ensure their share of the global 'cake'. This is a primary rationalisation for entering into the race.

A second rationalisation attempts to still the concern of developing countries and workers who fear for their jobs. Through the medium of international trade and the emergence of a more 'rational' international division of labour, as technological improvements take place, all actors will gain. In particular, if the advanced economies increase their output through the introduction of new technologies, so will the absolute size of the global cake increase and some of this new wealth will 'trickle' down to poorer, less industrialised, nations. Indeed, as new economic activities arise in the industrial countries so the pace of technology transfer to developing countries will increase and this will further accelerate their pace of industrialisation. Thus, rather than block industrialisation in developing countries, the reverse is the case. Even if the technological revolution turns out to be primarily in the advanced economies so that the technology gap increases, developing countries will gain.

A global approach

Globally, the situation is that much of the world economy is furiously competing for jobs while attempting to increase labour productivity. On the face of it, this appears a somewhat frightening scenario even though economic theory teaches that this could lead to an all round improvement in global welfare. While history shows this optimism to be broadly justified in the long term, the distributional and transitional consequences can be complex and uneven depending both on the detailed way in which particular innovations are introduced and the highly interrelated world economic system.

Most efforts to evaluate the impact of new technologies have been at a sectoral or national level, for example to examine the effects of new technology on the relocation of a particular activity (such as textile production) or the overall effects on employment in a particular locality. Such detailed studies are extremely valuable but cannot account for many of the secondary and indirect effects of technical change. Because of the interconnectedness of the modern world economy, wherever, or in whatever sector, new technologies are introduced, the rest of the world economy will be affected. Innovations in motor vehicle production in Japan, for example, affect the motor industry in rich North America and poor Asia. There are also interactions across sectors since within countries and internationally there is competition for labour and, more especially finance. This means that innovations in one sector can, in principle, affect production, employment and incomes in every other worldwide.

The idea of 'trickle down' was noted above. The reverse argument—that the industrialisation of developing economies leads to a 'trickle up' to industrial countries—is at least as reasonable, given the mounting debts and foreign ownership prevalent in much of the developing and industrial world. Despite this, for many developing countries engaging in the race to new technology and increased international competitiveness has become an act of faith, if not survival. On both counts this may be questioned. While the conventional wisdom underlying the desire to export suggests that all parties to international trade gain from the exchange, there appear to be both theoretical and empirical departures from this 'rule'. In addition, the distribution of gains from trade through technical change is anomalous. It depends in part on how labour saving or capital saving the new technology is, and, as noted above, the empirical evidence for this is not clear. In the short run the benefits of innovation may be exported away.

The effects of technical change on growth also need to be carefully considered. Economic theory teaches that only through constant technical change can the long-run rate of economic growth exceed the rate of growth of population. This desire for 'modernisation' too is part of the rationale behind the present rush to embrace new technologies. But the theory also shows that the imperative for labour displacing technical change only arises when *all* existing labour is fully employed with the existing technology. Clearly this is not the case in the world at large since there is massive unemployment and underemployment in most developing countries, and in the last years unemployment has risen to unprecedented levels in many industrial countries also. In the world at large then, the rationale is questionable. The spread of existing, or even more labour intensive techniques, might provide a greater boost to *global* welfare seeking mainly short term and local gains. Such observations are generally not appealing to the actors caught up in the global race to new technology. But questions are certainly asked with respect to some developing countries; especially whether new technology could not be used in a better way to solve global employment problems?

Two further issues must be accounted for, the increasing pace of global change and governments' efforts to control it. Although technological innovations in the past have always directly or indirectly impacted on the entire world economy, the speed at which transmission mechanisms operate today is much increased, and largely because of new technology. Each new wave of technological innovation has seen the industrialisation of further countries and regions. Increasingly the world has become a global market place and, especially with the growth of international firms, an international production system through which finance and knowhow can move with increasing rapidity.

In this situation, a 'devil take the hindmost' race to implement new technology, the world economy may even restructure into decline. So long as old activities are replaced by new, then the world economy experiences a process of 'creative destruction' which is on balance beneficial. But if creative destruction becomes cumulative destruction because the rate of closing of old plants, in conjunction with improving technology, is not matched by increased investment, then the level of employment, demand, international trade and global output will fall. Clearly then, something has gone awry in the global economy.

In the present situation most governments of nations, regions and cities are encouraging existing firms to introduce new technologies or attempting to attract 'high tech' enterprises into their communities, afraid that if they do not, then they will be competed out of existence by more successful neighbours. Governments are falling over each other to give away their resources, revoking welfare measures, shifting the burden of taxes and providing incentives to innovating or exporting industries or tariffs against imports: some measures are designed to make the economy more competitive; others are efforts to bolster failing industries against external competition. Socialist as well as market economies increasingly emphasise the importance of innovation and competition and with this the role of international and domestic markets.

Even as there is a general appeal to the 'magic of the marketplace', there are innumerable efforts by governments, corporations and labour organisations to manipulate the situation. The actions they initiate are typically self-interested and uncoordinated carrying the risk that governments are not only unable to limit the hardships caused by the working through of international market forces, but they may even make the situation worse.

Historically, the breakthroughs which have led to new waves of technical change have generally been the result of 'serendipity'. Even today there are few unambiguous links between research and development and economic success—between scientific endeavour and the commercial exploitation of technologies there are barely comprehended multiple and complex interactions. Nevertheless, scientific discovery and innovation is a far more directed process than in the past, and is becoming better understood. Thus it should, in the future be possible to better anticipate the unwanted consequences of serendipitous technical change and, more importantly, be possible to create technologies which address a wider spectrum of social and economic goals and ease their application.

The unavoidable agenda

For many reasons then much greater attention should be paid to the global character of any new technological revolution. This would be the case even were the technological revolution not taking place against the backcloth of a global economic 'crisis' which has been characterised variously by a slowdown in economic growth and trade, militarisation and mounting debts in many developing and industrial countries, high unemployment and inflation, and, ironically, a slowdown in aggregate productivity increases. Although the causal links between this global crisis and the imperative for technical change are not well understood, many theories (such as some of the 'long wave') draw a connection. Consequently, even though we omit the overarching issues of the crisis from our agenda there are many points of contact.

From this discussion comes a number of rather specific questions to be addressed in this book. These are:

- What is information technology, what sectors and what countries are in a position to implement the technology, and on what timescale?
- What will be the effect on labour and capital productivity; will the technology create or destroy jobs, where and what kind?
- What is the relative importance of the indirect versus the direct effect of the technology? How important are intersectoral and international processes?

- How will the technology affect the 'pecking order' of nations? Will it close or widen the growing gap between rich and poor countries?
- How will the pattern of specialisation be affected? What will be the result for production structures and commodity dependence?
- Can all countries gain in a 'devil take the hindmost race' to implement new technology? If countries engage in a trade war, will short run tactics undermine potential long-term gains?
- Will the new technology create wealth but destroy jobs? What will be the impact on the distribution of income between capital and labour, or between different kinds of labour?
- Can domestic and international social policy foster the potential gains and alleviate the potential inequities arising from the new technology?
- How can the technology be used to confront the development needs of low income countries? Do combinations of existing and new technologies offer a more fruitful approach?

There are related issues which we shall not address here except in passing. Apart from the world economic crisis, there are questions of the relationship of new technology to life styles, to political systems, democracy and social justice. Ultimately, these questions override our agenda but, nevertheless we would argue that they cannot be answered without a better appreciation of the economic potential and hazards of new technology.

We should add one final question. Are the uncertainties in data so great that they prevent any of the above questions being satisfactorily answered? Or, to rephrase this in a more positive way, can we, despite the uncertainties make some rather firm statements about the global impact of information technology on employment and income distribution?

Methodology

The last question is obviously critical for the methodology to be used. For our study we employ a combination of sectoral analysis and macroeconomic computer modelling. From the sector studies we can obtain an approximate estimate of changes in factor inputs (labour, capital and intermediate goods) arising from the introduction of new technology. We can also make estimates of how this varies across different sectors and economies and how rapid these changes might be. With a macroeconomic model we then can calculate both the direct and indirect effect across sectors and economies of a variety of different assumptions about new technology and also make some assessment of the effects of government policy. In short, we can ask a number of 'what if . . .' questions about the new technology.

But the uncertainties in data and theory mean we should limit our expectations of the approach. The discussion above shows that there is as yet no consensus on where, by whom and when new technologies will be implemented. Although the body of empirical evidence as to their potential and practice in the more industrialised countries is expanding, there is much less data for the developing and socialist economies. A major problem in reviewing the impact of new technology is that it is strongly influenced by the factors noted above, which in turn affect other contextual factors such as the availability of resources and knowhow, traditions of technical change, relative advantage, size of firm or locational choices. In this situation no single effect can be identified and generalisations become less useful. Often, individual studies are extremely detailed, indeed almost overly so if one wishes to extract a broad picture.

For the present study we have made a schematic interpolation based on available research, both at the micro and aggregate level and especially on those data that reflect the overall *sectoral* impact of information technology. From sector studies, data have been systematically compressed into a form suitable for the macro-economic model. First, countries and sectors are subdivided according to a first appraisal of their potential for implementing the new technology. Thus countries are divided according to their level of industrialisation and their political economy and subsectors classed as advanced, intermediate or basic in terms of their level of technological sophistication. From these empirical studies we have then extracted data which, though they are gross generalisations, enable a set of distinctive hypotheses about factor productivities across countries and sectors to be made.

Clearly, all studies of the impact of new technology on employment must assess the effect on factor productivity. But this is only a first step for a global evaluation. In an increasingly market oriented world system, competitiveness depends among other things on the prices of labour, capital and intermediate goods, taxes and subsidies. Changes in technology can affect all these variables. The impact on demand of improved competitiveness in turn depends on how great is the resultant shift in demand (as a result of parallel changes in the product or as a result of increased competitiveness) and on what happens in competing markets for commodities and factors at home and abroad.

Any economic model to study these issues must compromise between the amount of detail (such as how many processes to account for in the study of a particular industry), the scope (such as whether to take account of intersectoral and international effects or the number of alternatives considered). The present study has sacrificed detail in order to clarify discussion of the latter. In using a global model to explore the issues we have tried to build a bridge between empirical studies of local and sectoral effects and system wide phenomena addressed by economic theory. Standard theories of international trade provide a number of powerful theorems about the mutual gains from international economic exchanges. But, given the present diversity of economic structures in the world, it is unlikely that these theorems alone provide generalisations sufficient to cope with the present and future diversity among countries. Rather the many 'paradoxes' accepted in the literature suggest that counter example and ambiguity are themselves the norm. This is especially the case with respect to the impact on international income distribution of technical change, and especially the labour saving technical change associated with information technology. By combining theory and data some more concrete statements may be made. We have used a model of the world economy which is sufficiently detailed to begin to address these questions. Although our model is relatively simple we have endeavoured to take account of the very great differences between countries, their technology, income distribution and markets. But, because the empirical data on this new technology is ambiguous, and several alternatives appear for its future use, we have left out detail to preserve flexibility. While the alternatives together do not fit neatly into any single theory of technical change, a number of distinctive experiments with the model allow us to examine the various possibilities.

In presenting our study we are well aware of the considerable controversy which surrounds attempts to estimate the global or macroeconomic impacts of new technology. The approach has its detractors and supporters. Our view is that there are lessons to be learned from an earlier debate surrounding 'appropriate' technology. The arguments for and against this approach raged for over ten years amongst development economists and planners before some degree of concensus began to emerge. However, by this time the actual concept and much of its potential value had faded from the planners' agenda, to be replaced by more pressing issues such as mounting national debts and the challenge of new technologies. In support of our approach we should emphasise the limitations of a purely micro-economic approach. First, such studies inevitably fail to embrace a wide enough context—ignoring shifts in factor prices, demand, indirect and multiplier effects, for example. Second, the new Industrial Revolution is clearly having an impact on most sectors in the major economies—and through them on the whole world economy— thus even national economy wide studies may be limited unless they can be related to the wider context of the global problematique. Third, although generalisations are dangerous, not least because of the many intersectoral and international differences which must be taken into account—we suggest there is a need to take broad aggregations in order to establish the 'stylised facts' which ultimately form the basis of economic theory and public policy. Finally, it is worth reiterating that our aim is not to develop a set of scenarios which extrapolate technical change to the future but to use these as a base from which to suggest directions which *ought* to be taken if desirable social objectives are to be met.

We believe then that it is of value to make a contribution to the discussion of the impacts of information technology on employment and income of distribution *now*, whilst there is still an opportunity of acting upon any conclusions raised by such research in this field. We consider that the alternative technology routes examined can provide a basis for discussion and policy development.

Organisation of the book

The book begins with an overview of the development of information technology and, in particular, its impact on employment. Chapter 2 deals with some of the hypotheses which emerge from the discussion in the literature on technology, employment and development. Chapter 3 details the empirical evidence regarding the employment and investment consequences of information technology and tabulates our findings according to appropriate types of economy and primary, industrial and service activities. In Chapter 4 these data are discussed in the light of theories of economic change and so transformed into a form suitable for our model experiments. The main details of the model and its relevance to the issues in hand are given in Chapter 5. Chapters 6 to 8 give the results of our calculations as to the impact of three distinct technology 'routes' and possible reactions by firms and governments to the tendencies foreseen. Finally, in Chapter 9 we summarise our findings and use these to outline a tentative profile of technological change and the responses of the world economy over the next decades.

2   Who holds the cards?

This chapter explains why we believe that we should be looking at information technology as a radical force for change in the world economy. In particular it aims to show how much the technology is based on science and is knowledge-intensive and how the disposition of resources and experience in this field has already led to its being dominated by the advanced industrialised countries. This concentration—which even amongst the advanced economies is beginning to separate out into a race involving very few horses—is reinforced when we consider that the production and application of the technology is dominated by a very small number of very large firms.

In keeping with its radical status, information technology is also challenging many conventional economic and technical structures. It is not only knowledge-intensive but requires new (and still evolving) skills both to produce it and support it in its various manifestations. Unlike the first Industrial Revolution which had a clear geographical focus, the IT revolution is characterised by a strong international—and transnational —element, with researchers in many countries pushing forward the technological frontiers and with the transnational corporations diffusing it rapidly throughout the world. Much of the financial impetus behind this wave of change comes not from the conventional financial institutions or centres but from a new venture capital industry fuelling a strong entrepreneurial faith in 'high technology' enterprises.

The consequence of the rapid emergence of the technology and the evolution of new structures to support and exploit it is that the world economy—already in a state of considerable agitation as a result of post-war developments in world trade—now faces a major new challenge. Whilst this may appear to be a technological revolution spawned in the advanced industrialised countries and likely to benefit them particularly, we suggest that the very novelty of the technology, and its considerable power and flexibility, may also open up new opportunities for both industrialised and industrialising nations alike.

It is increasingly clear, from evidence from many countries and examples in many sectors, that information technology (IT) can make a major contribution to improved productivity; this is likely to have a major impact on international competitiveness. Rather as in the first Industrial Revolution, rapid shifts in productivity and the opening up of markets for new products may dramatically alter the balance of relationships in world trade. The possible benefits to those who succeed in this—and the costs to those who fail—have been the driving forces behind the strong support which IT development and application has received from most developed country governments (and increasingly, from governments in newly-industrialising countries such as Brazil, India, Korea). In the UK, for example, the Labour government of 1978 committed an initial £300 m to IT support; this figure has since risen to around £1,000 m, with an annual expenditure of about £200 m. It is justified in statements like this from the Department of Industry: 'if British firms do not seize the opportunities which microelectronics offers, the effects will not fall on them alone: inevitably, Britain's capability as an exporting nation will also be affected. Therefore the UK cannot afford to let its manufacturing industries miss the microelectronics boat. . . .' Similar projects can be found in most countries within the OECD; expenditure on direct support for information technology production and application now runs into several billion pounds in Europe alone—and this does not take into account the provisions being made under programmes aimed towards developing the so-called 'fifth generation' computer (see later).

This is no longer a developed country phenomenon only. As Sigurdson and Grandstrand (1984) found in their survey of South-East Asian NICs there is a strong emphasis on growth led by IT and backed by extensive government policies in fields like manpower development as well as direct industrial support. Similar findings have been reported for Latin America (see Cortes (1984), Tigre (1983), for example) and for India (see Bhargava (1981)).

The issue of international competitiveness is complex, but one of the key components is the potential which IT has for changing the pattern of comparative advantage between nations. This comes from a combination of factors—reduced labour input required, reduced skill input, improved product design, quality, reduced lead times on design and delivery, improved process control, reduced unit costs in production and so on. It is likely that there will be different sectoral and national impacts and that some economic groups will gain at the expense of others. Since changes in sectors of individual economies are communicated to the rest of the world through domestic and international markets, a change in the technology of this magnitude will lead to changes in the structure of production and the distribution of income in all economies.

Access to new technologies and the ability to make use of them varies between countries. Compared with a decade ago the ability of some developing countries to assimilate new techniques has increased greatly.

However this change is still confined to rather few economies—the NICs —who are responsible for the bulk of R & D and the production of capital goods in the developing countries. Even amongst the developed countries evidence suggests that there are also significant variations in the ability to create and adopt new production techniques. These differences arise partly from the directions which R & D has taken (e.g. oriented towards military rather than industrial spending) and partly from social and economic structures. Thus the differences which arise between developed and developing countries may also arise within these groups— once again confirming the role of technical change as a major force for change.

A feature of new technologies such as IT is that, in addition to employing a different composition of capital and labour from existing techniques, they also employ a different composition of skills. Thus the introduction of new technologies in a given sector is likely to affect relative levels of employment and the distribution of incomes among different categories of labour as well as between labour and capital. Within the different types of economy too the fact that new technologies may impact differently on sectors (in which there is a varying input of capital and skills) means that a similar process of polarisation to that going on between developed and developing countries could also take place in the pattern of domestic distribution of incomes.

We are, of course, aware of the importance of theories of international trade in helping to explain the problem of competitiveness and particularly the significant role which the transnational corporations play. In the context of information technology, TNCs have several key functions— as providers of finance, suppliers/transfer agents for technology and— most important, as we shall shortly see—as producers of information technology itself. Nevertheless, the focus of our attention is primarily on the issues raised by the technology itself and consideration of these wider aspects lies beyond the scope of our book.

Our discussion involves, first, a review of the technology itself and the justification for applying the adjective 'revolutionary' to it. This, we argue, is principally because of the potential which IT has for changing the balance of factor inputs to production. We go on to examine some of the implications for capital and skilled and unskilled labour inputs in particular, since these three are central to our model and it is through changes in them that we assume information technology to have its effect.

The technological revolution: a concentration of knowledge

Electronics as a science traces its roots back to the last century and to the work of pioneers such as Maxwell, Faraday, Hertz, Weber and Gauss. From their work it became possible to understand and predict the behaviour and properties of flowing electrons and to postulate a number of possible uses for such phenomena. These included complex and high speed switching—as in controls, in sequencing (as in telecommunications) and information processing where the 'on/off' positions of switches in combination could be used to represent numbers and letters in arithmetical calculations. Most of the major components of todays IT-computers, digital telephone systems, etc. were thus foreseen in outline before the turn of the century; what held scientists back from developing their thoughts was the absence of a suitable technology to harness the properties of electronics.

The valve was invented in 1904 by Fleming and the triode valve by De Forrest in 1906; both inventions combined the science of electronics with the manufacturing technology of light bulbs to make available a vehicle for exploiting the properties of electronics. A number of applications industries soon began to grow up—telecommunications, wireless telegraphy, consumer electronics, industrial controls and military equipment. Synergistic development of these industries continued throughout the early part of this century, with considerable impetus being given by the military requirements of the Second World War which led to the invention of radar and of 'intellegent' controls for gunnery systems. Despite major advances in the technology of valve design and manufacture, however, there were major limitations to their use as the basis for electronics application. In particular these were:

1. Reliability. (Like light bulbs, valves were fragile and prone to failure at unpredictable intervals. A major problem with any complex piece of equipment using many valves was the need to carry many spares and to supervise its operation closely in order to be able to spot where and when valves needed replacing.)
2. High power consumption.
3. High heat generation (and therefore the need for cooling systems) because most of the power consumed was dissipated as heat.
4. Size (especially in applications where many valves would be required).
5. Cost (being relatively complex components they were costly to make although developments in manufacturing techniques eased this problem considerably).

The transistor, invented at Bell Labs in late 1947, essentially reproduced all the basic characteristics of valves in terms of their electronics properties —but without the above limitations. They were small, relatively simple in design (although initially very complex to make), and used very little power (thus reducing the heat generation problem as well). Significantly, they relied on different physical principles—the flow of electrons in certain solids (known as semiconductors) as opposed to through gases; this move into 'solid state' physics offered an important new departure point for novel applications and devices. Once the initial teething troubles had been sorted out, the transistor quickly took hold of the electronics and associated industries as a replacement for the valve; by the early 1950s production was in full swing and growth began to accelerate, both in terms of market expansion and of technological development. We do not have the space to discuss in detail the many factors which contributed to the very rapid rise and expansion of the electronics industry, particularly in the USA (but see Braun and Macdonald (1978) for an excellent account); in outline these were:

- Close synergistic links with key user industries, particularly tele-communications, consumer electronics and computing. These links meant that regular, large orders were being placed—but also, that user needs were constantly posing new challenges to technological development in the industry.
- Military procurement—as with other industries, this meant regular, large contracts but these were usually on a cost–plus basis; the essential difference was that developments in technology did not have to be tailored to a commercial price and so much of the fundamental development work of key electronic components and systems was carried out in this way, to diffuse much later as spin-off to the civilian sector. The pressure was increased with the growth of world tension surrounding the Cold War in the late 1950s and again with the Kennedy initiative to the space programme to put a man on the moon by the end of the 1960s; both had a major, long-term influence on the industry.
- Entry of highly skilled and motivated manpower to the industry. As nuclear physics had been during the 1930s and 1940s, so electronics became the key area for research work in the 1950s and 1960s. This attracted high quality manpower—which could expect to receive the significant rewards of a rapidly growing industry. One consequence of this was high mobility amongst these skilled workers—which con-siderably assisted technology transfer between firms and led in the

longer term to the geographical concentration of the industry in places like Silicon Valley.

- Associated with this was the phenomenon of spin-off industry. The massive investments in R & D in electronics and related industries led to many researchers setting up their own businesses to exploit particular ideas; coupled with venture capital sources which were available at the time, a number of growth areas for new businesses could be identified. Again, there was some geographical concentration of these, close to the key centres of electronics development—Stanford in California or Route 128 in Boston, close to MIT, for example. These small businesses were often dominated by an innovation rather than a business development ethos, ploughing a higher-than-average proportion of profits back into R & D (often in turn spawning further spin-off companies). The effects of such small businesses on the traditional market structure of electronics were dramatic; over a twenty year period some of the biggest names in valve electronics were forced out of business altogether by rapidly growing technologically based small firms like Motorola and Texas Instruments (TI).

The overall effect of this was to give the electronics and related industries a rapid growth rate and a highly innovative profile. A cycle of rapid new product development emerged, with high profits being ploughed back into R & D leading to novel products which in turn led back to further market gains. It is possible during this period of rapid growth to isolate some milestones of technical development, but overall the pattern must be seen as a *continuous* growth fuelled by the equally rapid growth in demand for electronics and related products. In the early 1960s the integrated circuit was invented at Texas Instruments; this enabled several different components to be made on the same piece of semiconducting material rather than connected together externally as had previously been the case. This offered significant advantages in aspects like reliability and speed of operation, but the key contribution of this innovation was that it opened the door to *miniaturisation*; significantly, one of the first major customers for ICs was the hearing aid industry, although its exploitation and development had much more to do with the major military projects such as the control systems for the Minuteman missiles in the USA. Growth was very fast, with new process technology quickly making possible high levels of integration; the first design produced by Kilby at TI in 1959 had a handful of components on a chip but by 1980 components counts exceeded one million on certain types of chip.

With the rise in power and integration came a move towards specialist circuits, tailored for particular uses such as memories, input/output handling chips for computers, etc. Thus it was almost inevitable that at some stage a circuit would be designed which combined the basic information processing functions of a computer on a single chip; this happened in 1971 when the Intel company was approached by a Japanese calculator manufacturer. The subsequent product, designed by Hoff, was the first microprocessor: since then the range and complexity of integrated circuits has been considerably enhanced and there is now a very wide spectrum of choice to suit most applications. More recent has been the development of semi-custom circuits which are mass produced as standards and then tailored to user designs at a late stage in the production process; this is cheaper than a special purpose designed circuit, and has opened up the electronics application field to a host of smaller specialist companies.

Overall growth in the industry has been very rapid and thus far Moore's Law—which states that the complexity doubles and the costs per chip halve every five years—has more or less held true (although there are signs of a slowing down in the pace of change as we approach the theoretical limits of electronics technology.

To a large extent these changes in the electronics industry have been paralleled by similar events in the key user industries of telecommunications and computing. In particular there was a close and synergistic link between these sectors, based largely on the fact that they were all concerned with applying the information handling and processing capabilities of electronics. This convergence led to the emergence of the concept of 'information technology' (IT) as a resultant technological stream; IT continues to develop and more recent contributing streams include opto-electronics and artificial intelligence (see Figure 2.1).

Currently the world IT industry is growing at between 20 and 30 per cent and is on target to achieve a market potential of around $300 billion by 1990. It is characterised by extensive competition between a relatively small number of firms within the advanced developed countries—and the scale of investment required to maintain R & D and production innovation is forcing even the largest of them into some form of joint venture. State intervention and involvement in the IT industry is widespread, both in R & D support through the education system and in subsidies, procurement and even ownership of manufacturing facilities. The effect of these trends is to concentrate the world IT *producing* industry in a handful of countries which are competing in increasingly strategic fashion (Bessant, 1984). Indeed the various projects in the race to build the so-called 'fifth generation' computer have been seen by some as the first shots in what might become a world trade war with IT as the battleground.

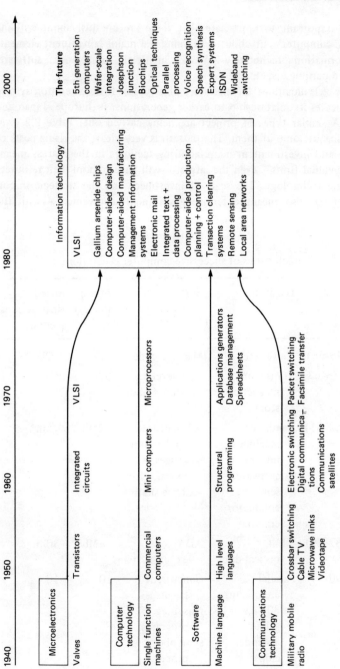

Figure 2.1 Convergent streams in information technology

It is important to appreciate that these are not just about building a 'super computer' but about developing the major constituent elements of information technology—VLSI, artificial intelligence software, advanced peripherals, etc.

Table 2.1 illustrates the character of a typical fifth generation system and indicates its relationship to earlier generations. In Europe, Japan and the USA similar types of project are being carried out; Table 2.2 gives an outline of some of them. The pattern is very clear; the rising costs of R & D and investment in manufacturing facilities in these areas means that individual firms—even the largest—will have to pool their resources and share technology. The scale of investment and the strategic importance of IT also means extensive government involvement—with the

Table 2.1   Characteristics of successive computer generations

Generation	Hardware	Software	Storage (bytes)	Speed (instructions/ second)
1st (1946–56)	Valves etc.	Machine code	2k	2k
2nd (1956–63)	Transistors, magnetic store	High level e.g. Fortran, Cobol	32k	200k
3rd (1963–81)	Family of machines, integrated software, semi- conductor circuits	Advanced applications langauges, e.g. Pascal, Lisp., Time-sharing	2Mb	5m
4th (1982–89)	VLSI, optical discs	ADA expert systems	8Mb	30m
5th (1990-)	Parallel architecture 30 i.c.s or less, gallium arsenide chips	Concurrent languages, reasoning programs, symbolic processing	10	10

Table 2.2   Examples of some fifth generation projects

Country	Project	Funds and timescale
Japan	VLSI-joint development by MITI and major semiconductor firms	1976–1980 £160 m
	Basic technologies for next generation (including bio-electronics)	£450 m over 10 years
	Optoelectronics scheme Mobile robots Picture processing	? £40 m
	National Superspeed Computer Project, principal aim to make a computer 1,000 times faster than the 1981 fastest (Cray-1)	£133 m over 8 years
	Fifth Generation project, based at Institute of New Generation Computer Technology, backed by MITI and all major electronics firms	£600–900 m over 10 years (£1.5 1982, £10 m 1983, £20 m 1984)
USA	Microelectronics and Computer Technology Corporation. Venture by 13 major IT firms (not IBM or ATT). Based at Austin, Texas, 255 staff laboratory. Projects include:	£50 m per year starting 1984
	— artificial intelligence	£10 m p.a.
	— CAD/CAM for VLSI	£7 m p.a.
	— software development	£5 m p.a.
	— chip packaging	£5 m p.a.
	Semiconductor Research Corporation Venture of 23 major IT firms (not ATT) Contracts placed with 30 universities Targets: 1987 1 m bit RAM 1990 4 m bit 1996 16 m bit	£20 m in 1984
	Department of Defence Advanced Project on Strategic Computing and Survivability. Aim to develop high performance software for multiprocessor	£750 m over 10 years

Table 2.2 (*cont.*)

Country	Project	Funds and timescale
USA	applications. Further application before Congress for artificial intelligence project.	£650 m
Europe	ESPRIT–European Strategic Programme of Research on Information Technology Funded jointly by EEC and 12 major firms. Five main activities: – VLSI – software engineering – man/machine interface – intelligent knowledge based systems	£1,000 m over 5 years with an initial £15 m for pilot projects, main projects start 1984

result that there are now clear national/continental concentrations in the field of IT.

Such strategic competition can only be justified on the basis of expected market rewards; as Rada (1980) points out, the scale of investment which IT producers have to make in R & D and production facilities can only be recouped by securing worldwide markets for their products. This is well illustrated by recent figures for the telecommunications industry. The new generation of telephone exchanges are highly sophisticated digital switching systems offering a wide range of options and a basic building block of any future information infrastructure. Entry into this area is costly but essential for future participation in the world information order. There are currently around sixteen major systems on the market, whose combined development costs were around $6 billion; they are competing for a share of a total world market estimated at around $12 billion—but with about half of this effectively closed because of preferential procurement by countries with indigenous production capacity.

This pattern is repeated throughout the information technology industry; in semiconductors, in manufacturing applications such as computer-aided design (CAD) and computer-aided manufacturing (CAM) equipment, in software and in office/service sector products. In each case there is a rising investment requirement—both in terms of direct financial investment and in terms of intellectual/equipment resources—which is forcing even the largest firms like IBM into joint ventures to spread the costs and risks. And in each case these investments are being undertaken with an eye to the massive and as yet largely untapped market potential of IT applications on a worldwide basis. For this reason we believe that it is in the area of IT *application* that the major impacts will be felt by most countries. It also involves a central role for both the transnational corporations as agencies for the diffusion of the technology and for the international financial community for its funding.

The application potential

Quite apart from the strong supply-side pressure for the adoption of IT there is considerable motivation provided by the technology itself. As Freeman (1982) and others have pointed out. IT represents a major 'heartland' technology in much the same way as steam power, the railways, electricity and the motor car did in earlier periods. Such technological developments are seen as key starting points for surges of innovations in products and processes; recently there has been much interest shown in so-called Kondratiev waves which relate such innovations to economic activity and identify a cyclic pattern with a period of around forty-five to fifty years (Freeman *et al*., 1982). This 'long wave' theory is particularly useful in the current discussion of employment and the relationship which it bears to technology and we will refer to it again shortly.

For the present we need to address the question of why IT is classed in the same way as preceding heartland technologies. The answer lies in the fact that information must be seen as a central component of most human activity—both at work and at leisure. For example, if we examine the typical activities which go on in manufacturing industry, we arrive at the list in Table 2.3 below:

Table 2.3 Typical activities in manufacturing

— controlled movement of materials, components, products
— control of process variables
— control of operations like shaping, cutting, mixing, moulding, etc.
— control of assembly—of components, sub-assemblies, etc.
— control of quality at all stages of manufacture via testing, inspection, analysis, etc.
— control of the organisation of production—via stock control, production, control, etc.
— organisation and planning via purchasing, scheduling, monitoring, etc.
— control of support functions such as personnel, marketing, administration, etc.
— organisation of pre- and post-production activities, such as design, R & D, marketing, etc.

The key feature of all of these is that a large proportion of them involve information activity of one kind or another. The word 'control', for example, features regularly; control is effected in the following way. Information about the state of a system—whether the contents of a reactor or the number of items produced per hour on a production line—is fed to the controller. Here it is compared with information about what the state of the process ought to be—and if there is a need to respond to a discrepancy, information is fed back from the controller to an actuator in the system to change something to bring it back into line with expectations. This simple control loop is the basis of all control activities—and it can be quickly appreciated that its operation is almost entirely based on information. In particular, information is *transmitted* between different elements in the system, *stored* in the controller (in the form of the set of expectations about how the system ought to behave) and *processed* in the controller when making the comparison between what is actually happening and what ought, and again when deciding what corrective action to take.

If we were to analyse any of the activities featured in Table 2.3 we would find them reducible to a combination of information storage/ retrieval, transmission or processing; thus it is clear that any technology which offers to make dramatic improvements in the way in which we carry out these information activities is likely to find major application right across the industrial spectrum. If we perform a similar analysis to that of Table 2.3 on activities within the service sector—banking, insurance, retailing, office work, etc.—we would find an even higher level of information activity. Most of what takes place in an office involves processing (of data, text, etc.), storage and retrieval (in other words, filing) and communication (by mail, telephone, telex, or whatever)—essentially information transmission and reception. Banking, for example, is a business based upon the manipulation of information; money is a symbol for information about transactions between people and organisations—and so almost all of what takes place in a bank—recording debits and credits, processing cheques between institutions, preparing statements (information) about the status of accounts, etc.—can be classed as information activity.

There have been attempts to develop an alternative to the Standard Industrial Classification analysis of the economy which reflect the information content of work—some pioneering research was done by Machlup (1962) and Porat (1977), and recent studies have been made by Mandeville *et al.* (1983). Although this is a complex issue it is clear that information activity is a major component of all industrial/service sector operations —and thus that IT will have considerable potential impact.

The transition from potential to actual application is beginning to accelerate—as statistics for a wide range of IT applications bear out (Bessant, 1984). Growth rates for technologies like local area networks, robotics and computer-aided design are all well over 20 per cent per annum, and the pace of change will be further increased as it is fuelled by new technological developments.

The trend towards integration

In the future the trend is increasingly likely to be towards *integration* of systems—what might be termed 'second generation' automation. As Kaplinsky (1984) points out, it is possible to identify several different spheres of activity in manufacturing or service sectors (see Figure 2.2).

In the past automation has taken place within these spheres, first combining discrete elements and then bringing together sub-systems into complex systems. This can be illustrated with the case of metalworking machine tools; in the earliest stage each operation—cutting, grinding, milling, drilling, etc.—would be carried out on a single machine under human operator control. The next step was to produce automatic tools working under numerical control but still carrying out only a single function. After this came computer control which would allow different operations to be carried out by changing the program, for example as in a CNC machining centre. This was followed by direct numerical control in which individual computer controlled tools were linked to a central computer supplying information about the entire activities of the shopfloor —scheduling, production control, etc.

The next stage in this sequence relies on the fact that information is a common parameter in all industrial and service sector activities. Thus IT provides the opportunity to integrate activities *between* spheres as well as within them. In the case of our machine tools this might take the form of a flexible manufacturing system in which the activities of co-ordination-production control, stock control, scheduling, materials management and handling, etc. are added to the production sphere.

This could go further to the concept of CAD/CAM (computer aided design and manufacture) in which the design stage produces information which is directly fed as control programs to the production and co-ordinating spheres. The eventual outcome is that the entire factory behaves as if it were a single machine—extremely complex but in essence governed only by its inputs.

Very similar patterns can be observed in the service sector, for example in the case of the integrated office of the future, combining origination and

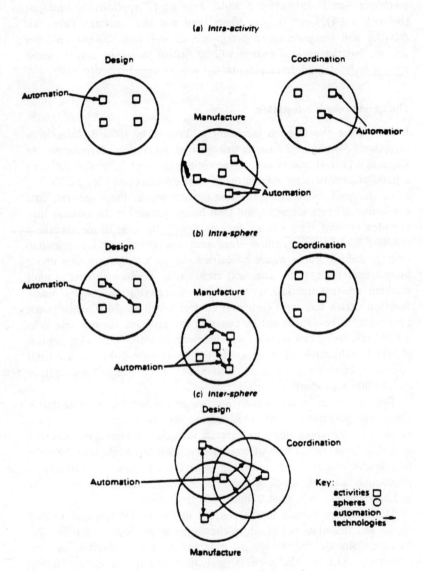

Figure 2.2   Integration of spheres of activity in manufacturing
Source: Kaplinsky (1984).

processing of data, text, images, voice etc. with communication and storage/retrieval. Figure 2.3 illustrates this.

New methodologies

It should be pointed out that the pattern at present is still some way from such fully integrated systems; as Zisman (1978), for example, argues, we are still in a phase which could more accurately be termed 'office mechanisation' where the emphasis is on replacing old technology —such as typewriters—with new—such as word processors. The real shifts in productivity and efficiency will come when we move from simply doing what we always have done but a little better to a point where we make full use of the range of new opportunities and facilities which IT offers. Similar views are expressed in the manufacturing context where the pattern at present is one of 'islands of automation' in a sea of conventional technology—and where the emphasis is on exploring new ways of working to get the best out of advanced manufacturing technology, and on solving the major problems posed by integration.

It is important to place these changes in context; as well as a technological revolution a radical shift is taking place in terms of management thinking about how production is organised. Writers such as Kaplinsky (1984) and Perez-Perez (1985) talk about a paradigm shift in manufacturing

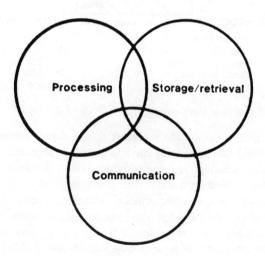

Figure 2.3 Integration of office-type activities

to what they term 'systemofacture'—an approach which combines the various elements of advanced manufacturing technology within an integrated framework like that described above and involving a much more systematic approach to production planning and management. Similarly, Halevi (1980) uses the term 'HAL-automation' derived from the Hebrew word meaning 'all-embracing' to describe it.

These ideas may not in themselves be new—concepts like 'group technology', for example, which essentially means grouping different machines in a cell related to a particular family of products so as to ensure maximum utilisation date back to the 1950s. What is new is the combination of these concepts with technologies which make them workable and highly productive. So the palette of choice for the systems designer of the factory of the future is extensive, drawing on hardware, software and a range of methodologies. The significance of this is that it becomes possible to select the most appropriate configuration to suit any kind of production activity or product range—whether small batch or high volume and operate in an economically viable fashion. Figure 2.4 below illustrates this.

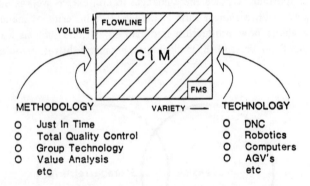

Figure 2.4 Choices in the design of the factory of the future

Without doubt one of the strongest driving forces behind this combined technological/methodological approach has been the example of Japanese manufacturing. The success story is well documented in terms of penetration of Western markets with a range of goods from motorcycles and cars through consumer electronics to, increasingly semiconductors and computer systems. Whilst it has also been appreciated for some time that Japanese factories were somehow 'different', it is only recently that systematic analysis (such as presented by Schonberger, 1982) has indicated the nature of this difference.

The essence of the Japanese approach is embodied in a total systems approach to production which includes:

- use of advanced technologies on a rapid replacement cycle
- flexible working practices and multi-skilled labour
- emphasis on quality management emplified by the concepts of 'zero defects' and 'total quality control' and a general consciousness of the product instilled via participative work practices, quality circles, etc.
- emphasis on planned systems which are highly responsive and flexible, exemplified by the concept of 'just in time' (JIT) scheduling.

One of the most important features of the Japanese approach is embodied in the concept of 'just in time' materials management. Initially developed in the Toyota company, this approach means that components are not stocked but delivered where and when they are needed directly to the shopfloor. This depends on the production system flowing smoothly and able to respond quickly and flexibly to change: this covers all activities, from the physical manufacturing operations, through the management control and planning procedures right up to the supplier network. Such an integrated approach makes it possible for a manufacturer of, say, machine tools, to plan his production for the next day on the previous day—and the system will respond flexibly and smoothly to this. The contrast with the traditional approach which may involve lead times of several months on the supply of components, delays and waiting time between operations on the shop floor—due to maintenance, need to reset machines, or whatever—high costs of buffer stock maintenance and work-in-progress inventory levels, etc. is very clear. It is also significant to note that this implies the extension of the integration model described earlier to the sphere of activities outside the firm— its links with suppliers.

The Japanese approach brings batch manufacture very close to continous processing; in particular it reduces the amount and cost of inventory to a minimum, which makes a major contribution to reducing manufacturing costs. Whilst it has so far been most graphically demonstrated in large volume batch industries—such as motor vehicles, consumer electronics and machine tools, there is a growing belief that suitably adapted variants are applicable to much smaller batch work. Thus far developments in flexible manufacturing technology in Japan have tended to concentrate on semi-dedicated flexibility around large batches or families of parts—an approach which has proved very successful as examples such as the Fujitsu Fanuc or Yamazaki factories demonstrate to visiting Westerners. However emphasis is now shifting to a much higher level of flexibility which will permit economic manufacture of very small batches and one-offs; the combination of this technology with the above production management philosophy may well pose major challenges to the traditional concepts of economies of scale.

Similar patterns can be found in the service sector; we have already mentioned the changes likely to emerge in the office of the future as currently discrete systems become integrated. Accompanying these will be a change in work organisation and practice with often radically different structures and the distinct possibility of remote working via a network rather than a single physical location.

In other areas the change is likely to be equally dramatic; for example, the present trends in banking and retailing automation are increasingly blurring the lines between these activities. Highly integrated systems for electronic funds transfer, advanced distribution networks and similar buyer/supplier relationships to those described above will all act to change the whole character and mode of operation of the service sector.

From the above we can see that the pattern of technological change due to IT has been rapid and dramatic—and as such may well deserve the title 'revolutionary'. However there are a number of important diffusion factors affecting the rate and direction in which information technology is spreading, and it is to these that we now turn.

General trends in the diffusion of IT

Before proceeding with our sectoral analysis, it will be useful to examine briefly the main enabling and constraining factors affecting the pattern of diffusion in different sectors. As we have already seen, there are strong technological and market forces at work on the supply side that are forcing the rate and direction of change. These have been accelerated in many cases by the involvement of the state in various programmes designed to promote both the development and adoption of information technologies and their applications. Significantly this trend is not confined to the developed world; many of the NICs are now actively pursuing informatics policies, some of which—such as the establishment of a Brazilian minicomputer industry—have been successful in meeting their objectives (although there are major questions about the effect this has on other social priorities); see, for example Tigre (1982), Cortes (1984), and Perez-Perez (1985) for a discussion of Latin American policies.

The overall effect of these is to generate a strong 'technology push' towards adoption of information technology in all sectors and most countries. The degree to which there is a corresponding 'need pull' is more variable, however, and this partly explains the differential pattern of diffusion reported in studies such as that of Northcott *et al.* (1985). As we have already noted, most activities involve some form of information component, but this 'information intensity' varies widely between sectors. So, for example, farming has a much lower level than, say, banking where almost all the activity in a financial transaction involves information processing, storage/retrieval or transmission. Thus, *a priori*, we would expect there to be more 'need pull' in information intensive sectors—and there does appear to be a growing correlation for this in the empirical data available.

That said, there are still major differences between—and often within—sectors in their adoption of IT which are due to specific factors such as skills shortages, lack of finance, incompatability with existing infrastructures, etc. The evidence available of diffusion factors is still fairly limited (see Bessant (1982) for a discussion of some of this) but there does seem to be broad agreement on the key determinants.

Costs of new equipment are the most commonly reported barrier, although this is much more of a problem in manufacturing applications than in services. The difficulty appears to be not so much the high and rising costs of equipment/systems as the incompatibility with organisational arrangements for accounting and investment appraisal. For example, a flexible manufacturing system (FMS) costing £10 m will not fit any kind of traditional payback calculation (such as the expectation of it paying for itself within two years). Yet taking into account the significant *capital* savings involved in such an integrated system, the possibility of increased output through working a third shift, the higher levels of plant utilisation not only implied by the FMS itself but also its up and downstream effects on the overall pattern of production organisation, and the likelihood of increased competitiveness due to shorter lead times and better customer service, such an investment can be justified. The need to shift to a more 'strategic' and long-term approach to investment appraisal has been mentioned by several commentators (e.g. Parkinson, 1984) and is one of the factors to which the relative success of the Japanese in the early adoption of new manufacturing technologies is attributed.

Skills shortages are also commonly reported as factors slowing the rate of diffusion (see Arnold and Senker (1982) and Northcott *et al.* (1985) for example). One of the major difficulties here is that it is difficult to identify clearly which skills are in short supply and to link this with policies for education and training, although again, there does seem to be a correlation between the relative success of countries like Japan and

West Germany in the use of information technologies and their consistent and extensive investment in training.

The most serious shortages at present are at the high level end—electronics engineers, systems analysts and applications engineers. Evidence suggests that there is considerable regional variation in the availability of this resource with serious shortfalls in many countries. For example, in the UK the total demand for electronic engineers far exceeds the supply from the higher education system; it was recently estimated that one firm could absorb the entire annual output of graduates for the next three years. Such shortages inevitably introduce other distortions; high wage levels and labour mobility often result and this has the effect of 'starving' smaller firms of suitable resources because they cannot attract and retain graduates in the face of better offers from larger firms—or increasingly, from overseas. This problem is, potentially, a serious threat to the NICs, although early evidence suggests that the output of suitable graduates from local universities and technical high schools is increasingly able to meet indigenous needs, at least in the application if not the development of IT.

In many ways a more serious problem is in the technician/maintenance/supervisory area where a mixture of old and new skills in flexible combinations is required. Here the need for 'local' knowledge and experience of industrial processes is an important component of the skills infrastructure, and it is at this level that developing countries may be in a less favourable position.

Most forecasts of future skills requirements make the point that although some traditional skills will no longer be required, changes are likely to be incremental, with a gradual broadening of capabilities and responsibilities, and a shift from active intervention in production processes to more of a supervisory/diagnostic role. One new group of skills which has been consistently identified and relates as much to the service as to the manufacturing sector, is that of information management. It is difficult to be explicit about the nature of this requirement but in general it involves the set of skills associated with managing the proliferating supply of data and information, and the technologies designed to manipulate them. As Macdonald (1983) points out, our understanding of this field is very weak and there is a real danger of organisations becoming less efficient as a result of widespread use of IT. He attempts to relate this to Liebenstein's concept of x-efficiency, and argues strongly for more attention to be paid to developing understanding of the economics of information usage.

This leads to the third, much more general, group of factors influencing diffusion. These relate to the infrastructural capacity to support IT applications and include such elements as suitable and stable power supplies, availability of high integrity telecommunications (for data transmission), existence of a technical support and maintenance/repair capability and other technical considerations. However it also relates to what might be termed the organisational compatability issues—that is, the degree to which the new technology fits in with the existing arrangements, attitudes etc. within the firm. It appears that in all sectors there is considerable lag between technological capability and the organisational ability to adapt to it; the increasing length of time taken to reach best practice performance in systems using advanced manufacturing technology provides an illustration of this (Bessant, 1985). For example:

- In research on the diffusion of CAD, Arnold and Senker (1982) found that in a sample of forty-four installations the average time taken to reach best practice performance was two years. Even in the case of turnkey packages there were significant problems in learning to get the most out of the technology.
- In a study of the adoption of industrial robots in the UK, Fleck (1984) reported that in a sample of 137 cases over a third (44 per cent) experienced initial failure and half of these abandoned robots altogether as a result of this.
- Although the diffusion of advanced computer-based management aids such as Materials Requirements Planning (MRP) is growing rapidly, a number of recent studies (*Technology*, 9 April 1984) have suggested that in very few of these installations are firms getting the full potential benefit. In the case of the MRP2 system suppliers grade users according to their capabilities and estimate that there are only twenty-five grade A users, that is, able to get the full potential from their system, in the whole of the USA.
- In studies of the adoption of FMS and CAD/CAM facilities, Voss (1984) reports that although 86 per cent experienced productivity gains, only just over half (57 per cent) were able to achieve the full benefits of reduced lead times, parts flexibility and quality improvements.

This suggests that in addition to adoption emphasis should be placed on how IT-based systems are actually *implemented*. We will examine differences in the international diffusion pattern in the next chapter.

IT and employment

Before we proceed to our analysis of the implications for different groups in the world economy, it will be useful to review briefly the general issues of technology and employment. In particular it is important to see this in an historical context since in many ways the present concern about IT is only the latest stage in a process which has been going on ever since man first began to use tools. The pattern of improving labour productivity in the agricultural sector in the UK during the late eighteenth century, largely due to increasing mechanisation is often advanced as one of the major contributors to the first Industrial Revolution. This not only made it possible to serve the needs of a growing domestic and export market but it also released a labour force to supply the newly-industrialising cities. Within the growing manufacturing sector early generations of machinery were relatively unsophisticated and labour intensive; nevertheless the rapid expansion in markets led to a massive increase in the rate of invention and innovation. Consequently productivity began to increase in the manufacturing sector—in some cases in quite spectacular fashion—and this began to affect the overall structure of employment, both in terms of skills and quantity of labour required. Concern in the late nineteenth century was not only for the availability of work but also for its quality; the Luddites were essentially protesting about the deskilling of their craft as weavers and textile workers by the introduction of new machinery.

As we have already noted, the effects of technology on employment cannot be separated from a wider economic context, and this is demonstrated in the pattern of events in the early twentieth century. Instead of employment continuing to decline as technological substitution increased, other factors intervened—the growth in world markets, development of new industries, the First World War and so on. The effect was to balance out some of the employment effects and commentators began to see a cyclic pattern in both economic growth and employment patterns.

Nevertheless the trend towards technological substitution continued with the bulk of the impact coming in the manufacturing sector. Here the economic incentives to innovate led to a steady stream of changes in both the actual operations and in the way the working process was organised—the Ford production lines or the concept of 'scientific management' being good examples of influential innovations of the latter type. One feature of this continuing development of technology was that the range of tasks which could be substituted grew rapidly and provoked growing concern about employment implications. The two types of innovation tended to be mutually reinforcing; new forms of work organisation tended towards increasing the division of labour and standardisation of tasks. In turn these highly fragmented standard operations lent themselves to some form of mechanisation, with a corresponding impact on employment levels. With growing experience in mechanisation technology it became possible to consider further aspects of the production process for change.

The period following the Second World War was characterised by a number of key advances in mechanisation technology linking different production operations together in production lines—transfer machinery, for example—and in permitting some form of programmable control, such as in the early numerical control machine tools (although the concept of programmable machines went back to the nineteenth century and the Jacquard looms of the weaving industry). In parallel with these developments came the growth of a school of commentary about the employment impacts—both qualitative and quantitative—of such change; amongst well-known writers in this field were Bright (1958) and Blauner (1964). This led to the first employment scares of the 1950s when it looked as though 'machines might be taking over'; this was followed by a second crisis period in the early 1960s as the first generation of commercially available mainframe computers were deployed in manufacturing industry amongst the larger firms. However, in both cases the pattern of world economic expansion, especially during the 1960s countered the worst employment effects (although there was a secular trend towards diminishing employment in the manufacturing sector).

Although, as Sadler (1980) points out, the fears of these early commentators proved largely groundless, they were not wrong in their general assessment of the potential impact of technology on employment but only in their judgement about the rate of change. If we examine the pattern of technological substitution up to the Second World War we find that the majority was based on sophisticated mechanisation; whilst this could replace manual labour involved in operation and manipulation and, with the crude generations of mechanical controllers available, some of the discretionary activities involved in machine control, it did not pose a major threat to employment. However advances made during the war in feedback controls—originally developed to improve naval gunnery—and in the technology of electronics and computing began to influence designers of production systems. Increasingly the focus shifted to complex machinery which could be controlled adaptively using advanced technologies; by the early 1960s the large-scale continuous process industries were already experimenting with mainframe computer control of entire plants. This distinction between 'automation' and 'mechanisation' is subtle but important; the former includes some component of discretionary decision-making, in other words, the controller 'thinks' about what it is doing and will do different things under different circumstances. This shift in thinking about control systems was crucial in its employment implications; whereas substitution up till then had been on the basis of physical strength and manipulative skills, the pattern now moved to include even high level intellectual skills. In many cases the technology improved on human abilities, for example, in oil refineries it was as much the speed of response and the ability to control interdependent variables which computer control offered as the direct labour savings which made this technology attractive.

IT fits into this picture at a critical stage; by the 1970s the trend in manufacturing was clearly one of increasing capital intensity and declining labour intensity. As the amount invested per head increased, so productivity rose. Industries like petrochemicals became characterised by large complex plants with high productivity supervised rather than operated by a small and highly flexible workforce. This indicated the direction in which other industries were likely to go, but the transition was limited by the availability of suitable technology at a suitable price. Clearly the car industry's approach—of achieving near-continuity by extensive and costly investment in special purpose transfer machinery—was not viable for many industrial sectors, especially those concerned with small batch manufacture. The arrival of IT introduced a step change into this system, making possible a much faster and far-reaching changeover because it makes possible not only discrete automation of individual process stages but also of entire production systems, as we have already noted. This pattern is demonstrated by the case of flexible manufacturing systems; here the plant is able to operate at a high level of utilisation and efficiency because the computer can plan the optimum production schedule and respond quickly to changes and unplanned events such as breakdown or stock shortages. In turn this makes the manufacture of even very small batches an economic proposition, and one open to small firms.

To this change in the production process must be added the effects on products themselves which IT has had. Indeed, many commentators argue that the major employment impacts so far experienced with IT have come about because of what are essentially changes in product design (although they usually involve process change as well). Examples include watches, cash registers, calculating machines and telecommunications equipment, all of which have been considerably simplified through the use of integrated circuits instead of mechanical or electromechanical components. In this

Table 2.4 Examples of employment change due to product simplification

(a) Calculating machines (Olivetti)

		Average labour input
1960	Divisumma range	9 hours
1975	Logos 50	5
1975–	Integrated circuit based (including printer—i.e. more sophisticated)	0.5
1960	Audit 24	33
1970	All electronic	13

(b) Television sets (Japanese)

	Total employed in Japanese firms	
	1972	1976
Hitachi	9,000	4,300
National Panasonic	9,875	3,900
Sony	4,498	2,278
All 7 major producers	48,000	25,000
Sets produced	8.4 m	10.5 m

Source: OECD.

process the assembly stage becomes simplified reducing both the labour input and the time required to produce what is a more reliable and often higher performance product. (Some examples are given in Table 2.4.) Although it can be argued that the rapid fall-off in manufacturing employment in many developed countries has been largely due to recessionary factors, it seems likely that the effect of IT—whilst not necessarily the direct cause of labour displacement—will be to reduce the need to re-employ workers when economies pick up again. This is certainly the case in manufacturing where the role of IT can be seen as accelerating what are clear long term trends; many commentators now argue that the percentage of employment in manufacturing in the USA and other developed countries may well fall below 10 per cent by the year 2000.

So far we have only mentioned manufacturing employment where the trend of technological substitution has been present for some time. In the service sector the picture in employment terms gives cause for concern because the threat from technology has emerged suddenly and it may have a discontinuous effect, bringing in its wake serious dislocations in the labour market. The first evidence of a growing trend towards substitution and an increased emphasis on productivity can be seen in the pattern of 'jobless growth' which has been observed by many researchers in key service sector industries such as banking and insurance. Here the growth in the industry has not been matched by employment increase; the implication is that these businesses are becoming more efficiently organised and technologically based. In so far as it is possible to measure productivity in the service sector (always a contentious issue) it appears that its growth has been much slower than in manufacturing and agriculture; certainly there have been strenuous efforts on the part of suppliers of new technologies to relate this to the relatively low levels of capital expenditure per head in the service sector. This suggests a growing pressure on service sector employers to seek technological solutions in their future growth plans.

More serious as a threat to employment is the nature of the technological change involved. Most service sector work in fields like banking and insurance is centred on information-generation, storage/retrieval, manipulation, transmission and so on; clearly any technology which promises to make radical improvements in information activities will have a major impact. As with manufacturing the pattern is increasingly one of integration in which processing, communication and storage/retrieval activities become combined into systems based on network technology. For example, the 'office of the future' will have an integrated workstation at which the operator can call up files from any database available to the firm—whether locally held or on the other side of the world. Processing of information—whether text, data, image, voice or whatever —can be carried out and the results stored or transmitted via electronic mail systems to anywhere in the world. The implications for speed, efficiency, reliability, etc. are considerable, but clearly the structure and volume of employment is also likely to undergo major change. Similar integration occurs in other fields, for example, the elimination of cash transactions as banks and retailers join together in electronic funds transfer systems.

Whilst these scenarios are still some way off becoming reality, the technological direction is clear and change is only being limited by economic and infrastructural barriers; in general terms some change in employment as a consequence of the emergence of IT in the service sector must be anticipated. Clearly not all parts of the service sector will be affected to the same degree; those less information intensive such as welfare, health care and other public services will remain largely dependent on labour rather than capital. However a serious political question is raised regarding the provision of these services; if they are to grow in order to 'mop up' labour displaced from elsewhere in the economy (i.e. manufacturing and information intensive services) then some way of paying for this must be found since these are not wealth creating services. The evidence from many countries pursuing monetarist policies (such as the USA) is that the reverse is happening and that the public service sector is being cut back as a source of employment. This may have the effect of removing one of the compensating mechanisms in the economy which might have helped in the societal adaptation to information technology.

Another point often advanced by optimists in dealing with the employment question raised by IT is that although it displaces labour it also has the potential for job creation via new products based on the new opportunities which the technology opens up. This is a seductive argument; certainly there is something attractive about the idea of 'smokestack' industries being left to the robots whilst people find a happier and healthier working environment in the bright new 'sunrise industries' of electronics and related advanced technologies. And on the face of it there is some evidence of job creation in these fields, especially in the field of computers and semiconductor fabrication. The difficulty is that there is a clear mismatch in terms of both numbers and skill levels involved in jobs lost and created. On the one hand, most jobs lost are relatively low skilled and in large numbers from labour intensive manufacturing and some service sectors. On the other, new jobs are being created for highly skilled staff and in small numbers; for example, the new plants for producing integrated circuits will typically employ a few hundred people, most of them women (who have greater manual dexterity for precision operations) and skilled technicians, whereas much manufacturing employment has gone in places like steelworks and engineering plants typically employing several thousand unskilled or semi-skilled men. It is often possible to see this pattern of change within the same firm; one UK manufacturer of digital telecommunications equipment has exploited the potential of semi-automated assembly technology and product improvement via IT to the point where it now takes only 100 men to assemble their telephone exchanges where before several thousand were employed. At the same time they have *increased* their recruitment at the level of graduate engineers and designers so that the 100 production workers are backed by around 1,000 design and development staff. During the period in which this structural shift has taken place the company has seen rapid market growth, even during the recession.

Such shifts are not confined to new products; the biggest growth in the service sectors has come, not surprisingly in the field of computer services. Yet despite growth rates per annum of around 30-40 per cent employment growth has been slight—in the UK, of less than 1 per cent during 1982, for example. Again, within this growth there is a growing shift in the structure of employment with the best prospects for the highly skilled analyst/engineer level and with actual decline for the lowest skill level of operator.

The pattern of imbalance is exacerbated when the geographical factor is considered; the new jobs and new industries are not being created in the same place as the old industries are dying. Many commentators fear a growing polarisation of societies as a result of this; in the UK a recent newspaper article contrasted two towns of similar size but on opposite sides of this divide. Workington, in the industrial north-west, is in decline, its major industries of steel and shipbuilding closed and its population declining; unemployment stands at around 18 per cent, despite efforts by central and local government to improve the picture via regional aid grants, investment allowances and rate reductions for potential industrial investors. Wokingham, in the prosperous south, close to the 'sunrise belt' along the route of the M4 motorway out of London has small, high technology industry and services such as software development as its major employers; population is growing rapidly and industrial investment is having to be curtailed because of a lack of suitable space. Unemployment is less than 4 per cent and there is no regional or national aid in the area.

This is not a phenomenon confined to the UK; similar patterns can be found in Europe and in the USA and reflect a substantial change in social structure which is at least partly due to information technology. If we look more widely afield it is clear that the question of employment prospects—and the distribution of that employment in terms of both skills and geographical location—is becoming an issue of central importance. For example, there is growing concern that the growth of many Far Eastern economies may be affected by the decision of multinational firms in electronics and related fields to relocate their assembly operations in the developed world now that suitable automated assembly equipment is available which can produce higher quality at lower costs than the traditional labour intensive routes which made use of low labour cost developing countries like Singapore, the Philippines, Taiwan and Korea. We will return to this theme shortly.

All of the above might appear to indicate that IT is the job-killing villain of the late twentieth century. This is certainly not the case; it is important to see it in the context of other forces which also act on the overall levels of employment. There is little doubt that most jobs lost during the 1980 recession went as a result of a lack of competitiveness rather than as a consequence of technology, although, as we have seen, it may well be that as production picks up, so technology rather than people is used to cope with the increased demand. Similarly, it is not just technological hardware which affects employment; as the Japanese experience demonstrates clearly, labour requirements can be cut dramatically simply by making use of alternative approaches to work organisation and production management. Figures for the labour input in the US and Japanese car industry confirm this, with the majority of the difference accounted for by the fact that the Japanese approach the problem of manufacturing in a different fashion, rather than because they have a higher investment in new technology (see Abernathy *et al.* 1983).

Another area in which job losses have been serious—and where much of the regional differences arise—is in rationalisation and concentration strategies which involve not only closing plants but also opening larger, more modern ones elsewhere. Here again the role of IT is not directly causal, although it certainly acts to facilitate the planning and management of rationalised operations.

Thus the overall impact of IT must be seen as exacerbating trends already present in most economies, rather than playing a major role in reducing employment. There are clear exceptions, where the information intensity is high and where, as a consequence, IT has a major direct impact. But, equally, there are also examples where the demands which IT poses for new skills mean that employment is actually created, as Ayres and Miller (1983) pointed out in their study of robots, and as Leontief and Duchin (1985) predict for the US economy as a whole in the late 1990s.

We suggest that the real questions are not so much associated with absolute impacts on employment as with the distribution of these effects. That is, which sectors/occupation categories/countries etc. are going to be more or less affected by the impact of IT? We will consider briefly the qualitative impacts below and then move on to examine the international implications.

Qualitative impact on employment

It is important to remember that even where IT has no direct impact on the numbers employed, there are likely to be qualitative changes, in levels of skill employed, in work organisation and so on. Most commentators agree that few occupations will remain untouched completely by new technology, although the actual impact will depend principally on the information content of the task involved. Thus the character of work in offices and banks may shift away from direct information handling and communication and stress instead the customer contact and service aspects. Similarly in manufacturing we are seeing a shift away from the direct involvement in the plant to a role for operators and supervisors which is more one of management by exception—a 'policeman' role in which action is only taken when something goes wrong.

There are a number of views about the likely impact on skills requirements of IT but the consensus is that there will be an increase in demand for high level skills and a corresponding fall-off in demand for traditional, craft-type skills (Senker *et al.* 1980, Cross 1983). Importantly, in plants employing high levels of automated equipment, the demand will also increase for flexibility, where workers will move between different tasks and take on responsibility for larger elements of the production process—in contrast to earlier trends towards high division of labour. Generally speaking, however, the impact is one of increasing capital substitution for labour with an accompanying shift from direct to indirect activities.

As we have already remarked, the pattern of change with IT involves a shift in skill levels across sectors, with new jobs being created to replace old ones destroyed by the use of the technology. This is rarely a purely lateral shift, however; the employment trends suggest an overall increase in skill levels being required in the new industries.

In terms of work organisation there are also growing shifts towards a capital-intensive model like that found at present in the large-scale process industries such as petrochemicals. Here the high cost of capital is recouped by continuous running with short breaks at long intervals such as annual maintenance shutdown and by minimal manning in a largely supervisory capacity. Whilst this pattern can already be found in most of the major process industries—glass, cement, steel, food and drink, etc.—other sectors such as engineering and almost all of the service sector are only beginning to enter the transitional phase.

This has been the subject of a number of studies. Emerging from these is the point that arguments about 'technological determinism' (Braverman, 1974) do not necessarily hold in the case of IT. Rather there appears to be a range of choices available regarding the design of production systems and patterns of work organisation; some writers have begun to talk about IT as a 'malleable' technology—i.e. one which can be shaped to suit a variety of different circumstances and needs. Sorge *et al.* (1982) for example, comment in their research on CNC machine tools,

> . . . all our results serve to stress the extreme malleability of CNC technology. There is no effect of CNC use as such . . . the malleability of CNC technology shows in the fact that its technical specification in detail and its organisational and labour conditions are closely adjusted to company and departmental strategies, existing production engineering and organisation strategies and manpower policies . . .

This view is confirmed in many other types of IT application—for examples, see Winch (1983).

The fact that different firms even using the same technology exhibit different responses to the problems of job design and work organisation is not really surprising. It reflects differences in attitudes, strategies and other components of the firm's current position. What is significant is, as Wilkinson (1983) points out, this is very much a *political* process involving negotiations between different actors with different degrees of power and influence within the organisation. In turn this suggests that decision-making about the pattern of skills requirement, job design and work organisation will increasingly enter the realms of what Child (1977) has called 'strategic choice' on the part of the key actors involved. Evidence is beginning to emerge which suggests that there is a correlation between the pattern of work organisation selected and the increases in productivity obtained through the use of new technology; in other words, success may not be determined so much by the adoption of new technology as by the way in which that technology is actually implemented (Bessant, Lamming and Arnold, 1984).

This conclusion—that there is no pre-determined 'best' way of using information technology but rather a range of possibilities—also has significance in our discussion of the future diffusion in the international context. The possibilities opened up by this wide range of choice, for example, that the technology can save on skills and capital under certain circumstances mean that information technology might be something which could be used to support small-scale, decentralised activities within developing countries, in addition to its probable use in the advanced, industrialised world. We shall return to this theme shortly.

Alternative trends

Inevitably there is a spectrum of views regarding the possible international implications of IT; for example, Kaplinsky identifies four major lines of argument about the impact of IT on patterns of comparative advantage. Whilst there is undoubtedly considerable pessimism about the prospects of the developing world benefiting from what is essentially a technical revolution bred in and for the developed world, some commentators have identified niches within this paradigm which look more hopeful. Many writers believe that some of the newly-industrialising countries such as India, Brazil, Venezuela and several of the Far Eastern economies may be in a position to make use of 'leapfrog' strategies, going for advanced generations of IT-based capital goods ahead of developed country competitors which may still be tied to existing generations of investment. Further, the organisational requirements for new production paradigms may be easier to achieve in newly-industrialising countries than in those countries with long-established patterns and practices (see, for example, Perez-Perez, 1985). Support for this also comes from economists such as Soete and Jacobsson who argue that the technology systems of such countries may already be strong enough to permit them to engage successfully in the *production* of some items of new technology (see Soete in Sigurdson and Grandstrand (1982), and Jacobsson (1982)). As Rada and others point out, however, such capabilities are confined to a relatively small group of 'sophisticated' NICs; for most LDCs the possibilities of applying the technology under these conditions appears limited.

An alternative which is currently the focus of considerable interest is the prospect of utilising the flexibility of IT to develop locally adapted variants which can be integrated into established and traditional patterns of economic activity within LDCs. Such 'blending' approaches address local priorities and problems such as skill shortages and energy/raw material conservation rather than those of the advanced developed countries. A growing number of examples have been identified, utilising a wide spread of advanced technologies (including biotechnology and solar) in addition to IT (see Bhalla and James (1984), and von Weizsäcker *et al.*, 1984).

Although there is criticism that such approaches represent little more than a repackaging of the old 'appropriate technology' solutions to developing country needs, it appears that they are symptomatic of a more aggressive and informed stance on the part of developing countries towards new technologies as initiatives such as UNIDO's microelectronics and biotechnology programmes and the regular publication of a 'Monitor' covering recent technological and market trends in these fields, bear out. The UN Centre for Science and Technology for Development (UNCSTD) have also embarked upon a programme called 'ATAS—Advanced Technology Alert System' which aims to provide at least a background to the new technologies in order to inform and assist decision-makers in developing countries; their first issue covered tissue culture, the second deals with automation technologies based on microelectronics and subsequent issues are scheduled to cover software technology, advanced information systems, lasers and optoelectronics.

In general there is consensus that any developing country response to the challenge of IT and other major new technologies will depend on some form of early warning/technical intelligence systems—a point made by Morehouse (1981) and Sigurdson and Jacobsson (1983), amongst others. But it is significant that amongst some developing countries the new technologies are not only being seen as a potential threat but also a possible opportunity for development.

Despite the optimistic note sounded by some of these workers it must be said that hitherto the diffusion of IT has largely taken place in the high income developed countries. More seriously, as Kaplinsky points out (1985), it is diffusing rapidly into those technology-intensive sectors in which the NICs hope to specialise in the future and this may undermine their longer-term industrialisation strategies. This may have a knock-on effect; if the middle income NICs are prevented from climbing the technological ladder in terms of products, then they will not vacate the lower rungs to permit low income less developed countries to carry through a programme of industrial growth.

From the evidence so far available it is difficult to be certain about anything except the technological trends and capabilities. For the rest it appears that, at least for a short time period, there may be choice available about who uses IT and how. The tide is running strongly in support of reinforcing existing trade patterns and constraining the development of the Third World by erosion of comparative advantages based on cheap labour or raw materials. Nevertheless some possibilities do exist for developing countries to exploit the benefits of IT, and to use its more appropriate properties, such as skill and capital savings, to achieve a more competitive position.

This leads us to the purpose of our book. Given that there is still some room to manœuvre with respect to IT, it is a matter of some urgency that a range of different possible futures are explored in order to generate suitable policy responses to the challenge which IT is now posing. Such explorations must clearly involve expert judgement, opinion and experience, and above all, be located within the context of a particular country's culture and societal organisation. But they also require some information input—however crude—based on a synthesis of the somewhat patchy empirical evidence currently available. The next chapter attempts to provide such an overview of the available empirical evidence about the employment implications of IT for different sectors and for different economic groups.

3 The game so far: experience with applications of information technology

This chapter reviews some of the empirical evidence about the employment effects associated with information technology. From this some general sectoral patterns are derived which will be used in the computer model. As we have already seen, the field of discussion for this subject is wide and well-populated. However we shall concentrate on the growing body of recent empirical evidence on the qualitative and quantitative effects on employment. Although the majority of these studies have been carried out in developed countries we suggest that for our macro-level modelling purposes it is possible to extrapolate the general trends observed in these studies which, when combined with contextual data on other economic groups, will enable us to make some generalisations and predictions about the likely pattern of employment effects associated with information technology on a world-scale. Detailed discussion of the issues affecting specific countries and sectors in the developed world can be found in a number of sources (see for example, Bessant and Dickson (1982), Kaplinsky (1985), Freeman and Guy (1984)).

One of the main problems in trying to review the impact of information technology on employment is that it is influenced to a considerable extent by a variety of contextual factors such as size of firm, industrial sector, tradition of technical change, availability of resources, patterns of relative advantage and so on. Thus it becomes impossible to talk of a *single* effect of IT as such: any discussion must include some form of disaggregation. In its turn this poses problems because of the highly specific nature of the data involved. The studies are often almost too rich in detail to permit widespread generalisation. There are many good examples of such research covering a number of different disaggregated perspectives on the qualitative and quantitative impact at the level of the firm, in selected geographical regions, relating to specific elements of information technology, within particular employment groups, within sectors and subsectors and so on.

Very few attempts have been made to develop and apply more *general* models relating employment and information technology. The difficulties associated with such exercises are considered in the next chapter. Probably the first of these was the study commissioned by the Austrian government in 1979 to develop a model which could be used to explore a number of different possible future scenarios relating IT, employment and general quality of life. This report (1981) involved a systematic application of input–output analysis across all the major sectors in the Austrian economy; the resulting data was integrated with expert discussion, Delphi-panel forecasting and other types of qualitative work aimed at generating coherent scenarios for the future. Having constructed such a model, it was possible to carry out a series of experiments examining the effects of different factors including faster or slower diffusion rates, and the influence of different policy measures.

A more recent contribution—inspired in large measure by the Austrian work—has been that of Leontief and Duchin (1985) on the USA. This involves a highly complex model for all sectors using data from eighty-nine economic branches and fifty-three occupational groups; it also incorporates a novel feature in that it relates inputs and outputs in different time periods by computing the demand for capital goods in each sector. The forecasts so far reported cover two time periods—to 1990 and 2000—and develop three basic scenarios relating to different levels of technical change.

As with the Austrian study, the purpose is as much heuristic as predictive, with the emphasis being placed on the use of the resulting scenarios as fuel for expert discussion amongst policy-makers as to what kinds of action should be taken in order to arrive at the most desirable of possible futures. A similar, albeit qualitative, exercise is currently being carried out in the UK by the National Economic Development Office (1985) where the aim is to identify 'weak signals' about possible futures early enough to be able to make an input into the policy processes which can shape those futures.

The model which we are using in this book derives from one developed by Cole and colleagues (1982); this formed the basis of a study which attempted to deal with international as well as national dimensions. It concluded that there were likely to be very significant international and national employment and distributional effects associated with technological change.

Kaplinsky (1985) discusses various types of research on employment and new technology and identifies three levels; meta, macro and micro. The first refers to those studies 'concerned with the broad sweeps of history'; these include the important strands of debate surrounding the 'long wave' school of thought and particularly the attempt to integrate the concept of 'heartland' technologies such as microelectronics (see Freeman *et al.*, 1982 for a discussion of this).

At the macro-level he considers several types of aggregated study, from the very broad (such as the EEC's FAST—Forecasting and Assessment in Science and Technology—programme), to the regionally, technologically or sectorally specific and at the micro-level he looks at firm and plant level studies. As might be expected, each level of analysis has its strengths and weaknesses and the obvious conclusion from his review is that the picture is far from complete, with many gaps in coverage, methodology and analysis remaining. Perhaps the most significant point is his recommendation that we attempt to incorporate several analytical perspectives; 'suitably adjusted for individual quality and coherence, each of the levels of discourse is relevant to our wider concern with the impact of microelectronics-related innovations on employment'.

For our purposes in this book we have attempted a very crude interpolation of available research evidence, taken mostly from macro and micro level studies. In particular we have used data which reflects the general *sectoral* impact of information technology. An early version of this was presented in a study for UNITAR (1980); this indicated the likely patterns of change associated with the application of IT in both products and processes. An attempt was also made to look at the differential pattern likely to be experienced in various world economic groups.

Our present model uses this data in a slightly more compact form: we have amalgamated the wide range of sectors into eight basic groups. The reasons for this are twofold: first, the model would quickly become enormously complex and unwieldy if we attempted to simulate the high variety of the real world by including data on every industrial sector. Since our intention is not to mirror the real world exactly but rather to give an indication of emerging trends and to permit some questioning and examination of alternative scenarios, we feel this aggregation is justified. Second, the trends within the field of information technology application are not really specific to individual sectors but tend to be concentrated in larger groups of sectors which share a common pattern of diffusion and impact. These sector groupings which we have chosen are:

   (i) agriculture (including fisheries and forestry);
  (ii) extractive industries (mining, quarrying, etc.);
 (iii) basic manufacturing (traditional industries such as textiles, foundries, simple food processing, etc.);
 (iv) intermediate manufacturing (medium scale, medium technology sectors such as consumer electrical goods, engineering, etc.);
  (v) advanced manufacturing (sectors based on or about to experience major change in the direction of advanced technology such as aerospace, electronics, pharmaceuticals, petrochemicals and large

scale process industries. This group also reflects the high growth areas of manufacturing industry);
(vi)   basic services (traditional service activities with high labour intensity such as tourism, catering, cleaning, etc.);
(vii) advanced services (including sectors with growing sophistication in services offered and technology/capital employed—e.g. banking, retailing);
(viii) utilities—power, telecommunications, etc.

Each of these sectors is examined in terms of the likely impacts which information technology will have on capital and labour inputs (both in a qualitative and, where suitable data exists, in a quantitative sense). Comment is also made about the likely patterns of change associated with different economic groups in the world economy. This information is used to update the original UNITAR estimates (see Cole, 1982) and provides the raw material for inputs to the model, discussed in Chapter 4.

Agriculture

This sector has been characterised by extensive productivity improvement over a long period of time. Much of this is due to relatively high levels of investment in equipment. For most developed countries there is a pattern of low employment or jobless growth in this sector (see, for example, Rothwell and Zegveld, 1981) but there has also been steady growth in productivity. In the UK, for example, between 1953 and 1975 employment declined by 50 per cent but productivity grew by 160 per cent. Although nowhere near so well-developed, there are signs that these trends are beginning to emerge in developing countries as well. The vast majority of these productivity improvements have been due to mechanisation, improvements in farm organisation, planning and methods and in economies of scale: the picture is now becoming complex as a result of the increasing trend towards subsidised production amongst major producing countries such as the EEC and against this background it is becoming difficult to determine realistic efficiencies or measure productivity.

The role of information technology must be seen as being largely peripheral to these changes in the agricultural sector: it will certainly have a small impact but this will chiefly be to continue trends established with earlier generations of mechanisation and improvement. In product terms the most likely impact will be on the quality of produce as a result of improvements in information and control systems: in particular automated 'black-box' portable instrumentation and anaysis equipment will reduce the need for sending produce samples away to laboratories for testing.

A number of applications also exist which further the sophistication of farm equipment such as tractors and materials handling plant. For large farms the expense of robot tractors running under computer control can be justified and these have been used successfully in the large grain farms in the USA. Special purpose equipment offers considerable scope—an example is the Loctronic potato grader. Basically an elevator sorting system, this reduces the manpower requirements and also improves the working conditions for the operators. Instead of sorting by hand the operator sits in a booth watching the elevator on a TV monitor: sorting is carried out by 'tagging' different sizes via an X-ray probe arrangement. The low cost of the electronics coupled with the performance and maintenance improvements make such systems competitive with conventional methods in those situations where labour availability is poor. A further advantage to equipment of this type is the relatively high reliability even under the arduous conditions normally encountered in farming. If breakdown should occur, maintenance is simplified through modular design and is carried out on a replacement rather than repair basis.

Other direct applications include specialised control systems for farm operations such as crop spraying, irrigation, milking shed, feed regulation and produce handling systems. More important than these operations-specific applications, however, are the increasing number of farm management aids based around computer systems. These range from simple accounting and general management packages to sophisticated farm-related software for crop planning, livestock management and so on. In the future it is possible that expert systems (computer systems which incorporate a large database of knowledge about the subject and a set of programs which enable them to make judgements and decisions in similar fashion to human experts) will be employed to assist with farm management by bringing to bear large information databases and helping to make available knowledge about best practice. Also important in the future will be farm networks linking farmers with suppliers of materials, chemicals and feedstuffs and with the relevant markets for their produce. (For examples of other applications of computer technology in agriculture with particular reference to developing countries, see *The Use of Computers for National Development; A Bibliography*, Heyden and Sons, London, 1981.)

One other area in which considerable progress is already being made is in the field of remote sensing, that is, in the use of satellites and other remote systems for monitoring changing patterns of climate, cultivation, migration etc. Examples of agricultural and related uses include mapping the migration of pests such as locusts, the distribution of rainfall (as an input to crop planning) and the identification of breeding/spawning grounds in fisheries.

The implications of this pattern for employment are fairly clear: the trend towards overall decline or at least jobless growth will be perpetuated in all developed countries. Of greater significance will be the change in the structure of the workforce: with the increasing use of more sophisticated technology on the farm it will become necessary to place a premium on skilled manpower with the necessary flexibility to handle a wide range of applications. This may be significant in the future because agriculture has traditionally been one of the main employment areas for the unskilled: with increasing capital investment this sector is becoming more of an 'agricultural industry'. At higher levels we are also likely to see the continuing rise of the 'professional' farmer and a decline in the old patterns of land ownership and management associated with families and with historical factors.

The pattern for capital inputs has been one of rising investment and this again is pushing the sector into a more 'industrial' orientation. This trend results from a combination of factors, principal amongst which has been the concentrating effects of market structures and farming methods, which have also been influenced by national policies on subsidies. Resulting from this is a pattern of fewer, larger farms. In addition this trend towards 'industrialisation' of farming is exacerbated by pressure from suppliers of equipment, many of whom see a growth market in agriculture. For example, the poor health of the cars and commercial vehicles sectors has led to considerable investment by the major vehicle builders and component suppliers in the market for tractors and other equipment which are still profitable. In so far as information technology will have an impact it is likely to be indirect and towards improving the utilisation of such plant, for example, by improved farm management and planning systems. Once again, this is analogous to the production planning systems now common in manufacturing industry, many of which were introduced in order to obtain efficient utilisation of increasingly expensive plant.

Thus in overall terms the rising costs and use of equipment based on IT are offset by the improved utilisation and greater flexibility which becomes possible. The position regarding inputs into the model is thus one which reflects very small changes in the balance of factor inputs, with an overall decline in unskilled labour input and a much smaller increase in the use of skilled labour. With capital saving possibilities like those described above, it seems likely that there will be little or no change in the capital input figures.

To a large extent the same sort of picture emerges with fisheries and forestry where overall employment has tended to decline and where capital investment particularly in forestry has risen.

In terms of differences between economic groups, the preceding analysis refers principally to those economies where mechanisation is well-advanced and where the process of substitution of labour with capital has been going on for some time. For developing countries the pattern is likely to differ because of the nature of the agricultural sector: clearly the adoption of even 'conventional' mechanisation may be slowed because of the relatively low cost of labour and the fact that there may be strong pressure to retain agriculture as a major employer in economies which are otherwise underdeveloped. The problem here is that such policies may ultimately have a negative effect, for example, if they lead to exhaustion of the soil: in this connection it may well be that 'strategic' use of information technology to assist with agricultural management may be appropriate, for example, through the use of expert systems.

An interesting experiment along these lines was recently carried out by the UK software house, CAP, in Swaziland. In this demonstration project they equipped a Land Rover with a variety of 'ruggedised' IT equipment —computers, slow-scan TV, miniature satellite dish aerial, telecommunications software and modems, etc.—which was then driven around to remote locations. Here, operating only on battery power, a variety of relevant tasks were carried out; population censuses, health checks, crop moisture analysis, etc. The intention was to demonstrate the extensive range of tasks which could be performed by the same equipment and the fact that, at relatively low cost, this could be made available to developing countries. Emphasis was placed on local ability to support and maintain all the technology used by employing standard components and simple, easy replacement, low-cost modules.

For the newly industrialising countries the pattern is somewhat different: there is a need to develop the agricultural infrastructure to support a growing urban population and there is also the skills and technological support infrastructure which would be able to permit entry into widespread use of advanced agricultural technology. Given that the trend towards mechanisation is less developed than in the OECD countries, it may be argued that the NICs are in a strong position to 'leapfrog' and go for the most advanced generations of equipment—which may well incorporate IT. For the moment, however, the pattern is generally following the 'traditional' mechanisation route and there is little use of IT except in marginal applications. In the longer term, we expect to see a major shift in the balance between skilled and unskilled labour inputs and a rise in the capital input reflecting the changes in the nature of agriculture and the effect of such technological 'leapfrogging'.

The case of many of the resource exporting countries is also somewhat different: here the capital costs of the new equipment are less likely to be a deterrent to adoption. The need to develop the agricultural sector in these countries and the problems of labour availability in some cases may mean that sophisticated technology provides one route for development without necessarily using labour intensive methods. For the moment we have assumed the pattern to be similar to the NICs and that future development will remain along broadly similar lines.

Extractive industries

Although the pattern in this sector is strongly influenced by fluctuations in the demand for coal, metals and other minerals on the world market, there has been a long-term trend towards increased mechanisation and a reduction in labour requirements, especially amongst direct workers. Rationalisation has also taken place on a large scale and the expected future pattern will be one of fewer sites with larger scale highly auto-mated and integrated operations.

The effects of information technology are likely to be significant in the longer term, but only as part of an overall development in the industry which has been taking place for some time already. In product terms there is likely to be little direct impact although some possibilities exist for improving product quality and differentiation through IT-based systems. The major impacts will be associated with process applications and will mainly come as the trend towards sophisticated automation begins to permit integration of operations and management systems. The typical objectives in this trend are well-illustrated by the UK Coal Board's MINOS (Mine Operating System) concept. Here the strategy is to automate underground operations as fully as possible with corres-ponding shifts in the labour pattern and then to link these operations to a sophisticated management and distribution system on the surface. MINOS components include:

- fully-automated cutting and face development systems;
- remote guidance and monitoring;
- environmental maintenance/management systems (including air circula-tion, power supplies, etc.);

- integrated transporation systems (both on and below surface);
- advanced safety features (including provision for fire, transportation equipment and other hazard types);
- advanced mine management systems (including planning systems, distribution network systems and production control).

Table 3.1 indicates the extent of investment so far in these systems; hitherto these have been installed on a piecemeal basis but a totally integrated version of MINOS, fully configured with all components was due to come on-line in the Yorkshire coalfields (especially the £1 bn Selby development) from 1984 onwards.

Table 3.1 Components of MINOS installed (1984)

MIDAS Shearer guidance systems	20
FIDO Face-work monitoring systems	31
IMPACT Machinery monitoring systems	9
Electronically-controlled transport systems	44
Electronically-controlled coal preparation	16
Environmental monitoring systems	5
Integrated management information systems	20

It is important to see that the role of IT in the development of such systems is largely a *facilitating* one in the control area. The equipment for most of these tasks has already been available and in use for some time: what IT has provided is the necessary 'intelligence' network to make the systems work together as an integrated whole with a communicating hierarchy of computers acting as a 'central nervous system'.

In the longer term there is likely to be a more extensive use of expert systems in this field, particularly associated with surveying and prospecting work. (One of the most successful early generation of expert system computers has been developed in the USA for such work: called 'PROSPECTOR', it has used the combined experience and knowledge of a large group of geologists and has successfully predicted the existence and location of rich mineral deposits in unexplored areas.)

As with agriculture, remote sensing technologies are likely to become increasingly important in the prospecting field, especially with the opening up of deep sea mining and the extension of work in geographically remote and hostile areas. Also associated with this kind of work will be an increase in the use of telechiric devices such as robots, able to carry out complex manipulations in hostile environments; much of the present Japanese

Advanced Robotics project is aimed at developing heavy duty robots with sensory capabilities for this kind of application.

The likely pattern of employment change in the mining sector will be one of steady decline but it must be emphasised that the vast majority of lost jobs will be due to the extension of a long-term trend towards rationalisation and increasing capital intensity rather than any specific feature of IT. As Rothwell and Zegveld point out, the UK mining industry lost around 60 per cent of its labour force (=427,000 jobs) between 1952 and 1972 and this steady decline is reflected elsewhere. Figures for the MINOS system suggest that further reductions will take place: estimates indicate that changes will include:

- face working teams cut from twenty-two to fifteen with an expected doubling of productivity per shift and reduced downtime;
- transport labour requirements reduced by 50 per cent;
- preparation plant requirements reduced by 25 per cent.

A more serious threat is seen by many as coming in the indirect labour area with the reorganisation and rationalisation of operations into a smaller number of highly automated and integrated plants. In this connection IT may have a greater impact in areas like office automation, production planning and control and other activities which are predominantly routine in nature.

Overall, though, the quantitative changes due to IT will be marginal in comparison with those due to rationalisation with closure of operations and concentration of activities. The qualitative changes are likely to be more significant: of those who remain in employment the requirement will almost certainly be for higher levels of skill and greater flexibility. In order to operate a sophisticated system like MINOS with a small team of men per shift it is essential that there is flexible decentralised operational autonomy and this will mean a shift towards the pattern found at the moment in capital intensive process industries. This is likely to mean that the unskilled manual worker will disappear to be replaced by a multi-skilled shift team carrying out supervision of automated direct operations. On the surface and in other indirect activities the change in structure is likely to be less dramatic but will involve a reduction in numbers and a rise in skill level: in particular basic clerical grade skills will no longer be required.

It should be stressed, however, that these changes will not take place overnight; rather, as with agriculture, the pattern will be one of continuing increase in capital intensity. So far the direct effects of IT on employment have been minimal although we expect the picture to change in the longer term with a greater impact; this is reflected in the inputs to the model.

The picture for capital inputs is complex; although the cost of systems such as MINOS is high, the resulting integration of operations (and the implied economies of scale) often involves capital saving. Operating costs also improve, with higher productivity and the possible working of difficult or low yielding deposits. Overall we suggest that there will be a slight increase in capital input, but that this will be offset by labour savings in the unskilled area.

In terms of regional variations in the pattern it must be said that of all sectors extractive industries represent the most homogeneous group. With ownership concentrated in the hands of a small number of trans-national organisations, levels of technology tend to be high throughout the world.

Basic manufacturing

This group of sectors covers what are generally considered to be 'traditional' industries, fundamental to the early stages of industrial development in any economy—textiles, metal casting and forging, basic processing of food and simple chemicals etc. They can be grouped together because they represent industries which are fairly easy to enter: the process technology is well established and does not have to be high cost or complex and is widely available. More important perhaps, is the fact that the skills requirement is relatively low. It is not only the relatively easy entry conditions which makes these industries the first stages in industrialisation however; the range of products involved are often important elements of industrial infrastructure. For example, the castings industry is an essential element to support development of an engineering sector.

As we have already seen in Chapter 2, the pattern of world trade in such basic items is in a state of flux with technology providing one of the major shaping forces on the emerging pattern. IT is opening up major new opportunities in terms of flexibility, quality and unit costs of production in the field of such basic products, and there is considerable speculation as to whether it will be the developed or developing world which exploits these to regain or maintain competitive advantage. This issue is discussed extensively elsewhere (see, for example, Kaplinsky (1982), Hoffman and Rush (1983), Boon (1982), Morehouse (1981), Sigurdson and Jacobsson (1983)).

In terms of the direct impacts of IT on employment in these sectors, most of the evidence so far comes from the developed countries who have been early adopters. The general pattern is very much along the lines set out in the preceding chapter, with moves towards computer-integrated manufacturing taking place at all levels. In the case of foundries, for example, the trend is towards considerable integration of activities and increasing flexibility—all facilitated by the use of IT. IT has made possible new kinds of foundry equipment which can work far more productively and to higher quality and precision than traditional labour intensive methods (see Bessant, 1984 for a fuller discussion of these). An example of the kind of change in foundry technology which has taken place is the integrated continuous casting line. Traditionally metal casting is a batch operation; moulds are made, metal melted and poured and then the casting is removed from the mould and dressed to remove unwanted metal. With the new generation of microprocessor controlled production lines, all these stages can be integrated so that mould making (to a standard pattern), melting, pouring, knock-out (separating mould from casting) and fettling and finishing are all carried out on a continuous flow basis. The line has a high capacity but a very low labour requirement, essentially concerned with process supervision rather than operation. Although this small team is of relatively high calibre and skill, the bulk of the experience and skills input to the process is embodied in the control program for the microprocessor. Other advantages of an integrated system include significant space saving (because the line replaces a number of discrete operations), increased throughput (because handling is on a flow rather than batch basis), ease of planning and scheduling (and better materials management and utilisation) and high and reproducible quality.

This kind of arrangement is best suited to volume production such as for the vehicle industry where the quality and technology requirements are continuing to rise. Other IT applications are more suited to the smaller batch specialist type of foundry; here the principle of embodying skills in a black box is important to ensure the high tolerances and reproducable quality. Also important is the advantage of flexibility which having a programmable system offers; this means that changeover to different batches can be effected quickly and economically. Recent attention in the steel castings industry, for example, has focused on the development of flexible manufacturing systems using automated pouring, robot fettling and handling linked to novel and automated mould-making processes for small batches.

Thus far the foundry sector has not yet achieved full computer-integrated manufacturing capability, however. Use of computer-aided design is far less well-developed except in large foundries, often tied to major producers such as in the automobile industry where is it used to prepare dies for pressure-casting. The diffusion of computer-based production management aids, such as materials requirements planning, production control, etc., is also relatively slow, again with the exception of the major foundries in the automotive and aerospace sectors. Thus the pattern reflects the relatively traditional orientation of the industry in that the major impacts come from embodied technology, often originating outside the industry rather than in disembodied form.

The overall impact of IT is to reduce the labour input at both skilled and unskilled level, and to raise the capital intensity and concentration. One other important feature of such innovations is that they are often capital saving; although expensive, they integrate the process to the point where for a fixed or higher level of output, fewer stages are required. This reduces not only the costs of the plant to perform the manufacturing operations but also has an impact on machine utilisation and overall plant planning and scheduling with consequent reductions in inventory levels.

In the food and drink processing industry a similar pattern can be found, although the actual rate of technological change is much more rapid. This can in part be explained by the fact that in the developed countries the industry is highly concentrated and very competitive— placing an emphasis on unit cost reduction, quality assurance and increasing flexibility in the face of a demanding retailing sector (which is also highly concentrated and thus powerful in purchasing power) (Burns *et al.*, 1983). The impact of IT is significant as it represents a much more general change across the entire sector, covering batch and continuous process plants and large and small firms. (See Bessant and Lamming, 1983 for a review of this.)

IT can have an impact on three levels; at the first it is purely a passive technology, reporting on the state of plant or operations as a *monitoring* system. This may take the form of a discrete display or a sensor connected remotely to a computer collecting and collating the information from the whole plant and displaying it in aggregated or analysed form. Next there is the stage at which—often in addition to monitoring—the technology is used to intervene in the process, that is, it performs a *control* function. This may be a simple sequencing activity over time, or it may involve a complex control algorithm with demands for the computer to perform complicated mathematical work within a fraction of a second. It can be adaptive, working out the optimal response to changing conditions, or it can have responses pre-programmed in. Once again, control may be local and discrete or it may be centralised, run from a remote computer facility.

Finally there is the possibility of a distributed network, in which discrete monitoring and control of individual plant operations takes place but information is also sent remotely to a central supervisory computer. This monitors progress throughout the plant and, where necessary, can send overriding control instructions back to the individual units. Such integrated systems correspond to the computer-integrated pattern described earlier.

The food and drink processing industry is no exception to this pattern; indeed, its very density and range of activities suggests that it will be a major user of IT. This is confirmed by the little evidence which we have for the diffusion of the technology; in recent research in the UK the food and drink industry was the second largest user of IT, only just behind the electrical/electronics industry itself (see Table 3.2).

One other factor contributes strongly to the potential for widespread application of IT; unlike many other technologies it exists in both embodied and disembodied form. Thus it can be retro-fitted to existing plant, installed to provide a completely new function (such as computer-based material management) or it can be fitted as part of a total investment package in a new machine or plant. Because it is not necessarily tied to the capital replacement cycle (which, for items like baking ovens in the food industry can be as long as 15–20 years) its potential rate of diffusion is enhanced. Its cost may be high when combined with a new plant or when a major integrated plant control system is required but it can equally be very low for a standard application for which software is already available; thus a device like a programmable logic controller will be able to manage control of a single variable like temperature in a cooker for as little as £1,000, including sensors and actuator. Table 3.A, in the appendix at the end of this chapter, lists some examples which demonstrate how IT has been used in monitoring, controlling and in integrated networked systems. As with most manufacturing innovation, the motives for usage vary and IT systems have been installed for reasons such as those given in Table 3.3; the important point to note is that labour saving is only one of these and by no means the dominant force behind the moves in automation in the industry.

In terms of the impact on employment, IT is exacerbating trends already present to improve productivity and rationalise operations; Table 3.4 gives figures for one major UK firm showing the reduction in numbers of plants, employees and products in the range and the increase in capital investment, much of it in highly-automated plant using IT. In another study (Leach and Shutt, 1985), similar data is presented for rationalisation of the packaging operations in a food company's plants,

Table 3.2 Use of microprocessors in UK manufacturing industry by sector*

Sector	1982 % using	Percentage of their processes†	1981 % using
Electrical/electronic/ instrument engineering	85	31	60
Food and drink	75	31	56
Mechanical engineering	72	19	53
Vehicles	70	25	52
Paper and printing	70	41	50
Chemicals/ metals	69	24	50
Other metal goods	55	27	40
Other manu- facturing	54	26	40
Textiles	47	23	31
Clothing	38	20	21
Average	65	27	

The distribution by firm size of usage in the Food and Drink sector‡

Size range (employees)	1982 %	1981 %
20–49	15	16
50–99	17	17
100–199	16	18
200–499	26	25
500–999	28	26
1,000+	24	24

*Based on two surveys of statistically balanced samples of firms in 1981 and in 1982; 1,200 firms in each sample, 200 in each of six size ranges representing all manufacturing.

†The purpose of the percentage of their processes figure is to show how much of the industry has been affected by IT.

‡This demonstrates that it is mainly the large firms which are making use of the technology.

Source: PSI 1982, 1984.

Table 3.3   Motives for use of IT in the food and drink industry

---

Energy saving
Raw material saving
Labour saving (skilled and unskilled)
Quality improvement at all stages in production
More accurate control (of all stages in production)
Greater process integration
Faster throughput times
Better plant utilisation (e.g. through reduced set up times)
Improved reliability
Improved flexibility (plant able to make wider range of products)

---

where rationalisation of distribution led to closure of some sites and opening of new concentrated centres with a high level of investment in automated equipment. The overall effect was to reduce labour input required
by both closure of sites and technological change facilitated by IT;
typically the latter investments in new packaging machinery cut the
labour requirement by two-thirds (from about 390 per packing line
to 117).

Because of the highly concentrated nature of the food and drink
processing industry in the developed world, these changes are likely to
diffuse rapidly. In the case of developing countries the picture is less
clear. Potentially there is, as with foundries, a relatively low entry barrier
to using IT-based automated plants since the majority of the skills input
is embodied in 'black-box' microprocessor controls. The major difficulty
is the relatively high capital cost but this must be offset against the capital
savings which often accrue by moving to a more integrated processing
operation.

In the case of textiles, similar patterns can again be found with a trend
towards integrated manufacturing and with change taking place in large
increments within particular spheres of manufacturing activity. Much of
the textile industry in developed countries is now highly automated and
rates of innovation tend to be high. There is the added advantage that,
like machine tools, there is a tradition of programability—via Jacquard
techniques—which the computer industry has exploited systematically,
building up close user/supplier links (Rothwell, 1976). With IT the major
impacts are likely to come from process automation; examples include:

• computer aided design;
• mill monitors;

Table 3.4 Productivity improvement pattern for a major UK food and drink firm

	1977	1978	1979	1980	1981	1982	1983
Total output (tonnes)	144,625	154,516	151,991	149,149	150,374	150,992	135,934
Number of employees	8,836	8,565	8,436	7,314	6,664	6,155	5,376
Productivity (tonnes/ employee)	16.4	18.0	18.0	20.4	22.6	24.5	25.3
Number of products in range	63	60	55	46	33	31	29
Capital investment (£m)	5.4	5.6	7.7	11.8	19.3	36.8	35.3

- multiphase looms;
- ink jet printing of carpets;
- dyeing control;
- shift away from centralised digital control to distributed local systems, incorporating monitoring, fault detection and on-line analysis.

Despite the fact that labour still accounts for around a third of the total costs it is doubtful whether IT will be responsible for any further major losses of jobs. Most employment changes have come about as a result of import penetration mostly from NICs and developing countries. Where IT is introduced, however, there are clear improvements in productivity e.g. automated mill monitoring reduces supervisory labour requirement by around 50 per cent. More significant are the capital savings—modern high speed looms can replace several slower old looms and substitution figures as high as ten to one have been reported.

The clothing and footwear industries are also good examples of basic industries: import penetration of DC markets, especially from NICs in the Far East, has been massive. In shoes, for example, 40 per cent of the US, 50 per cent of the UK and almost all of the West German market is accounted for by imports (Kaplinsky, 1979). The majority of this competition is based on low labour cost comparative advantage (although there is a small tradition of high grade leatherwork in some NICs). Equally, Table 3.5 shows the extent to which LDCs have been successful in penetrating DC markets.

The impact on employment in developed countries has been serious and, as in our earlier examples, has led to various kinds of economic counter-attack. Technical change could play a major role; as Hoffman and Rush (1980) point out, the implications for developing countries are clear:

> it is arguable that the newly-industrialising countries have the economic strength and technological capacity to adapt to rapid change and competition in the world economy. It is equally plausible, however, that for some of these countries, the nature of their integration into the world economy will prove problematic. Export-oriented economies solely dependent on cheap labour may lose their comparative advantage in a relatively short time, with potentially severe balance-of-payments and employment effects . . .

However, it is important to note that unlike the preceding sectors the rate of diffusion of new technology in the garments industry is slow and this suggests that there are major technological problems still to be solved.

Table 3.5 Imports of clothing into selected developed countries

Year	EEC (10)		US		Canada		Japan	
	Imports US$ bn.	% of total imports	Imports US$ bn.	% of total imports	Imports US$ bn.	% of total imports	Imports US$ bn.	% of total imports
1963	0.14	17.9	0.11	28.2	0.01	16.6	0.0	0.0
1970	0.35	13.8	0.67	52.8	0.06	35.3	0.05	55.5
1973	1.18	20.3	1.49	68.7	0.15	45.4	0.42	73.6
1976	2.68	27.7	2.91	80.3	0.43	58.9	0.58	73.4
1977	3.00	26.9	3.30	80.1	0.34	55.7	0.59	67.8
1978	3.52	25.7	4.37	80.6	0.36	61.0	0.85	68.5
1979	4.80	27.0	5.06	82.4	0.42	57.5	1.17	65.0
1980	5.83	28.7	5.82	83.8	0.43	60.5	0.85	55.5
1981	5.43	30.6	6.71	82.6	0.55	65.4	1.13	62.7

Source: Hoffman and Rush, 1984

For example, much of the work involved in making garments requires handling of soft and indefinitely shaped materials—unsuitable operations for automated techniques such as robotics. Given the growing R & D commitment by equipment suppliers anxious to enter this potentially large market, these seem likely to be only short-term barriers. We believe that in the long term the pattern will be essentially similar to foundries or textiles.

In terms of inputs to our model, the present position is one in which IT has been/is being used to defend existing markets. By the end of the century one scenario would see it being widely used by the advanced developed countries to recapture markets lost to developing countries. The effect of IT has been to facilitate major technical change and process integration and thus there is a relatively large decline in unskilled labour requirement—often as high as 50 per cent. At the same time the structure of employment is changing to reflect shifts towards higher and more flexible skills and towards indirect rather than direct activities. Thus we expect a slight increase in the skilled labour input.

Changes in capital inputs are harder to assess. One the one hand there is the steep rise in the capital cost of new plant of high sophistication. On the other there is considerable capital saving made possible through process integration and associated benefits such as space saving, improved utilisation, greater flexibility and so on. Operating costs are generally reduced and the benefits of scale economy can be achieved with smaller plants but higher utilisation—a consequence of the increased flexibility. On balance we suggest that there will only be a minimal change in the capital input figures.

The longer term figures for the advanced economies reflect the fact that whilst present changes have been dramatic, the trend will probably see a relative slowdown in productivity growth. In this connection the strategies adopted by developing and industrialising countries may well be of major importance because these countries may be able to exploit advanced technology to retain their share of developed country markets. Indeed, the sales of automated and integrated equipment in sectors like foundries have been growing at a much faster rate in NICs like Brazil and Korea than in the developed countries and there is growing concern in European firms about the possible entry of these countries into the higher added value markets for greater precision and quality goods. At present the rate of change has not had a major impact on employment but by the late 1990s the picture for the NICs could be much closer to the present advanced economies group.

For the less industrialised developing countries the problem is one of access: if they, like the NICs, can overcome the capital cost problems (and to a lesser extent, the skilled labour shortage), they could pursue an aggressive policy in these industries. If, on the other hand, they retain their present position which is largely unaffected by IT, then by the late 1990s the indirect effects on their employment as a result of declining international competitiveness may be serious. The case of the resource exporting countries is probably closer to that of the NICs since they have better access to capital resources.

Advanced manufacturing

Under this heading we consider the technologically advanced industries in terms of products and processes; this list of sectors includes pharmaceuticals, electronics, aerospace, medical and other precision engineering. Although involving widely differing products, production processes and scale of operations, these industries share a number of characteristics, chief amongst which are their high capital and knowledge intensity and the relatively high complexity and added value of their output. Also included in this group are the high volume, capital intensive industries such as petrochemicals and steelmaking (although it is recognised that there is some overlap here with more basic industries).

In general the pattern amongst such advanced industries is increasingly becoming dominated by very large transnational corporations which have the advantages of being able to choose from different locations for operational activities and to switch production and marketing capabilities quickly to exploit worldwide markets. In this way they are able to generate the income necessary to support the high levels of R & D and investment in new production capacity.

Characteristic of this pattern is a high rate of innovation and the early adoption of new manufacturing technologies. Thus it is in these industries that we see the most evidence of the trend towards computer-integrated manufacturing; the 'islands of automation' referred to in the previous chapter are closest to forming continents within industries like aerospace and electronics. Significantly these changes are not just taking place in terms of embodied technologies but across a wide spectrum of choices which also include alternative production methodologies, principally those emerging from the Japanese experience such as JIT ('just-in-time') scheduling and total quality control.

One of the interesting consequences of these changes is a gradual erosion of the boundaries between what used to be 'batch' or 'continuous/ flow' processes; as firms approach full computer-integrated manufacturing, so the possibilities emerge for achieving an optimal production pattern which embraces the major advantages of continuous flow processing even in small batch work. Amongst these we might consider:

- ease of production planning and scheduling to avoid or minimise down time and ensure maximum plant utilistation;
- scope for varying the end product rapidly to meet changing market demands, i.e. a high degree of flexibility;
- constant throughput allowing for maintenance of quality at consistent levels;
- because most problems occur in start-up or shutdown, continuously operating plants tend to be more reliable and amenable to planned maintenance;
- stockholding is confined to the beginning and end of the process, so the costs of holding buffer stocks can be eliminated;
- the relatively straightforward layout allows for considerable process integration and rationalisation. Introduction of automated control is also facilitated: consequently continuous plant tends to be capital rather than labour intensive.

Clearly these are ideal characteristics: in practice continuous plants also have their disadvantages and problems. Still, it can be argued that they represent a more cost-effective model for production than does batch processing which tends to have higher labour intensity, costs of stocks and buffer stocks, problems in planning and scheduling, problems of inefficient utilisation of plant because of down-time, resetting time and so on.

Much manufacturing innovation over the past century has been devoted to methods of making batch processing resemble continuous processing more closely; few industries could be described as 'naturally' flow-oriented. In some cases this has been made possible through a particular item of technology—the tunnel kiln in the refractory industry or continuous casting and rolling plant in the steel industry are examples. In others it has involved a change in philosophy—the most notable examples being the ideas of Ford and Sloan in their development of the concept of mass production for the automobile industry. Over a period of time these two streams converge to give us the kind of plants with which we are familiar today. The car plant with its high volume assembly operations using sophisticated special purpose transfer machinery is an excellent example of how the marriage of technology and production philosophy combines to produce near continuous operation in what was once a batch engineering sector.

The emergence of IT has opened up many new options in the control of production plant and processes and in the management of operations: it also permits hierarchical and integrated control of whole operations and sites. However the majority of IT applications have so far tended to be in discrete automation of individual items of plant or process: the 'second wave'—that of automating entire production *systems*—has, arguably, still to break in many countries.

The other major change which such moves towards integrated automation based on IT is making is in the idea of scale economies. If batch plants can operate efficiently with high rates of utilisation and flexibility, then the traditional advantages of scale may be eroded, or, as some commentators argue, replaced by 'economies of scope'. Such systems are able to respond rapidly to changing conditions, both within and outside the works. They can deal with small batches and short production runs where in a more traditional batch manufacturing works these quantities would not be economical to produce. The significance of this can be seen if we consider the high proportion of production which is presently carried out in batches of under 50 items in size. This also has clearly important implications for developing countries, concerned with smaller scale and decentralised manufacturing.

The consequence of this is that the potential benefits of automation are opened up to small batch manufacturers as well as to the volume producers who hitherto have been the only firms able to support the costs of development and use of dedicated special purpose machinery. With such a range of technical choice it becomes possible to match production needs and means much more closely. Firms working to very small batch sizes can achieve high utilisation of machinery and minimal work-in-progress inventory levels through investment in flexible manufacturing systems—complex arrangements of machine tools, automated handling systems under integrated computer control. The benefits of such approaches can be seen in a growing number of cases; for example, the Yamazaki machine tool plant in Japan employs 215 people and sixty-five machine tools and thirty-five robots operating in computer-integrated fashion. The benefits achieved in terms of flexibility, speed of response and overall savings in overheads mean that this plant manages an output which would normally require ten times the workforce in a conventional factory. The flexibility comes out strongly when we consider that whilst current output in sales is around $230 m it could be reduced to as little as $80 m without the need to lay off workers. Similar figures have been reported in the UK, for example, the SCAMP (600 Group Computer Automated Manufacturing Project) at Colchester, making a range of parts for one of its machine tool subsiduaries. The

plant involves a flexible manufacturing system configured around robots
and conveyors feeding a group technology arrangement of machine tools,
all under computer control. In a conventional plant the requirements
for making the small batches of around forty different parts would require
a dedicated machine shop and about twenty to thirty men plus maintenance staff. In SCAMP the whole operation is managed by two operators
whose main task is supervision rather than direct intervention.

In another case, the firm of Normalair–Garrett have made use of an
FMS for production of small batches of high precision components for the
aerospace industry. Their output per worker has risen to £209,000 per
year from £67,000 using conventional technology, whilst their stock turn
frequency—a measure of their ability to reduce costly inventory—has
increased from four times per year to twenty-four times (see Hatvany
(1982) for details of other FMS installations throughout the world).

At the other end of the scale firms with large batch sizes which would
traditionally have had to invest in expensive dedicated special purpose
machinery can now exploit the advantages of flexible automation. With
production lines under computer control, changes in product specifica-
tions do not require a complete new machine or long resetting operations
but can be handled under software control. Once again the major benefits
come in improved utilisation and in reductions in buffer stocks and
work-in-progress inventory levels (see Bessant (1985) for a review of the
various configurations of flexible manufacturing technology).

Given this range of technological choice, it is clear that much will
depend on the way in which production is organised. We emphasised
earlier the Japanese model because it is likely to be as important as IT
in changing the way in which manufacturing industry operates. Indeed
it seems likely that without this approach—or some locally adapted
variant to suit prevailing culture, the full benefits of even extensive investment in IT will not be realised. A systems-based technology requires
a total systems approach to its successful exploitation.

It would be wrong to give the impression that the Japanese system
is infallible or that it offers the best prescription for other economies.
Nevertheless, there is growing evidence that productivity improvements
in manufacturing are due as much to how new technology is used as to
the technology itself—and in this respect the Japanese philosophy appears
to have worked very efficiently.

One indicator of this change in production philosophy can be seen in
the growth of suppliers offering complete turnkey systems as packages
rather than selling discrete items of hardware. The growing concentration of the supply industry and the involvement of major firms such as

IBM and General Motors across a wide spectrum of new manufacturing technologies is also significant in this. Table 3.6 indicates some of the key new technologies in manufacturing and Table 3.7 gives an indication of the rate and extent of diffusion, using the example of industrial robots.

Table 3.6   New manufacturing technologies and their diffusion

Computer aided design	— Production design and analysis including graphic design, functional analysis, stress strain analysis, heat and material balances, simulation and modelling, data reduction and analysis and cost estimating of the proposed product or system to determine fitness of purpose and economically optimised production.
Customer order handling	— Record keeping, tracking and reporting on the status of individual customer orders, particularly when part of an integrated on-line system.
Production, material and inventory control	— Scheduling and information handling pertaining to material requirements planning, inventory control, facilities planning and order scheduling, particularly when related to an integrated on-line system.
Automated production	— Numerical and computer control of machine tools, lathes, milling, boring machines, pattern and fabric cutting, welding, brazing, plating, flow soldering, casting, flame cutting, spray painting and automated assembly (all of these exist and are under further development).
Automated material handling	— Integrated materials handling using computer operated conveyors, robotic units, etc.
Automated testing	— Automated inspection of machine parts, testing of electronic components, circuits and products, automated material inspection and grading using sensor based computer systems, pattern recognition.

Table 3.6 (*cont.*)

Automated packaging	— Computer implemented coordination of material and information in packaging, bottling, labelling and weighing systems.
Automated warehousing	— Computer implemented order picking and material handling for both work in progress inventory and finished goods inventory. Automated label reading, routing of packages, parcels, baggage in shipping, sorting and distribution centres.

Source: Scrimgeour, 1981.

Table 3.7   Diffusion of industrial robots

Country	1980	1981	1982	1983
Sweden	1,200	1,435	1,650	1,850
Japan	7,140	14,826	27,623 ·	43,619
USA	3,500	5,000	6,250	8,000
UK	371	713	1,152	1,753
W. Germany	1,133	2,300	3,500	4,800
Belgium	58	242	361	500
Italy	353	450	700	1,800
Total	13,755	24,966	41,236	62,322

Source: Jacobsson and Edquist, 1984.

If we now return to our 'advanced' industries we can begin to see a common pattern emerging. As we have suggested, some industries already have 'natural' flow characteristics which have led to their development as continuous processes—petrochemicals are a good example of this. Others, like cement, glass and steel, have been pushed into this by the high production volumes involved and by regular incremental technological change. Others, like the electronics or pharmaceutical industries or the aerospace sector began as batch processes making high value products in medium to low volume: here the shift towards automation and continuity has come from a concern with flexibility and quality, often linked to increasing volume and design sophistication (which may require

the precision offered by advanced control systems). At the extreme—
and the electronics industry is characteristic of this—the move towards
continuity makes possible economies of scale which in turn helps to
develop high volume markets which provide returns for further refine-
ments of the process development—essentially a self-reinforcing circle
which moves the industry rapidly from a small batch to a large semi-
continuous process one. Figure 3.1 indicates a rough split across the
industrial spectrum which shows the progress of continuity and control.

One-off	Small batch	Mass production	Flowline	Continuous
Jobbing	Precision	Components	Vehicles	Chemicals
Prototyping	engineering	Fasteners	Glass	Food
Repairs	Aerospace		Steel	
Technical			Cement	
service			Food	
Toolmaking			Brewing	
Forgings				
Foundries				
Engineering				

Figure 3.1 Spectrum of continuity and control

The employment and capital implications within this sector are clear;
the pattern is given by industries like petrochemicals. In overall numbers
employment has declined whilst capital investment has risen; during this
period major productivity increases have been made, although gains are
increasingly marginal and some writers (for example, Soete, 1982) have
suggested that further productivity gains in the developed countries
advanced industries will be increasingly difficult to make without substantial investment.

The change in the structure of employment is perhaps more significant,
involving a shift away from direct operator involvement and towards
indirect activities concerned with supervision and maintenance of what is
increasingly automated plant. The demands placed on this small process
management team are for high and flexible skills so that although overall
employment falls, the requirement for *skilled* labour may actually increase.

There is an important point associated with this: research has indicated
that the skills required for successful exploitation of IT are a composite
of existing trades, new trades (such as electronics technician) and a component of what might be termed 'local knowledge'. That is, knowledge
derived largely from experience of the precise nature of the processes
under control within the specific context of the particular plant (see
Cross (1983), Senker *et al.* (1980), Bessant and Verstoep (1984)). This

requires a dual system of training involving both external inputs and in-house, on-the-job components, and a higher investment per head in training. The selection of candidates for training in this fashion is strongly biased in favour of younger employees—the argument being that they are much more ready to accept and adapt to advanced manufacturing technology and they will repay the investment in their training by providing the firm with a valuable long-term resource. Taken with the early retirement programmes currently being used to reduce employment in manufacturing, the effect is to skew the age distribution of the workforce.

The pattern of industries exhibiting continuous or near continuous characteristics is likely to change significantly in the near future with the entry of advanced IT-based manufacturing systems; this will particularly affect the engineering industry and some other 'intermediate' sectors which involve assembly and machining operations. Whilst at present these are a long way from the petrochemicals type of image, the technological trajectory is clear (and is demonstrated most effectively in Japan); we can expect a gradual shedding of labour and a shift towards the smaller workforce with higher and flexible skills which is typical of the advanced sector at the moment.

For economic groups (1) and (2) the picture is likely to be one of increasingly significant change as we move into the 1990s. Employment will decline in those industries already oriented towards continuity, this displacement will be relatively small and gradual but in the engineering and related sectors relatively new to continuity it may be more rapid and serious. (Against this must be set the major job loss which has taken place during the recession; it seems likely that what will in fact happen is that as firms invest in new technology to meet rising demand on the upturn, they will not re-employ staff laid off.)

The position regarding capital inputs is more difficult to predict; certainly the cost of moving to continuous and flexible production is extremely high and to achieve maximum effect really requires the construction of totally new plant rather than modification of existing works. Against this very high capital cost must be set the contribution which advanced systems make to reducing the number of process stages for which plant is required (via integrated design), increased plant utilisation (via flexibility), space saving, reduction in stock and work-in-progress inventory levels and so on. These may well produce significant savings in the capital costs of new plant: at the very least the picture in balance is not likely to imply much of an increase in capital input per unit output.

The wider international picture is difficult to predict in the longer term because much depends on the strategy employed by the newly-industrialising countries. In the short term it is fairly certain that the capital and technology costs of such advanced technology will preclude its production outside of a small group of countries, principally those in the OECD. Indeed, there is a growing 'stringing out' of participants even within this 'club', with the competition resolving into three major components the USA, Japan and Western Europe. Examples of this pattern can be found in the wide range of IT production, for example, integrated circuits, telecommunications equipment and computers (see Table 3.8). The pattern is very clear; the rising costs of R & D and investment in manufacturing facilities in these areas means that individual firms, even the largest, will have to pool their resources and share technology. The scale of investment and the strategic importance of IT also means extensive government involvement—with the result that there are now clear national/continental concentrations in the field of IT. Some commentators argue that this lays the foundations for a growing international trade war in IT—of which the fierce battle between the USA and Japan on semiconductor products is just an early skirmish.

Table 3.8 Countries participating in advanced technology industries

(a) *World sales of semiconductors—leading firms*

Firm	Location	1980 ($m)	1983 ($m)
Texas Instruments	USA	1,580	1,310
Motorola	USA	1,100	1,500
National Semiconductor	USA	770	690
Nippon Electric	Japan	769	1,084
Hitachi	Japan		820
Toshiba	Japan	629	705
Intel	USA	575	685
Fairchild	USA	566	400
Philips	Netherlands	558	500
Siemens	West Germany	420	
Fujitsu	Japan	419	500
Signetics	USA	384	
Mostek	USA	330	
Matsushita	Japan	300	
Mitsubishi	Japan	254	

Table 3.8 (*cont.*)

Firm	Location	1980 ($m)	1983 ($m)
AEG-Telefunken	West Germany	196	
Thomson-CSF	France	190	
Sanyo	Japan	180	
SGS-Ates	Italy	150	
Plessey	UK	49	
Ferranti	UK	48	

(*b*) *World production and trade in integrated circuits ($bn) 1981/2*

Country	Production	Internal consumption	Exports		Imports
USA	9.3	7.52	(a) Europe	1.08	0.1
			(b) Japan	0.36	0.15
			(c) RoW	0.34	0.03
Japan	3.13	2.23	(a) RoW	0.28	–
			(b) Europe	0.17	–
			(c) USA	0.15	0.36
Europe	0.79	0.65	(a) USA	0.1	1.08
			(b) RoW	0.04	–
			(c) Japan	–	0.17
Rest of world	0.16	0.13	(a) USA	0.03	0.34
			(b) Japan	–	0.28
			(c) Europe	–	0.04

(*c*) *Major computer suppliers in Western Europe, 1982*

Supplier	Location	Sales $m
IBM	USA	9,747
Olivetti	Italy	1,310
Siemens	West Germany	1,270
CII/Honeywell/Bull	France	1,200
DEC	USA	1,041
ICL	UK	994

Table 3.8 (*cont.*)

Supplier	Location	Sales $m
Burroughs	USA	970
Sperry	USA	813
Nixdorf	West Germany	796
CDC	USA	794
Philips	Netherlands	787
NCR	USA	702
Hewlett-Packard	USA	694
CIT-Alcatel	France	517
Honeywell	USA	478

(*d*) *World computer suppliers, 1978*

Firm	Nationality	Sales $m
IBM	USA	17,072
Burroughs	USA	2,107
NCR	USA	1,932
CDC	USA	1,867
Hitachi	Japan	1,830
Sperry/Univac	USA	1,807
Toshiba	Japan	1,633
DEC	USA	1,437
Honeywell	USA	1,294
Fujitsu	Japan	1,247
CII/Honeywell/Bull	France	1,047
ICL	UK	1,019
Olivetti	Italy	789
Siemens	West Germany	703
Nippon EC	Japan	672
Philips	Netherlands	602
Nixdorf	West Germany	554
OKI	Japan	200
Mitsubishi	Japan	190

Sources: (a) 1980 figures, Datapost 1981.
(b) 1983 figures compiled from trade press.
(c) Logica/Datamation.
(d) G. Locksley (1981).

These arguments make it unlikely—even with the possible falls in costs facilitated by IT—that all but a handful of highly developed and relatively healthy economies will be able to participate in the short term in the development and expansion of advanced technological capacity. In the longer term, towards the mid-1990s, the picture may be different: much will depend on the strategic position adopted by developing countries, a point which we take up later in this book. For now it is important to note that entry to these advanced technology sectors (apart from as a direct consequence of TNC investment and location policy) will depend on three main factors:

- (i) Selection. It is extremely unlikely that *all* sectors could be catered for in newly-industrialising or resource exporting countries; success is likely to depend on choosing sectors in which there is already some experience and investment—such as petrochemicals in the resource exporting countries.

- (ii) Markets. As Rada (1981) points out, the cost of investment in R & D and equipment can only be offset by mobilising very large markets; it is their ability to mobilise *worldwide* markets which gives TNCs so much of an advantage—and one which IT may actually help significantly. However, some NIC groupings—notably Latin America and the Far East—may be in a position to develop regional markets of a large enough size to make such investment possible, provided the necessary economic and political unity could be achieved.

- (iii) Strategic planning. Unlike earlier generations of technology, the present advanced stage cannot be approached on the basis of a piecemeal industrial policy; rather it has to be conceived as a long term strategic development which will take many years to achieve fruition, and which will involve the systematic creation of a new industrial infrastructure. Thus some major government commitment needs to be made towards new technology.

Whilst the concept of 'appropriate' technology is no longer fashionable, the focus of discussion has begun to shift towards the idea of integration of traditional and new manufacturing technologies. (See for example, Bhalla and James (1984), or von Weizsäcker *et al*. (1983).) The argument is that whilst developing countries are severely limited in their abilities to use advanced technologies because of resource constaints on capital, skills and suitable technology, there may be niches in which suitable applications of IT can be used, in many cases exploiting its properties in skill and capital saving to overcome the very obstacles which traditionally limit LDCs technological capabilities. Despite the growing evidence of this trend in basic and intermediate manufacturing sectors, we believe there is little scope for entry into the advanced type of industry that we have described in this section. Indeed, for many poor countries the matter can really be of academic interest only since there is little industrial development in these countries in the advanced area. Present inputs to production are likely to change only very slightly; the interesting question is how far these countries are able to go in development strategies based on acquiring advanced sectors in the future (apart from those established by transnational corporations). It seems most probable that the advanced economies will dominate this field, although it is plausible that NICs and resource exporting countries might enter before the turn of the century. For the remainder of the less industrialised developing countries it is possible to construct a scenario which sees them exploiting the sort of 'blending' route described above. Our experiments with the model suggest that this would have dramatic implications in terms of employment and income distribution but it must be said that the likelihood of this being achieved in practice is limited. We discuss this theme in more detail in later chapters.

Assuming that advanced manufacturing systems based on IT are used by 1990 there is likely to be significant displacement of labour at both skilled and unskilled levels as a 'leap-frog' jump is made from skilled manual machining to highly automated plant. The skilled labour input decline is likely to be balanced by a growth in demand for high level flexible skills—although in practice those displaced will not necessarily be the same people as those taken on in the new industries.

Capital inputs will resemble the advanced country pattern, with rising costs offset by capital savings from various process changes and improved utilisation.

Intermediate manufacturing

This grouping covers those industries which lie between advanced and basic. They represent industries which in the short term are less susceptible to import penetration from LDCs because of the higher requirements for skills, technology and capital. At the same time they have not yet reached the point in production technology where they move into *systems* based automation of the kind discussed earlier. As a group they are clearly heterogeneous and as such it is difficult to make many general statements about the likely impacts of IT. However, in very broad terms we expect the kinds of changes to involve elements such as:

- improved process monitoring and control at the discrete machine/process loop level;
- improved control of production and use of production management software such as scheduling, planning, stock control and material requirements planning packages—but again on a discrete rather than an integrated basis;
- improved quality management through better process control, use of automated test equipment, etc. but again, not an integrated total quality control system;
- improved flexibility and ability to work to smaller batches and reduce setting times—but confined to individual machines or plant elements;
- use of CAD and CAM techniques but not full-scale CIM.

The employment and capital implications of this follow the trends which we have already identified with a steady substitution of capital for labour —a process which IT has accelerated rather than caused. A typical sector undergoing such change is motor vehicle components; the pattern within this sector has been one of steadily increasing competition for a share of what is a largely static market. Emphasis has been placed on maintaining competitiveness by offering higher technology and quality products and by reducing manufacturing costs through the use of advanced manufacturing technologies and novel production management techniques.

One example is a UK-based manufacturer of pistons who has adopted an extensive new technology investment strategy, costing around £6m. per year for the past three years, in order to protect its position. They have moved from a labour intensive operation involving extensive discrete machining stages to a systems approach which operates on a flow–line basis incorporating advanced machine tools, each capable of carrying out a number of operations. The lines are under computer control which has reduced the setting up time from several days to a matter of three or four hours—which has a dramatic effect on flexibility. Labour savings of around 60 per cent have been made and the remaining workers are multi-skilled and responsible for an entire section of line rather than for a single machine. Their flexibility extends to the point where they can be moved to any line or point on that line without difficulty. This level of flexibility is being further enhanced by an investment programme in stand-alone computer controlled machine tools to handle the very small batches of specialist customer orders; these will be manned by skilled machinists but again they will be trained to operate all the machines and to move freely between them. In all operations the company is moving from the traditional motor industry pattern of two shifts to a three shifts, semi-continuous system such as is common in the chemical and process industries.

In certain key sectors, such as toys or instruments, the ability of IT to impact on product design as well as process technology has a multiplicative effect on employment levels. This comes about because of the possibilities for component substitution, product simplification, design for manufacturer, etc. and the overall effect is to reduce the number of assembly operations required. In the early days of the 'microelectronics revolution' there is no doubt that the labour displacement associated with this was dramatic: see Hines and Searle (1980) for some examples. But it must be remembered that such changes were exceptional in terms of the speed with which they arrived and the applicability of the technology; the more typical picture is one in which such changes take place gradually and labour is displaced with each new generation of products in incremental fashion rather than as a step change.

In qualitative terms there is a continuing restructuring of the labour input, with most of the job loss occurring at the unskilled/semi-skilled end of the labour market, such as in assembly operations of a simple, repetitive type. At the same time there is a smaller shift towards higher and more flexible skills requirements to meet the changing nature of technology and production and with a shift to indirect work like supervision and maintenance rather than direct operation.

In terms of our inputs to the model the role of IT is significant. Whilst recession and rationalisation have been the major causes of unemployment so far, the firms which have survived have tended to invest in sophisticated plant rather than in taking on new labour to meet any expected rise in demand. This gives a pattern of declining unskilled labour input and minor increase in skilled labour input. Capital inputs are likely to rise slightly, but again, the change is slight because the higher costs of new technology must be offset against the savings in capital and the changes in scale economies offered by IT.

The long-term picture is not expected to differ markedly, except that the amount of unskilled labour 'slack' in the system will have disappeared and thus the rate of decline will slow. We anticipate that the sector will gradually move to the advanced manufacturing pattern, with a slowing down in productivity growth as technological and organisational limits of best practice productivity are approached.

The above comments apply principally to the advanced countries; for less industrialised developing economies the implications of such moves towards IT are indirect but serious. With the moves towards automated, capital intensive production in developed countries, the cheap assembly

base in developing countries becomes less attractive and DC based manufacturers may be tempted to relocate production in their own countries.
At the same time such LDCs would be unlikely—at least in the short
term—to be able to access such sophisticated production technology
to set up their own competing production facilities because of the skills
and capital cost required to do so. By the year 2000 this picture may have
changed—particularly if suitable embodied control software and low cost
modular hardware units become available. How far they would be able to
recover markets or exploit opportunities is a more serious question.

The NICs are in a much stronger position and it seems likely that many
of them could exploit the present generations of IT-based production
technology to advantage. At present this trend is only beginning to emerge,
but by the year 2000 such a 'leap-frog' strategy could bring considerable
benefits to their programme of industrialisation. As before, the case of
the resource exporters is ambiguous; for those sectors in which they have
a traditional manufacturing presence such strategies might be open to
them. But on the whole their economies are based on resource endow-
ment rather than a highly developed or rapidly growing industrial infrastructure.

Basic services

The service sector currently accounts for between 30 and 40 per cent of
employment in most developed countries and is generally accepted to be
the major growth sector. (See Table 3.9.) It is clearly difficult to treat
in aggregate form so we have chosen to separate out two classes of activity;
those which will be affected by IT, and those which will be largely unaffected by it. In the former case we are concerned with information-
based activities such as banking, insurance, travel and office services,
and in the latter we are dealing with those services which still require
a largely personal input. These might typically include welfare work,
hotel and catering activities, cleaning and other services, etc.

The extent to which IT will affect these is limited to a contribution
to improved management and planning rather than in direct improvements to the services themselves. We do not expect to see robot teachers
or nurses in the short term, but we do expect to see considerable growth
in network systems which offer relatively low-cost routes to improving
activities such as:

● planning and scheduling;
● filing and record keeping;

Table 3.9   Distribution of employment in developed countries:
employment impact and implications of IT (percentage
in each sector)

Country	Agriculture		Manufacturing		Services	
	1968	1978	1968	1978	1968	1978
Japan	19.8	11.7	34.6	35.0	45.6	53.3
USA	5.1	3.7	35.4	31.2	59.4	65.1
UK	3.5	2.7	45.2	39.6	51.3	57.7
France	15.8	9.2	39.5	37.1	44.7	53.7
W. Germany	9.9	6.5	47.1	45.0	43.0	48.5

Source: Eaton and Smithers, 1982.

● updating and exchange of information;
● interdepartmental/area communications.

Employment impact and implications of IT

In terms of capital inputs to this sector, we expect there to be very little
increase since the nature of the sector is that it is labour rather than
capital intensive. Delivery of services will continue to be predominantly
dependent on people. However, strategies aimed at rationalising the use of
manpower and improving its value for the community's money are likely
to have the effect of pushing up capital/labour ratios, which will give the
impression of an increase in capital intensity. This type of pattern is
already visible in many developed countries, where social welfare cutbacks
have become common and where the usual effect is a reduction in manpower disposed in those sectors hit by the cuts.

For similar reasons, the direct effect of IT on employment is likely to
be minimal although the effects of rationalisation may be significant,
and such rationalisation may be the product of the use of IT in planning
and scheduling for efficient operation. There may also be a small shift
in the structure of employment towards the higher skills end of the
labour market in order to provide personnel to operate and use IT-based
systems—but we expect this change to be very small. Most of the employment impact will come in the clerical grades—filing clerks, typists and
related staff, but it is important to offset any potential labour displacement by the growing nature of the sector, such that relocation rather
than redundancy may be the future pattern.

It is very difficult to estimate what the relative employment effects due to technology, rationalisation and other influences will be; for our purposes we have considered the main determinant of the employment impact of IT to be the cost of labour relative to the provision of this class of services. Thus, in developing countries where this is low, we expect there to be almost no impact of IT in the short term and only a gradual increase as we approach the turn of the century. By contrast the group 1 and 2 countries may experience some displacement, particularly where pressures to improve efficiency dominate. An example of this is the UK Department of Health and Social Security which proposes a ten-year investment programme in IT, to improve efficiency and management; this will result in an estimated reduction in the workforce of around 25,000 jobs. This will involve an investment of around £700 m in seventy large computers, 3,000 microcomputers and 30,000 terminals over the next ten years. The system is expected to save around £1,900 m and to improve efficiency in a number of services, such as the processing of claims in the social security system. (*Computertalk*, 7 November 1983.)

As far as capital inputs are concerned, the same will hold true; in groups 1 and 2 we expect there to be a gradual rise in the capital input and a fall in the labour input whereas in developing countries the reverse will be true. Over time the NICs may experience rising wage rates such that they are pushed into a capital rather than labour intensive mode of operation—but we do not expect this to happen until late in the century.

The exception to the above pattern may be the resource exporting countries which have a rapidly rising standard of living and an associated demand for personal services, but which may well move along a capital-intensive rather than labour-intensive route to meet these needs.

Advanced services

Within this group we include those service sector activities which are likely to experience substantial change as a result of their high information content. Examples include banking, insurance, office work and administration in local and national government. There are a number of important reasons for expecting major change in these areas, including:

- They represent most of the growth areas in the service sector of developed and developing economies and account for a large proportion of employment.
- Levels of investment per head have tended to be low; given that the rate of productivity growth in services is far less than for manufacturing or

services, it is likely that increases will be sought through the use of efficiency improving new technology rather than by employment growth. This argument has been strongly pushed by major suppliers on automated systems;

- Most of these sectors are large and profitable and are seen as potential growth markets by the technology supply industry. Since, in the case of IT, this is dominated by large and sophisticated companies with significant experience and resources in marketing and distribution, it is likely that there will be strong supply side pressure to innovate.
- The information content of most service sector activities is very high and thus there is a strong potential application of IT in a wide variety of areas.
- The units of technology are readily available and at much lower cost than manufacturing systems. More important, in the case of items like word processors, they can be installed with minimal disruption in an incremental system development strategy which permits rapid progress up the learning curve with minimal risk of technology rejection.

Growth has been rapid here especially in banking, retailing and in office applications. The main applications have been point-of-sale (POS) systems in retailing, automated telling machinery (ATM) in banks and word processors and database systems in office/administrative activity. All of these sectors have been characterised by a very strong supply side push to move into new technology and it is significant once again to note the dominance of major firms with other IT interests. Associated with this has been the somewhat misleading argument regarding productivity and technology in the service sector.

In essence this says that there is a relationship between investment per head and productivity; figures for agricultural investment of $40,000 per head are related to a 200 per cent increase in productivity since the Second World War, in manufacturing of $30,000 per head giving a 100 per cent increase and in services only $2,500 per head being used to explain the low (around 5 per cent) growth in productivity. While plausible, this ignores the fact that growth is much more complex than a simple technological factor. It also takes no account of non-quantifiable factors like quality. IT can certainly increase the amount of information generated but there is nothing to suggest that even major capital investment can *of itself* improve quality: more of the same does not necessarily equate to better.

In the office automation field this approach is beginning to give way to a more realistic appraisal of what the technology can and cannot do and the moves which need to be made on the way to the integrated office of the future. Table 3.10 indicates the present distribution of technologies, from which it can be seen that reprographics still dominate the field. By the 1990s this is expected to fall to around 20 per cent and the bulk of concentration around 50 per cent will be in text generation and transmission equipment. The figures are for the UK but are comparable with those for most of Europe, falling between the more advanced West Germany and the less advanced smaller countries: for the USA the rate of diffusion has been faster.

Table 3.10 Office products in current use in the UK

Equipment	In use		Planned
	KFI study	PSI study	
Photocopiers	97.6	98	
Electronic typewriters	85.5	81	
Word processors	78.9	62	18.8
Microcomputers	77.5	79	
PBX (advanced)		60	28.3
Intelligent workstations		29	16.4
Local area networks		15	16.1
Electronic mail		12	15.0
Telex machines		78	
Microfilm/fiche		64	
Viewdata/videotex		19	

Sources: PSI study, 250 firms, all sizes, 1982; KFI study 255 large firms, 1982.

Three areas of office automation can be identified—communication, storage/retrieval and processing of information (whether text, data, image or voice). The longer-term picture will see these integrated into the office of the future—but there are major problems still to be overcome, including the standardisation of communications.

The overall market for office automation products was worth around £3 bn in 1982 and is expected to form about 15 per cent of the future IT market, especially as the convergence with telecommunications develops and multi-function workstation terminals covering text, voice, data, and picture transmission become available. The market is expected to grow at around 15 per cent per year.

In terms of the pattern of technological development the most significant factor has been the above-mentioned convergence with telecommunications and particularly in the field of Local Area Networks (LANs) which allow multi-user systems, access to shared resources and common databases, etc. Although there are some prototype systems in use, usually based on advanced PBX systems, the difficulties of standards and network compatibility have still to be resolved. Indeed, in several European studies, the point has been repeatedly made that after financial considerations, the biggest barrier to using IT is the lack of standards and compatability.

What is taking place here is essentially the same trend towards integration which we have already seen in the context of manufacturing. The pattern is also going through some clearly identifiable stages, although at a much more rapid pace than in manufacturing. The first stage involves the discrete substitution of old technology, such as typewriters, with information technology based products, such as word processors. In essence such 'office mechanisation' as Zisman (1980) calls it, is simply doing what is already done a little better through the use of IT. Productivity can be improved—but whether being able to produce five times as much printed paper at the end of the day is a benefit or not still depends on the quality of what has actually been said on the paper; this lack of information management skills is a major limitation to the efficient use of many items of IT (see Macdonald (1983) for an extension of this criticism).

The second stage—and the present limit of experience and application —corresponds to the 'islands of automation' idea in manufacturing, where some parts of some organisations are making use of integrated workstations linked to some form of local area network. Many of these activities are in the way of being demonstration projects but they do represent the most advanced configurations so far achieved. They are beginning to move away from the mechanisation paradigm in that they facilitate not just doing what we already do better but also totally new ways of working. Their limitation is organisational rather than technological in that the necessary information management skills to make full use of their potential have yet to evolve. Full office automation in the 'office of the future' will require radically different approaches to administrative procedures as well as new technology—and few commentators expect it to arrive before the late 1990s.

In banking automation the field of ATM (automated telling machinery) is growing rapidly with a market worth round $2.5 bn from banks, building

Table 3.11 Distribution of ATM worldwide

Country	1975	1977	1981	1995
USA		6,300	25,400	90,000
Europe	3,800		11,000	(17,000)*
Japan			27,000	

*1982 figure.

societies and other financial agencies. Table 3.11 gives some idea of this
rapid growth in several countries. In terms of the use of such systems,
UK evidence indicates near exponential growth in the number of withdrawals being made: 80 million in 1981, 150 million in 1982 and around
200 million in 1983. The pattern of supply is again dominated by IT
related firms, although one firm, Diebold, has specialised from the earliest
days in this technology and can be said to have pioneered its use. Table
3.12 indicates the market share distribution. There seems little doubt that
the growth will continue in numbers and that there will also be an expansion in the range of services offered; some US machines are already offering up to 125 different options. It also seems likely that other financial
institutions will be drawn into the use of 'through the wall' banking of
ths kind and that technology will increasingly become a competitive
weapon within the financial sector.

In the longer term the major development will be in electronic funds
transfer (EFT) so-called on-line banking. Such systems are theoretically

Table 3.12 Market share of ATM producers (1982)

Firm	USA %	Europe %
Diebold	47	
IBM	25	34
Docutel	19	8
NCR	6	17
Transac		12
Dassault		11
Chubb		5
Others	3	13

Sources: USA, Diebold; Europe, Battelle.

possible now but a number of problems remain to be solved, particularly in the area of getting agreement between major retailers and the banks to implement the system. Trials have been carried out in a variety of locations and activities—garages, restaurants, shops, etc. and recent announcements in the UK indicate that a major national level trial will take place shortly following agreement on standards and systems amongst the major banks and retailers.

Within banking operations the use of advanced IT systems and especially telecommunications networks continues to grow and international arrangements such as the SWIFT system for transfer payments and transactions will certainly develop. This has significant implications for development and participation in world trade; just as advanced nations will need to belong to the telecommunications network infrastructure, so they will need to make the necessary investments to participate in the financial one.

It is difficult to predict the pattern of future change in financial services because the potential which IT, particularly the opening up of various network services, may well change the whole nature of the sector. At present it is dominated in most countries by a relatively small number of large institutions—but with developments in viewdata and other systems many commentators believe the market will grow rapidly for specialist services and the delivery of these will be undertaken by a whole new generation of firms—thus increasing the overall competition within the sector. Whatever the outcome, the role of IT will be a central one.

In the area of retailing the diffusion of first-generation POS systems is well advanced and very few shops do not have some form of electronic system. These may be simple cash registers or they may carry advanced data capture and information display facilities. However the major development is now in bar code reading systems, usually involving laser scanning. This is widely used in the USA and in large European shops; a recent survey (NEDO, 1983) in the UK suggested that by 1985 about 1,000 retailers would be using the system. Much depends on the availability of coded products; at present around 70 per cent of European goods are bar-coded, with up to 90 per cent for some items. Investment levels amongst major retailers provide some indication of the speed with which such changes are likely to come. Table 3.13 indicates UK and US progress in adopting some of these technologies.

The rapid growth described in Table 3.13 is beginning to have significant employment effects. Although relatively few redundancies have so far been declared, it must be remembered that this part of the service sector is expanding. In general, the pattern is one of jobless growth, that is, expansion of activities without corresponding increases in employment.

Table 3.13 Examples of diffusion of IT in retailing

(a) *UK use of EPOS*

	1979	1980	1981	1982	1983	1985 (est.)
Number of stores	1	6	8	11	34	1,000

(b) *US use of laser scan*

	1980	1981	1982
Number of stores	22,000		
% of all food stores	7	21	31

Source: Kaplinsky (1985).

Figures for some UK banks confirm this; the growth in business (as measured by the total payment items) grew from £1.34 bn in 1970 to £3.12 bn in 1982—an increase of 135 per cent. But job growth has only run at 35 per cent, and in recent years has been sharply arrested, with business expanding at around 10–15 per cent per year and jobs by only 3–4 per cent.

In computer services, arguably the best growth prospect at present within the service sector, there is an even more marked slowdown in job growth. Although the computing services industry grew at 33 per cent for 1981/1982, the corresponding growth in employment was less than 1 per cent (*Computing*, 23 September 1982). In this case, as in the banks and other service sector fields, investment per head has risen sharply. Whilst there is some attempt to play down the employment effects of introducing new technologies, statements by relevant trade unions indicate cause for concern. In the banking case, for example, the union (BIFU) believe that the major impacts on employment are still to come, with the introduction of three key innovations. These are the CHAPS (Clearing House Automated Payments Systems) for same day clearance of large cheques, electronic payments at supermarket checkouts and cheque truncation—all of which are imminent (*Financial Times*, 15 February 1984).

In other sectors similar concerns are being expressed; Table 3.14 gives some examples of technologically-related redundancies which many believe to be the tip of the iceberg.

Qualitative shifts in employment structure are also likely to be significant, particularly in the case where clerical and routine office tasks are

Table 3.14 Examples of redundancies in the UK service sector due to technological change

(*a*) *Offices*:

Alfred Marks survey	– 13% decline in employment expected in 1984
Nalgo/Apex	– 30% decline in employment expected in 1984

(*b*) *Banks*:

NCR estimate that '90 per cent of all routine withdrawals will be made via ATM' by 1990; this is likely to contribute to jobless growth. For example, Barclays in 1982 grew 7 per cent but employment increase was less than 2 per cent.

(*c*) *Retailing*:

Extensive investment in POS systems—over £1 bn in the UK, for example. This tends to produce redundancies in 'behind-the-shop areas'—e.g. Tesco cut its DP workforce by 10 per cent (*Computing*, 19 January 1984); 'it is largely the development of POS and computerising the High St that has caused the recent cutbacks'.

(*d*) *Insurance*:

Commercial Union forecast a 15 per cent reduction (=7,000 jobs) between 1982 and 1984.

In 1982 Prudential declared 400 redundancies, many due to office automation.

(*e*) *Distribution*:

Grattan (mail order) cut 500 jobs between 1979 and 1981, largely attributable to productivity improvements gained by using word processing and viewdata systems.

Littlewoods expect 25 per cent (600 out of 2,320 staff) redundancies as a result of moving to IT-based systems (*Computing*, 3 December 1984).

automated. New skills in fields like information network management will be required; in general the pattern will once again be one of exchange of low for high level skills and of many for fewer.

Opinions vary between those who see the contribution of IT as essentially positive, releasing staff from routine and repetitive tasks and allowing them the opportunity to work in enriched and more satisfying roles —the typical example being the secretary vs. typist distinction. Others are more pessimistic arguing that the pattern will be one of increasing division of labour, tighter control over routine activities and labour displacement. To this must be added the fact that on any analysis the impact of IT will be disproportionately felt by women since the bulk of the clerical and related labour force in the service sector is female.

The inputs to our table for advanced economies reflect this general pattern with employment displacement and a shift in the structure of employment with some slowing down towards the end of the century. In principle the notion of the integrated, automated office is possible to imagine—essentially the service sector equivalent of advanced manufacturing systems. However in practice there is still a long way to go as we have already seen. Thus we do not expect a total decline in employment to the low levels found in manufacturing for at least twenty years and probably longer largely because of the social adjustment required. People expect services to be delivered by people and whilst there is growing acceptance of trends such as through-the-wall banking, it will be some time before total automation is accepted.

It is important to stress the *mobility* which information technology gives to the provision and delivery of services. Whereas location of manufacturing operations depends on a variety of geographical, physical and economic factors, the same is not true for services. Via information technology, in particular advanced telecommunications and satellite technology, it is possible to deliver services (such as banking) anywhere in the world. Further, the networking possibilities in information technology mean that the sources of such services can themselves by geographically dispersed; thus it is possible to envisage a decentralised financial community in the future rather than one concentrated on key centres such as London, New York or Tokyo. For this reason many commentators, such as Rada (1982), suggest that developing and newly-industrialising countries should concentrate on the service sector, exploiting this new mobility since it offers the chance to remove dependence on institutions long-established within the advanced industrialised countries.

However, the very transferability of services may act against the Third World; IT also facilitates the concentration of control over service provision and delivery because it eliminates the need for *local* activities such as branches of banks. Further, the rapid growth in international networks raises a number of issues about control over information as a national resource and in particular over what are called 'trans-border data flows'.

The key issue here seems to be that of infrastructural capacity; without a reliable telecommunications system it will be impossible to join the growing number of worldwide networks. Such investments are capital intensive but beyond this the extra costs of equipment for providing and delivering services are relatively low—a factor which again suggests that there may be opportunities for developing countries.

In the NICs the service sector is rapidly growing and there is considerable potential for IT applications and development of local strength (Maxwell, 1983; Rada, 1982). Unlike manufacturing technology, there appear to be fewer entry barriers and so we expect the position to resemble the advanced economies, although there may be a lag due to the less-well developed nature of the infrastructure involved. (Although, as we shall see in the next section, many of the newly-industrialised and resource exporting countries have made recent investments in state-of-the-art telecommunications facilities which might put them in a stronger position than many of the advanced industrialised countries.)

A similar pattern emerges for the resource exporters; in both cases we expect the impacts to be greater towards the end of the century. The impacts on less industrialised developing countries are more difficult to predict since there are opportunities for growth in the use of networked services. Nevertheless we expect that the impact will be slight in the short term, reflecting the low level of development of advanced service sectors in these countries.

Utilities

Under this heading we have grouped the major utilities—telecommunications, water, power, postal services, etc. Characteristic of all of these is the trend towards an overall improvement in the quality and range of services provided (especially in telecommunications) coupled with a steady and in some cases rapid increase in capital investment. As Moseley (1979) and others have shown, this is essentially a long term trend in which employment has declined steadily and concentration of plant and resources has grown. Accompanying this is an overall shift away from direct operating labour and towards indirect, supervisory and maintenance activities, often demanding a higher and more flexible range of skills.

Within this context, the influence of IT has been to accelerate this trend and in particular to facilitate the extension of the range of services. Applications of IT include better control systems of production plants, although proportionately the major impacts are likely to come in the improved management and distribution of such services.

The case of telecommunications is particularly important; this industry has been dramatically affected by the convergence of computing and communications and 'intelligent' systems are now being developed to cater for the full range of information types—voice, data, graphics, text and video. The current world telecommunications market is worth around $50 bn and is projected to grow to around $65 bn by 1987, with particularly fast growth in Asia (see Table 3.15). In the face of such large markets it is inevitable that there is strong competition. The pressure is compounded by the need to search for scale economies because of the high and rising costs of telecommunications equipment development; although component and hardware costs are generally low, software development is extremely expensive. For example, the latest ITT System 12 electronic switching system cost over $1 bn to develop and Northern Telecom of Canada spent over $700 m on their latest product.

Table 3.15a   Telecommunications market growth forecasts for the next ten years

Country	% growth	% market share
Asia	10	28
N. America	8	42
Latin America	8	3
Africa	8	1
Europe	7	25
Oceania	7	—

Source: A. D. Little (1982).

Gaining access to world markets is not straightforward in telecommunications, however; few countries allow free entry and most local telecommunications markets are dominated by PTTs which maintain a monopoly over much of the equipment market and tend to favour national suppliers. Developing countries are also becoming more selective and are trying to build up indigenous capability or at least acquire local manufacturing. Although there are signs—with deregulation in the USA

Table 3.15b Growth in telecommunications equipment markets
to 1987 ($ bn)

	1977	1982	1987
Switching systems	10.0	13.0	20.0
Transmission/local distribution	11.4	17.0	25.0
Terminals, mobile radio, private systems, etc.	9.0	15.1	20.3
Total	30.4	45.1	65.3

Source: A. D. Little (1982).

and liberalisation in the UK and Japan—of a breakup of the monopoly, it is still a restricted market. A recent OECD survey estimated that there were currently sixteen major systems on the world market whose combined development costs were around $6 bn. They were competing for a potential world market of $12 bn—but only half of this could be considered as truly open market, the rest being subject to national monopoly and preferential procurement.

The importance of telecommunications as a component of future infrastructure is illustrated by the conclusions to a recent report by the consultants, Logica: 'every W. European country will be obliged to undertake the massive initial investment to install these new networks—or risk losing its place in the ranks of the advanced industrialised countries'. Table 3.16 gives some figures for European investment which reinforce this: of perhaps greater significance is the changing role of the newly-industrialising countries which are now well to the fore in installing such systems. For example, the most recent major contracts for all-electronic exchanges have been in Mexico, Egypt, Saudi Arabia and Singapore, with others on order for the Caribbean, India and China (see Table 3.17). On the technology front there are several important developments; so far emphasis has been on digital switching systems. However recent interest has focused on the field of PBX (private branch exchanges) which dominate company-level communications. With advances in technology these have become, in effect, switching computers and many suppliers see them as the basic elements in the development of local area networks (LANs). Since something like 70 per cent of all business communications

Table 3.16 European investment by PTTs (converted
to US$) 1982

Country	Investment ($ m)	Investment per head ($)
UK	2,460	44
West Germany	5,843	95
France	3,520	65
Italy	2,760	49
Sweden	557	67
Spain	769	20
The Netherlands	561	39

Source: Logica.

Table 3.17 Recent contracts for all-electronic exchanges

Country	Supplier	Systems cost (approx.)
Saudi Arabia	Philips/Ericsson	$3 bn
Egypt	Siemens/CIT Alcatel	?
Jordan	CIT–Alcatel	$145 m
India	CIT–Alcatel	$200 m
Mexico	ITT System 12	?
Norway	ITT System 12	?
West Germany	mostly Siemens	$100 m
St. Vincent	System X (UK consortium of Plessey/GEC and others)	

Source: Financial Times.

take place within a thirty-mile radius, and most of that within the same
site, the market potential for LANs is considerable. A recent IDC survey
forecast for Western Europe that the present 3,000 LANs would increase
tenfold during 1984 and the population would be as high as 250,000 by
1987. More important, LANs are an essential part of the infrastructure for

integrated office automation; with long-range networks they will facilitate the full range of information transmission—voice, data, image, text and video.

There are major technical problems still to be resolved, the most significant of which is that of standardisation. Any network must have some standard way of getting information into, through and out of the network and a number of attempts at developing a standard protocol have been made. The International Standards Organisation has been trying to establish what is termed the Open Systems Standard (OSI) for world-wide use, with the aim of allowing information to be exchanged between computer systems regardless of manufacture or geographical locations. However there are problems in obtaining agreement between different nations and suppliers and there is a real danger that the proliferation of systems will lead to a twentieth-century equivalent of the Tower of Babel.

Apart from LANs considerable developments have been made in fields like cable and satellite systems, where the emphasis is on high speed/capacity/integrity systems—again designed to provide the infrastructure for the future information society.

Inputs to the model

The foregoing has presented a very brief overview of some of the empirical data regarding the employment implications of information technology. As we said at the outset, it is extremely difficult to generalise from the data because there is so much of it, but also because there are many gaps in the available evidence. However, the exercise does permit us to generate some working estimates for our computer model; these are presented in Tables 3B and 3C in the Appendix to this chapter.

The first presents a sectoral overview of the likely impacts on products and processes in a number of sectors and the second tries to fit this into our model of different world economic groups. Although it is recognised that such inputs have a very limited foundation, they are useful in helping generate some hypotheses for later discussion. As the work by Leontief and Duchin (1985) has shown, the process of obtaining accurate estimates in quantitative form is extremely difficult even for an advanced industrial country like the USA for which there are plenty of available statistics.

What we can observe with some confidence is the existence of trends within these sectors towards higher levels of integration and capital intensity and away from direct labour intensity. The convergence of information technologies is being mirrored by the convergence in the shape and production methodologies in most industrial service sectors.

In the case of Table 3B an attempt is made to indicate the extent to which particular sectors are likely to feel the impact of IT, and how this will affect both qualitative and quantitative aspects of employment. As this chapter has shown, most of these impacts will be felt in the manufacturing and service sectors, with a growing emphasis on the latter because of its high information content. This is reflected in the inputs which we have derived from this table for our model—a process which is described in the next chapters.

Table 3C takes this data a stage further and summarises the likely pattern across a number of different groups in the world economy. The issues covered include the impacts on employment levels, skills distribution and structure and capital intensity, together with a consideration of the likely entry barriers and diffusion problems. Our reservations about making generalisations from what is still patchy empirical data apply even more strongly here, since for many countries no attempt has yet been made to explore the implications of IT. The data in the tables for groups (1) and (2)—technologically progressive and declining economies—is least suspect because it is based on some reasonably consistent data from various case studies and surveys in the developed world. The picture for the NICs is also becoming gradually clearer as more empirical study is carried out; however, for many countries we have been forced to speculate about the impacts of IT. In some cases we have assumed an approximate similarity in behaviour towards the technology; for example, the resource exporting countries have been grouped together with the NICs. In others, such as is the case with the centrally planned economies, we have assumed that in certain sectors the rate of technological development is on a par with the group (1) and (2) economies. This would be true of sectors like electronics or aerospace, but less so of other sectors; for this reason we have assumed this group to be closest to the group (2) economies in terms of technological progress.

However, there are complications in this kind of simplification; in the case of centrally planned economies the pattern of production and work organisation is radically different from that in, say, Western economies—and this necessarily changes the nature of the entire innovation process. For example, the political importance of preserving 'full' employment by using labour-intensive production techniques may affect the rate of diffusion of labour-saving technologies based on IT.

A further limitation is that in grouping all the countries of the world into six categories we necessarily lose sight of the major differences between countries within those groups. For example, there is a growing stringing out of participants in the group (1) economies with the USA and

Japan leading the field but with many European economies beginning to slip behind in the race. Despite these limitations, the data provides a loose approximation to the real picture which can be used in our model to examine a number of different scenarios.

In the next chapter we concentrate on three scenarios for the future, based on this data. The first, which we have termed 'probable', assumes that the trends towards the dominance of the advanced industrialised countries will continue. The second—our 'plausible' scenario—assumes that the newly-industrialising and resource exporting countries are able to make use of the technology to accelerate their development and to 'leap-frog' the advanced industrialised countries in certain fields.

Finally we look at a 'possible' scenario, which explores what might happen if the attributes of information technology, particularly its flexibility and its potential for contributing 'economies of scope', are pressed into service within the less industrialised developing countries.

Appendix

Table 3A Examples of IT applications in the food and drink processing industry

---

(a) Monitoring

It should be stressed that monitoring is a very common application in all activities in food and drink manufacturing, from raw materials input through to packaging, storage and distribution. The following examples indicate the range of options: most of these are based on standard sensors and software. Monitoring is only limited in its application by the absence of suitable sensors for a particular duty. Examples include:

- Data-logging/energy monitoring systems: in their simplest form, IT systems can offer low cost ways of collecting information about energy usage, a vital first step towards identifying areas of high losses and setting priorities for improvement innovation. Such systems are essentially passive, they merely note what is going on but do not take any control action; in many systems however, it is possible to record data over a long period, say a week, and then display it in a form which has already been analysed by the system, e.g. for periods of peak demand.
- Diagnostic analyser, capable of monitoring up to 160 different plant conditions: sold as a 'black box' product for around £6,000 and has been widely used in food and drink processing plants.

Advantages include: simplicity and cost; improved plant reliability through condition monitoring; diagnostic skill saving; improved maintenance.

Table 3A (*cont.*)

(b) Process Control

The food and drink processing industry has a number of basically standard processes and operations for which a range of control loops and software is available, for example, in weighing, cooking, sequencing. Control hardware, as in the monitoring case, is widely available and selection depends largely on particular process requirements.

The trade-off is largely between complexity of requirements and cost; but, as with most applications of IT, it is the software element which is responsible for most of the cost. For this reason many suppliers now offer standard 'black box' packages which can be used for many different applications. The following examples are all process control automation projects using one of these standard packages, and the list indicates clearly the flexibility involved, and the range of sophistication and cost.

Date	Application*	Client	Cost (£'000)	No. of modules
1980	Chocolate moulding control	Confectioner 1	50	2
1981	Soft drinks blending	Drinks 1	30	1
1981	Hollow chocolate manufacture	Confectioner 1	170	4
1981	Chocolate moulding control	Confectioner 1	80	4
1981	Flour mill controls	Miller 1	90	11
1981	Chocolate moulding control	Confectioner 1	50	1
1981	Flour mill controls	Miller 1	51	2
1981	Packaging monitor	Confectioner 1	24	1
1981	Weigh and package control	Confectioner 1	100	7
1982	Refrigeration plant	Confectioner 1	67	1
1982	Chocolate manufacture	Confectioner 1	250	13
1983	Batch mixing, continuous cookery moulding and enrobing	Confectioner 1	335	5
1983	Chocolate moulding control	Confectioner 1	300	8
1983	Packaging and machine monitor	Tea & Coffee 1	67	1
1982	Malting house control	Brewer 1	15	1
1983	Grain handling	Brewer 1	15	2
1982	Keg filling	Brewer 2	15	1
1983	Keg filling extension	Brewer 2	15	1
1982	Malting house control	Brewer 3	10	1
1983	Coffee process plant	Tea & Coffee 2		
1983	Coffee process plant	Tea & Coffee 2		
1983	Tea blending plant	Tea & Coffee 3	60	
1983	Chocolate wrapping	Confectioner 1	32	1
1983	Flour milling	Miller 2	12	1

Date	Application*	Client	Cost (£'000)	No. of modules
1983	Bread mixing	Baker 1	20	2
1982	Flour milling	Miller 3	18	2
1982	Packaging	Packaging firm	18	
1983	Boiler control	Confectioner		2

*These are only food industry products. The total number of projects, based on the same set of modules, is around 120—indicating the very wide application potential.

(c) Integrated automation

Since the 1960s automation in food and drink processing using information technology has gone through three basic stages. In essence the change has come full circle, from the days when large, very expensive and technologically limited mainframe computers supervised the operation of large plant, through the period of micro-processor control of individual operations and plant items to the present position of integrated control. The difference now comes in the cost and sophistication of such overall control.

This type of automation is increasingly the norm amongst food and drink processors, and some recent examples of such total systems automation follow.

(i) *Frozen pizzas and comminuted meat products* (Findus, UK, part of Unilever/Nestle). (*Source: Food Processing*)
This plant, opened in 1983 cost around £30 million and is designed to produce around 20,000 tonnes/year; 5,000 of which is baked pizza bread and the remainder meat products. It is designed as an investment for the future, anticipating growth in frozen food, which has hitherto, been rapid.

UK (market size)	1960	£45 m
	1980	£850 m
	1983	£1,415 m

One consequence of this has been a design for extra capacity which has not yet been fully commited. The present plant is designed for 24 hour, 7 day working and considerable effort has gone into plant layout for efficiency and hygiene.

In the meat area, frozen blocks are delivered, weighed using micro-processor controlled weigh scales, checked for metal with an electronic detector and stored in a cold store. A Glafascan visual image analyser digitises pictures of the meat and a microprocessor calculates the fat/lean ratio. This information is then used to calculate the formulations to be used in later processing.

Prior to processing the meat is tempered, that is, allowed to thaw over a 20-hour controlled period; this stage is managed by a small PLC system. The route from here on is designed as an automatic

Table 3A (*cont.*)

flow-line, but through the use of computer controls and layout planning it is possible to retain a high flexibility in product range handled. In essence frozen meat goes in one end and finished beef-burgers come out the other.

Patties produced in this way are weigh and quality checked (including metal detection and optical scanning) via microprocessor controlled monitoring systems. They are then fast frozen for 20 minutes in another continuous flow line which leads to the packaging area. Once again, computer controls, advanced machinery and plant lay-out means that any one of the five lines can handle any product. Packaging is in flexible wrapping and then in cartons; these are then palletised and moved into cold store to await despatch. Most of the labour force (170 at present) are concentrated in this area where there is still considerable manual work.

There are two main products in the bakery area: traditional pizza bases and French bread style pizzas. However these products have been standardised as far as possible so that they are compatible with downstream automated processing lines. Dough is mixed in batches (under automated control) but beyond this point, all production is continuous. Dividing, moulding, pouring, baking and 2-stage cooking are all monitored via TV scan over conveyors and on a control loop mimic display on the control room VDU. The ovens are advanced design with microprocessor controls and full energy saving features such as preheating and recirculation.

Following cooking and final processing, the pizzas are frozen and packed in sachets on the packaging lines described earlier.

(*ii*) *Dairy* (intermediate size, main business in own-label supply to a major retailer chain). (*Source: Food Processing*)
Invested in major re-equipment as a stagewise programme costing around £10 m; component projects include:

£2.5 m	yoghurt plant
£2 m	cottage cheese plant
£3 m	fruit juice
£2.75 m	bottling plant
£2–3 m	new creamery (planned)

The bottling plant, commissioned in 1983 handles around 290,000 litres/day on a computerised bottling line running 800/hour. A micro-processor-based controller (Alfa-Lavel Alert) handles milk reception and controls:

— four milk reception pumps (working at 27,000 litres/hour each)
— two chillers
— seven storage silos (356,000 litres each)
— two pasteurisers
— four finished milk tanks.

(*ii*) *Dairy* (*cont.*)

In addition the system controls clean-in-place facilities for both the plant and delivery tankers.

The bottle filling lines are also under microprocessor control, covering handling and conveyor operations, optical scanning for breakages, crating, palletisation and lorry loading.

The whole plant is operated from a central control room, although attempts have been made to retain links with traditional processing departments. Thus the room is not continuously manned but used by operators as and when they need to have access.

(*iii*) *Other dairies*

A similar upgrading scheme, costing £24 m and covering six sites has been underway on behalf of a major national dairy products firm. This includes a fully-computerised hard cheese plant with what is currently the largest capacity in Europe (30,000 tonnes per year).

In another case, a major dairy has recently invested £3.1 m in a new creamery including a fully automatic cheesemaking facility which is computer controlled from milk reception through to cheese packaging and storage. This includes advanced process monitoring, production scheduling and automated clean-in-place equipment.

(*iv*) *Chocolate factory*

The projects in this case were part of a major five-year investment and upgrading programme which has cost around £150 m and is accompanied by a cut in the work-force of around 2,500 employees. Two major changes are involved—rationalisation (both of the number of sites and of the layout of operations on those remaining) and use of advanced automation technology.

Chocolate manufacture was traditionally a batch activity and the old plant had grown without reference to any clear production logic. One of the major changes has been to adapt this to semi-continuous operation, carried out on a single, long process line. This change, and particularly the automation of the packaging operations, required a simplification and modification in product type and range to suit automated manufacture. In particular, although the line has some flexibility, short-run items have been removed from the range; this is essentially similar to the car industry which also operates a semi-continuous process.

Raw materials are held in storage silos whose contents are monitored by a supervisory system: when ingredients are required, they are delivered via microprocessor controlled blending pumps to the mixing area. Recipes are stored in memory and overall production at this stage is under a network mini/microprocessor system: thus any one of the many mixers has autonomous control but overall operations and production control are handled by the supervisory minicomputer.

Cooking of both fillings and chocolate is effected, again under computer control and monitoring. Up to ten separate ingredients are

Table 3A (*cont.*)

monitored and controlled: each controller costs around £35,000. The chocolate is then tempered, a process which allows it to solidify in uniform crystalline state. The fillings are then 'robed', that is, covered in chocolate. Accurate process control is essential in all these stages in terms of parameter measurement (viscosity, weight, temperature, etc.), process sequencing, monitoring and quality control.

After chocolates have been produced they are conveyed to a packaging area. Here the traditional process was to pack and assort, using purpose-built programmable arms. Costing £1.6 m, there are twenty-four of these which pack sixty trays/minute, which is less (by twenty) than the manual line replaced. However the manning in the area was cut from forty to twenty per line, and (with 24-hour working), the number of lines is being reduced from ten to three.

Before final despatch the assortments are wrapped and weighed: in order to comply with EEC minimum weight legislation, it is necessary to provide accurate checks and this is accomplished using another microprocessor weighing system.

Overall plant management is handled by a central mini computer using data from the various process stages.

(*v*) *Canned soup manufacturer*
This plan uses a distributed microprocessor system to control and monitor various aspects of the plant's batch sequence processing operations. It is capable of handling up to 200 different recipes and thirty different mix cycles: at any time up to twenty-four of these recipes will be in production at the plant.

In the central control room an operator allocates recipes for the different production lines, and on the plant the process operator calls up the necessary batches of ingredients which are automatically delivered to the relevant mixing tanks.

The control system has a number of additional features including a heat balance module for temperature control, compensation for materials in transit, calibration for weighing operations and auto-mation self-test facilities. Overall operation is automatic and under alarm conditions the operator is presented with a concise analysis of problems and a predefined set of recovery options.

The system also features a process-monitoring function carrying information on plant efficiency, material usage, stock levels, batch recipe and mix cycle data. Amongst benefits offered by the system are:

− increased quality
− increased throughput
− energy saving
− high reliability
− flexibility and ease of set up

Overall system cost is around £23,000.

Elsewhere on the site, and supplied by other firms but software

integrated is a microprocessor controlled hydrostatic steriliser and
a supervisory controller for eleven wrapping machines for packing,
which costs around £1 m; it can cope with up to 650 operating
permutations of can size, labelling time, sterilisation conditions, etc.
In addition the system (based on a Philips PLC) offers:

- on-line monitoring
- self diagnostic routines
- flexibility
- energy saving (around £350,000 per annum)
- smooth process flow (no bottlenecks)

(*vi*) *Confectionery plant*
This case involved another chocolate factory and used five
microprocessor-based controllers to effect overall plant management.
Distribution of tasks was as follows:

- three units controlling process stages such as ingredients handling,
  product cooking, chocolate covering, packing, etc.
- one unit monitoring and controlling common site services—steam,
  water, electricity, etc.
- one unit as overall supervisory computer, looking after start-up
  and shut-down procedures and maintaining compatible throughput levels in different process areas. This supervisory unit also
  collects on-line management information including records of plant
  performance and material usage. There is a data link to the company mainframe computer to transfer historical data records for
  detailed analysis. The entire production process is controlled from
  a control room equipped with VDU displays and a keyboard; in
  addition data can be entered from the shop floor via fifteen
  terminals spread around the plant.

Table 3B　Summary of sectoral analysis of impact of IT-related techniques in advanced industrialised countries

Sector	Impact on products	Impact on processes
Agriculture	Minor (Mainly quality improvements.)	Minor (Mainly safety, reliability, efficiency improvements, replacement of scarce skills, improved management and control.)
Mining and quarrying	Minor (Mainly quality improvements.)	Minor (Mainly safety, transportation, access to difficult zones, elimination of hostile environments, improved management and control. Highly integrated systems planned.)
Food, drink and tobacco	Minor (Mainly quality and differentiation effects; possible cost reductions through reduced manufacture and distribution costs.)	Major (Mainly in finishing operations, packaging, storage, handling and distribution. Some process improvements, moves towards distributed control and management systems and highly integrated plants.)
Coal and petroleum products	Minor (Mainly improvements in quality differentiation.)	Minor (Industry already highly automated, little scope for major change. Trend now to optimise performance, mainly on energy saving. Use of distributed networks linking local dedicated microprocessor controllers to central production control and management systems based on mainframes. High levels of integration planned.)
Chemicals and allied products	Minor (Mainly improvements in quality and differentiation from more sophisticated process control.)	Minor (As above, industry already automated to a high degree and using relatively efficient controller technology. Rate of take-up likely likely to be slow as a result. Some basic applications in moving from batch to continuous operation made possible through this technology. General trend is towards

Table 3B (*cont.*)

Proportion of sector potentially affected	Potential employment impacts	
	Quantitative	Qualitative
Low	Minimal losses. Small improvement in labour productivity.	Skills level required likely to rise, need for multivalent skills e.g. mechanics/electricians.
Medium	Some losses mainly surface workers and in finishing. In some areas, labour productivity improvements of 100% or more (face work). Elsewhere up to 50% (preparation etc.).	Skills shift, need for more support personnel with higher and multivalent skills especially in maintenance.
Medium/High	Some losses mainly in finishing areas, may effect women disproportionately. Labour productivity in finishing can be improved up to *500%*. Labour saving as high as 80%.	Skills shift towards more specialisation, especially on support and administrative side.
Low	Minimal losses. Minimal changes in productivity due to low labour intensity.	Continuing trend towards high level skills and multiple skills trades; increasing need for maintenance and decreasing need for supervision. Decentralisation of large plants places considerable responsibility on remaining operators.
Medium/Low	Minimal losses. In finishing, large improvements (over 100%), in manufacture, low.	As above, with early reduction in supervisory staff as process automation of small batch operations becomes possible.

Table 3B (*cont.*)

Sector	Impact on products	Impact on processes
		highly integrated systems like those described above. Also some applications in materials handling and transport.)
Metals manufacture	Minor (Mainly quality and differentiation improvements.)	Minor (Industry already highly automated and has been using computer technology for over twenty years, microprocessor for ten. Applications are to increase accuracy and reliability, to cut-down time and to improve production control and scheduling. Smaller-scale operations, e.g. foundries, may apply on an individual machine basis, but overall impact is likely to be slight except where integrated casting lines are used in high volume foundries.)
Electrical	Minor (Improvements in quality and performance, especially in addition of features like displays and programmability. Character of internal construction likely to change significantly towards use of integrated circuits; may lead to more basic changes later.)	Minor (The bulk of changes are likely to come as a result of alterations in the product, e.g., the substitution of integrated circuits for wiring. Such trends may facilitate automatic assembly at a later stage.)
Shipbuilding	Minor (Improvements in safety and control and in systems for passenger handling and transit.)	Minor/major (Advances in mechanical engineering technology will influence this sector considerably in activities like cutting, shaping, drilling, etc. CAD techniques will also be used and robotics may appear in handling or repetitive welding tasks. Production control systems linked to order and stock systems will also be used.)

Table 3B (*cont.*)

Proportion of sector potentially affected	Potential employment impacts	
	Quantitative	Qualitative
Medium	Significant losses but due to other factors like rationalisation in the face of overcapacity. Labour productivity improvement low in general.	Major impacts likely in finishing rather than producer areas; trend will be towards increasing levels of operator discretion and responsibility. Skills requirement likely to rise and broaden.
Medium	Some losses mainly associated with import penetration. Jobs could rise if new product range can be locally produced—likely trend is towards foreign lead however. With automated assembly large (50–100%) improvements in labour productivity.	Main skill group affected is electrical trades, e.g., substitution of wiring with solid state leads to simplification of task and reduction to numbers required. When automatic assembly appears, this will deskill further and reduce labour needs. At the same time higher skill level is required to handle the additional component features— e.g. display or programming.
Medium	Losses due to new technology are likely to be insignificant compared to those arising from the world shipping decline and strong overseas competition. Labour productivity improvements as for mechanical engineering.	Replacement of some skill groups is likely, but these are difficult to identify; the one-off production mode in this sector means that human flexibility in task performance is valuable and may not be easy to duplicate on programmable systems economically.

Table 3B (*cont.*)

Sector	Impact on products	Impact on processes
Vehicles	Major/minor (Short-term product changes include additions for economy, safety, pollution control, and driver information. Later possibilities include cheaper and simpler designs, which may make vehicles less of a luxury product.)	Major/minor (Applications in design and pre-production work are likely to be concerned with quality and range improvement. Assembly will be the major area of impact with integrated flexible manufacturing systems the ultimate goal. Moves towards this have already been made and robots are more extensively used in this industry than any other. Production control and management systems will also develop towards integrated hierarchies using distributed control and communication between plants.)
Textiles	Minor (Improvements in quality, range, differentiation, possibly cost reduction through more efficient manufacture.)	Major/minor (Industry is already used to programmable operations and high rates of innovation. Computer systems already fairly common; likely trend will be towards dedicated control of individual machines via microprocessor linked through a distributed network to an information system monitoring production control, stock levels, order processing and similar functions.)

Table 3B (*cont.*)

Proportion of sector potentially affected	Potential employment impacts	
	Quantitative	Qualitative
		In general there will be a reduction in the need for supervisory skills and an increase in the level and number on maintenance and support.
Medium	Losses likely to be less than feared and related to cutting down present high manning levels and general production rationalisation. New technology introduction, when linked to labour-saving, is highly dependent on wage rates. Thus Swedish vehicle industry is far more automated than in the UK, for example. In certain areas significant improvements (over 20%) in labour productivity (e.g. on assembly tracks. In warehousing even higher (over 400%). Some applications put the overall possibility as high as 900%. Labour saving 20–95% depending on application.	Most impact will be in the assembly areas where the pattern will be replacement of unskilled and semi-skilled. In the design and tool-room activities, much of the transition to computer-aided operation had already taken place smoothly; here there has been a change in job character but little loss of jobs. Supervisor grades are likely to diminish in requirement, whilst there is already an acute shortage of maintenance and support personnel which is likely to increase in the short term. The skills requirement here particularly is for flexibility and multi-disciplinary expertise.
Medium	Some job losses in the finishing operations —warehousing, packing and others, Bulk of job loss as a result of mechanisation has already taken place; present rates of wastage will probably be sufficient to absorb new losses. Potentially significant improvement in labour	Major change is likely to be a shift towards a higher skills requirement at the expense of traditional craft abilities. Supervision needs will fall, maintenance needs will rise. Some operator displacement may take place but bulk of movement will be away from finishing and

Table 3B (*cont.*)

Sector	Impact on products	Impact on processes
Leather and fur	Minor (Slight improvements in quality.)	Minor (Improvements in process control in tanning, degreasing, etc. Some changes in materials handling and finishing; bulk of changes likely in production control and management.
Clothing and footwear	Minor (Improvements in range, quality, etc. Possible price reduction—at least to levels competitive with imports.)	Major/minor (There is considerable scope for automation in this sector, both in the direction of labour-saving and in process sophistication. Some work has already been done on flexible manufacturing systems but the major change so far has been the automated programmable sewing machine. Other applications include laser cutting and robot spraying of shoes. Widespread diffusion has yet to occur, however.)
Electronic components	Major (Innovation rates in this sector are high because of intense competition and rapidly growing markets.)	Major (Much of the product innovation requires development of new processes with higher accuracy, reliability, etc. Since they involve working to extremely fine tolerances, automated assembly and manufacturing and also quality control is being used to an increasing extent.)

Table 3B (*cont.*)

Proportion of sector potentially affected	Potential employment impacts	
	Quantitative	Qualitative
	productivity (100–200%) Labour savings as high as 80%.	handling areas.
Low	Mimimal Small improvements in labour productivity.	Gradual shift away from craft skills as more automation possibilities emerge. Growing need for higher levels of skill, especially in maintenance areas. Supervisory requirement will fall with improved production control.
High	Job losses in this sector are mainly due to overseas import penetration and not to new technology. However the economies of microelectronics make them an attractive option especially since they permit high quality product manufacture at low unit cost. Thus job loss trend is likely to continue. Significant improvements (over 200%) in labour productivity are possible with large labour savings (>50% in some cases).	With the advent of microprocessor-controls on sewing machines etc. there has been consider-able deskilling of many semi-skilled jobs. Demand for supervision is also likely to fall with introduction of production control systems but support in terms of programming and maintenance skills will be a growing need. Higher and multiple skills needed.
Medium	Losses here due to rationalisation and product integration balanced by overall growth in the industry. Picture complicated by worldwide location decisions (+ rapid changes in these) by transnational corpora-tions.	Considerable skill shift with production moving away from a labour intensive low skill operation and towards a highly automated, knowledge intensive one. New skills required include design, programming and maintenance of highly sophisticated machinery.

Table 3B (*cont.*)

Sector	Impact on products	Impact on processes
Electronic goods	Major/minor (Goods produced for the industrial market and particularly for the military have been sophisticated for some time and developments here are likely to be along the lines of incremental improvements only. Consumer goods, by contrast, will change considerably with a number of totally new products, e.g., toys, viewdata, video etc. Conventional ones will also improve in quality and price, e.g., hi-fi, T.V.)	Major/minor (The major change here is associated with replacement of individual components by i.c.s, with a dramatic simplification of the process of manufacture. Techniques such as automated assembly and quality control become possible and as the factory moves towards high volume automated production, so the potential for applying sophisticated and highly integrated information and control systems for orders, stock, etc., becomes greater. Changes in the low volume high quality field will be incremental in nature.)
Electronic computers	Minor/major (Microelectronics has made a wide range of options possible and the flexibility and choice for the user is large. Essentially all these changes are still based on the original concept and product, though the 'mechanics' now differ widely.)	Minor/major (As for the electronics industry.)
Commercial equipment	Major/minor (Major changes in the type and capability of product as a result of redesign and extensive	Major/minor (The situation here is similar to that in the electronics goods sector, with product changes making assembly automation possible and with simplification of the manufacturing process.

Table 3B (*cont.*)

Proportion of sector potentially affected	Potential employment impacts	
	Quantitative	Qualitative
High/Very High	Significant in high volume areas. Import penetration is largely on the basis of quality and cost and this had led to job loss on a large scale —e.g., in the T.V. industry. New technology will make products more competitive but is likely to cost jobs through automation to a high level. As above, major (over 100%) improvements in labour productivity. Labour savings 50–75% in some cases.	Skill shift here will be mainly towards a deskilling of the manufacturing operation through the use of automated assembly and quality control. Some new demand for support staff can be expected but again the supervisory element is likely to decline.
Medium	Considerable growth potential through market expansion; rise in product sophistication and increased use of automated assembly tempers this however. As above, major (over 100%) improvements in labour productivity. Labour savings 50–75% in some cases.	Skill shift linked to product sophistication and increasing use of automated assembly methods. Expected rise in demand for higher grade skills, for maintenance and support staff, for designers—especially in the front line of microelectronics application. Currently these skills are in very short supply. Corresponding fall in supervision and direct operator requirement.
High/Very High	Major changes in this sector; in the first place these arise from the new technology directly but a secondary effect can be observed in those	Shifts in the direction of deskilling as a result of automation in assembly and quality control. Fall in supervisor requirement with growth of production control

Table 3B (*cont.*)

Sector	Impact on products	Impact on processes
	components substitution—e.g. cash registers. Also on other products there will be a performance improvement and new features, e.g., displays.)	Additionally there will be improvements in quality control and in production information systems.)
Materials handling	Major/minor (Improvements in the control systems in this sector are possible through local microprocessors linked to larger information networks. This has a radical effect on the flexibility and performance of materials handling and also makes them suitable for integration into total input/output systems for management control. Lack of moving parts increases reliability and their programmable nature is important in extending the range of application.)	Major/minor (Systems themselves are not likely to change but the control elements will. Since the trend here is towards high levels of sophistication it is likely that this work will be contracted out to specialist firms at least in the short term. In operation, there is great scope for expansion into automated warehousing and materials transport.)
Aerospace	Minor (Improvements in safety and performance.)	Minor (Some further changes in production and design methods, e.g., use of CAD, CNC and FMS tools.)
Precision engineering	Major/minor (Improvements in existing products e.g., through display addition or greater accuracy. New	Major (Changes in the nature of product from mechanical to electronic mean that the industry as a whole must reorient itself. Simplification of product also makes automated

Table 3B (*cont.*)

Proportion of sector potentially affected	Potential employment impacts	
	Quantitative	Qualitative
	firms which are slow to switch their products and processes. Major improvements in labour productivity (as high as 500%) generally 50% or over largely due to change in product nature. Labour savings 50–75% or more in many cases.	systems; rise in design and maintenance areas needs. In general, higher and multiple skills needed.
Medium	Potential growth in this sector may generate jobs but these are likely to be in high-skill areas only, and may also lie outside the firms manufacturing the systems. In operation considerable job loss, through use of automated warehousing. Potentially high, though difficult to assess. Labour productivity changes— anywhere from 50–500%. Labour savings as high as 80%.	Some deskilling in the area of installation. Mainly growth in the demand for high level skills, especially in software development for control systems. In operation, deskilling and reduction in supervisor needs.
Low/medium	Minimal Main changes linked to state of market. Labour productivity changes as for mechanical engineering.	Shift to higher and different skills requirement—growth in design and support functions.
High	Significant Examples include the Swiss and German watch and clock industry. Shift to the Far East where	Major shifts in skills requirement. Deskilling of assembly and checking and need for a range of totally new skills.

Table 3B (*cont.*)

Sector	Impact on products	Impact on processes
	product concepts, —e.g., digital watches have had a major impact.)	assembly and checking possible and reduces unit cost of manufacture.)
Gas, electricity and water	Minor (Improvements in safety and quality of service.)	Minor (Some improvements in processing controls; major impact is likely in the administrative data processing supporting these industries. Some changes in test and maintenance patterns through use of new techniques made possible through microelectronics.)
Construction	Minor (Improvements in tendering, materials management, etc.)	Minor (Very little impact, mostly in the production control aspects of the industry and also in administrative data processing.)
Tele-communications	Major (Makes possible the revolution in communications with more extensive networks, faster, cheaper, more reliable contact and new possibilities like viewdata.)	Major (Switch to all-electronic switching technology simplifies product manufacture, installation and maintenance.)
Office sector	Major (Major improvements in productivity and	Major (Changes towards the automated office. Presently this focuses on

Table 3B (*cont.*)

Proportion of sector potentially affected	Potential employment impacts	
	Quantitative	Qualitative
	both low cost assembly and high technology product dominate. Major changes in labour productivity resulting from product design change—of the order of 250% in many cases. Labour savings over 50%.	
Low	Minimal Little change in labour productivity.	Some skill shifts, away from production and into maintenance and support. General increase in level of skills required.
Low	Minimal Little change.	Minimal
High/very high	Significant Fundamental change in the nature of product reduces labour requirements in assembly and operation by as much as 80%. Major changes in labour productivity—up to 200% reported and potentially bigger improvement in future. Labour savings of the order 50–80% in manufacture and figures for installation and maintenance.	Deskilling through automated assembly of simpler products. Changes also in maintenance and installation skills— again in a downward direction. Some reduction in telephone operators through increases in automatic dialling options. Supervisory require-ments also likely to diminish. Growth in demand for high level skills particularly in design.
High	Significant potential and some losses so far. Impact on women	Major changes in the character of jobs, with a shift towards all-round

Table 3B (*cont.*)

Sector	Impact on products	Impact on processes
	type of service/ activity carried out here. Also growing trend to home working at 'work stations').	word processing but other developments will include electronic mail, computer filing and video links. Major impacts expected once systems become integrated.)
Insurance, banking and finance	Major/minor (Short term improvements in service quality. Longer term may see widespread application of electronic funds transfer.)	Major/minor (Technology has accelerated the trend towards automation in this sector. Since information content is around 80% potential for computer application is considerable. Likely trend towards higher levels of integration of information systems and growth of networking.)
Retailing and distribution	Major/minor (Improvements in service and quality made possible through high levels of back-up automation.)	Major/minor (Improvements in stock handling, planning and scheduling systems, etc., will move the industry to a more efficient base. In the stores themselves point-of-sale systems will become increasingly common and will be integrated into total distribution control systems.)
Postal services	Major/minor (In short term, technology will assist introduction of mechanisation to improve speed and quality of service. Longer term may see	Major/minor (Mechanisation unlikely to make major changes, only improvements —e.g. optical character recognition systems for sorting. Electronic mail will alter whole structure and concept of postal system.)

Table 3B (*cont.*)

Proportion of sector potentially affected	Potential employment impacts	
	Quantitative	Qualitative
	is particularly acute. Predictions suggest losses in this area could be as high as 50%. Major improvements in labour productivity considerable —already 150–300% reported with further potential.	secretarial duties and away from single skills like filing and typing. In some cases managers are doing their own typing and text editing; in others there is a growth in the field of 'pool' working. Likely growth in demand for service engineers to maintain office systems.
Medium/High	Significant potential though little change as yet, mainly because of extensive growth in this sector. Some forecasts put the number of jobs at risk as high as 50%. As above in office labour productivity: similar for other information-linked activities.	Likely shifts towards higher skills and away from direct service involvement. Threat to women is marked in this sector. Growth in demand for data processing and support staff, losses in clerical and typing/general office work.
Medium/high	Potential losses are significant but no evidence of changes so far. Main loss areas will be in warehousing and stock control. Improvements in labour productivity particularly in warehousing (up to 500% has been reported).	Likely shift away from labour intensive stock operations with effect on clerical and handling staff. In shops reduction of checkout staff may be compensated by the need for on-shelf labelling and other duties. Overall some deskilling and demand for sophisticated planning staff—more software skills.
Medium/high	Slight in short term sector is in decline already and mechanisation losses have largely taken place or will be accounted for by natural wastage.	Shift already taking away from direct delivery and towards more mechanised systems. Likely growth in demand for higher skills in sorting and other machine operation and

Table 3B (*cont.*)

Sector	Impact on products	Impact on processes
	widespread use of electronic mail.)	
Transportation	Minor (Improvements in service, safety, availability, etc.)	Minor (Trends towards mechanisation are already advanced and this technology only offers incremental improvements. Major changes are likely in signalling and scheduling, in passenger handling—e.g., reservations and ticketing—and to a lesser extent in operation—e.g., driverless train systems.)

Table 3B (*cont.*)

Proportion of sector potentially affected	Potential employment impacts	
	Quantitative	Qualitative
	Longer term is difficult to predict and depends on speed of adoption of electronic mail. Major increases in labour productivity coupled with labour reductions in shifting to electronic mail.	development. Growth in maintenance needs.
Medium	Some losses are possible but these will depend on the behaviour of the travelling public. If use declines, then major redundancies can be expected. Many systems are purpose built, however and thus job losses can be minimised. Improvements of the order of 50–75% in labour productivity in support staff: less in operations.	Likely shift away from operation to support functions in operation e.g. maintenance. Some passenger administration —e.g., in booking halls —but scope for redployment in other activities. Rise in level of skills required, and particular growth in planning and scheduling areas.

Table 3C Differential impact on world economies

Sector	Technologically progressive (1)	Technologically declining (2)	Centrally planned (3)	Newly industrialising (4)	Resource exporting (5)	Less industrialised developing/other (6)
Agriculture	Widespread use as farming aid in future. Potential for solving skilled labour shortages.	As 1.	As 1 and 2 —linked to strong emphasis on mechanisation.	Lack of skills and availability of cheap labour. May adopt as part of general programme of mechanisation.	Lack of suitable skills base prevents short term application. Long term may see growing use to maximise farming efficiency.	Lack of skills and capital make adoption unlikely, in the short term.
Mining and quarrying	Widespread use to improve productivity and controllability.	As 1.	As 1.	Problems of capital and skill availability.	Growing use by multinationals in resource exporting countries. High capital cost and skills represent limitations.	As 4. This sector is dominated by a small group of large firms.
Food, drink and tobacco	Widespread use to improve controllability, productivity, materials saving and quality.	As 1.	As 1.	Problems of skilled labour and capital availability.	Use unlikely in short term. Problems of skills, availability and existing level of technology.	Problems of skilled labour and capital availability. Emphasis on labour intensive techniques.
Coal and petroleum products	Very widespread use due to capital intensive	As 1.	As 1.	Problems of capital and skills availability —but	Fairly widespread use at present: long term will see	Major restrictions on adoption due to skills and capital availability

	nature of the sector and need for controllability.			some NICs—e.g. Mexico—are in a very strong position to invest in high technology plant. To some extent high automation reduces skills requirements.	problems. high levels of sophitication and use of state-of-the-art plant. Role of multinationals in transferring technology is important here.
Chemicals and allied products	Widespread use for reasons given in preceding sector.	As 1.		Growing use but problems of skills shortages. Role of multinationals important here too.	As 4.
Metals manufacture	As above—aim is to make continuous process as controllable as possible.	As above.	As 2. E.g. USSR 5 Year Plan for steel industry is very similar to that put forward by many OECD countries regarding automation strategies in the future.	Considerable investment in capital intensive plant, often state-of-the-art purchases has led to high levels of sophistication in these groups. For example, Venezuela has largest electric plant in the world, and India, S. Korea etc. have considerable capacity. Skills problems resolved to some extent by use of high levels of automation or by using imported labour. Role of multinationals important.	Major limitations on capital and skill availability—adoption by other economies of sophisticated technology is likely to widen the gap between them and this group.
Mechanical engineering	Widespread use (and large potential for expansion into) of CNC and robotic	As 1 but likely to proceed at a slower	As 2.	Early adoption by NICs like Korea has helped in their exports	Problems of adoption (skills and capital) compounded by

Table 3C (*cont.*)

Sector	Technologically progressive (1)	Technologically declining (2)	Centrally planned (3)	Newly industrialising (4)	Resource exporting (5)	Less industrialised developing/other (6)
	technology in sophisticated flexible manufacturing systems: especially relevant to small batch operations.	rate.		of this type of technology. Problems of skills shortage at the software level. Good prospects.	in machinery will raise level of CNC usage. Skills shortage in software may be a problem.	threat this technology poses to existing batch manufacture using cheap but flexible human resources.
Instrumentation	Widespread use and development of new products and new markets.	As 1 but slower rate —still strongly tied to traditional technology	As 2.	Already making inroads into developed countries on low technology products. Switch to microelectronics is limited by skills and R & D shortage: role of multinationals is again significant.	Skills shortage precludes short-term use of microelectronics but bought-in systems plus imported labour may lay the foundations for indigenous industry.	Likely exclusion on the basis of R & D and skills availability.
Electrical goods	Widespread use.	Widespread use —rate of adoption depends on market acceptance.	As 2.	Growing penetration of developed country markets —unlikely to adopt sophisticated technology in short term due to skills and R & D limits.	Potential for indigenous manufacture in long term may bring emphasis on sophisticated technology. Present R & D	Excluded due to R & D, skill and capital shortages. Assembly work threatened through use of automated techniques in

(continued)		As 1.	Long term use however.	and skills limitation.	the developed countries.
Shipbuilding	Use in mechanical engineering operations— but limited by health of sector.	As 1. —strength of this sector may be an advantage.	Growth in strength of this group in this sector offers short term option to use this technology by importing it. Long-term indigenous skills can be developed. NICs like Korea and Brazil have already been very successful in this field.	Little direct involvement with this sector, thus limited adoption to be expected.	Skill and capital shortages and world slump in shipping preclude adoption.
Vehicles	Widespread use in both product and process.	As 1 (but at a much slower rate).	Growing industry likely to benefit from multinational involvement. Skills and R & D shortages are biggest problems.	Considerable R & D and skills shortages. Role of multinationals important.	Excluded on grounds of skills and R & D and capital savings.
Textiles	Widespread use to counter Third World import penetration—offers opportunity for considerable improvements in productivity to compete again with developing country low wage rates.	Unknown.	Advantages held by control of raw material resources being eroded by sophisticated synthetics plant. Role of multi-nationals is	As 4.	Excluded on grounds given above. Represents a threat in that developing world exports may lose their comparative

Table 3C (*cont.*)

Sector	Technologically progressive (1)	Technologically declining (2)	Centrally planned (3)	Newly industrialising (4)	Resource exporting (5)	Less industrialised developing/other (6)
				important. Skills and R & D shortages may be a problem though these can be imported.		advantage in using low cost but highly flexible human resources on old multi-purpose plant.
Leather and fur	Some use to improve quality and to automate where possible. Craft basis of these industries unlikely to change.		As 1 and 2.	Little change likely—craft basis will remain.	Little change	Excluded on grounds of cost, skills and other shortages.
Clothing and footwear	Widespread use in order to combat import penetration. Use of very high levels of sophistication which also improves raw materials usage, quality, product range, etc.		Unknown.	Depends on adaptability of industries—loss of comparative advantage on labour rates can be compensated for by early adoption. Problems of skill shortages especially on software.	Shortage of skills may push industry towards capital-intensive basis—and hence faster micro-electronics adoption.	Major threat since exclusion from the technology (for the above reasons) leaves only the comparative advantage of low labour and materials costs—a position which micro-electronics will erode.
Bricks, pottery, glass,	Widespread use, position as for other capital-intensive process		As 1 and 2.	Likely purchase of capital-intensive plant will bring high levels of auto-		Excluded due to resource and

cement	industries.		mation which may alleviate some skills shortage problems. Role of multinationals significant.		capital availability.
Timber and furniture	Small changes, sector remains largely craft based. Use of machinery will involve sophisticated controls.	As 1 and 2.	Little change	Little change	Little change.
Paper, printing, publishing	Paper manufacture, use as for process industries. Printing and publishing very widespread use and changes in the industry structure e.g. rise of Viewdata.	As 1 and 2.	Limitations on the availability of suitably developed infrastructure for communications coupled to skills shortages. Long-term need to participate in world business community likely to bring about early adoption.		Exclusion due to capital, skills availability and lack of communications infrastructure. Threat in long-term is increasing isolation due to exclusion from major communications networks.
Electronics components	Widespread use and switch to automated assembly in many areas. U.S., Japan likely to dominate but others carrying out R & D to develop their own.	As 1 and 2.	Capital and R & D intensive nature of this industry likely to exclude direct manufacture. Joint ventures or multinationals may be very significant, however. Some countries, e.g. India, are exceptions with considerable potential.		Excluded due to capital, skill and R & D resource shortage.
Electronic goods	Widespread use and growth of new markets for new 'intelligent' products. Use of automated assembly techniques.	As 1 and 2.	Established tradition of consumer goods manufacture likely to develop considerably. Wide-	Major potential for establishment for capital-intensive electronics based industry. Wide-	Major threat to employment in assembly through relocation and use of automated

Table 3C (*cont.*)

Sector	Technologically progressive (1)	Technologically declining (2)	Centrally planned (3)	Newly industrialising (4)	Resource exporting (5)	Less industrialised developing/other (6)
				spread application likely but skill shortage major problem.	spread application likely but skilled shortage major problem.	assembly. Skills, capital and R & D resource limitations preclude indigenous use.
Electronic computers	Widespread use and growth of new markets for new 'intelligent' products. Use of automated assembly techniques.		As 1 and 2.	Little direct manufacture possible due to R & D shortage. Considerable potential for multinational or joint venture operations. Exceptions are countries like Brazil with IT strategies based on indigenous computer industry.		Major threat to employment in assembly through relocation and use of automated assembly. Skills, capital and R & D resource limitations preclude indigenous use.
Commercial equipment	Widespread use and development of new materials for new products. Use of automated assembly increasing.		As 1 and 2.	Possibilities of capital intensive and highly automated plant to assemble equipment in this growing market. Skills and R & D shortage suggests multinational involvement likely in short-term.		Excluded on resource availability grounds and lack of experience in this field. Any assembly operations also likely to be relocated shortly.

Materials handling	Widespread use with considerable sophistication and flexibility—e.g. robot warehousing.	As 1 and 2.		As above.
Precision engineering	Widespread use and new product development e.g. watches. Use of automated assembly and deskilling as a consequence.	As 1 and 2.	Considerable opportunities for assembly as with digital watches. Skill and R & D shortages make multinational involvement most likely short-term option.	As above.
Aerospace industries	Widespread use in both product and process.	As 1 and 2.	Potential to make use of CNC experience to produce high quality work: considerable opportunity but skills and R & D shortage problems.	Excluded—lack of capital, skills, R & D.
Gas, electricity, water	Widespread use.	As 1 and 2.	As systems are installed, likely to use advanced equipment.	Unlikely—many services still poorly provided.
Construction	Low level of usage (except in planning, project control etc.)			
Telecommunications	Widespread use—an essential requirement for future society is cheap and flexible communications systems.	As 1 and 2.	Widespread use—evidence suggests considerable investment in modern systems. It will be essential for future trade to have a developed communications infrastructure—and telecommunications systems form the basis of this. R & D and skill costs means that these will be supplied from developed countries.	Excluded due to capital costs—this is significant because it reflects the Third world's long-term ability to participate on an equal footing.
Office sector	Widespread use, with longer-term shift out of offices and into home 'work-stations'. Major impacts on	As 1 and 2.	Depends on growth of office sector: in short term may well be introduced to cope with shortages	Excluded – costs – skills

Table 3C (*cont.*)

Sector	Technologically progressive (1)	Technologically declining (2)	Centrally planned (3)	Newly industrialising (4)	Resource exporting (5)	Less industrialised developing/other (6)
	employment expected.			of office skills. Long-term significant potential application with the use of industry.		
Banking, insurance, finance	As above in office sectors. Also use of EFT and other systems; likely rise in technological sophistication will be considerable.		Although banking and finance structure is different from capitalist economies, expect a similar pattern —with possible increased de-centralisation— in the use of technology.	Electronic transfer of money and information likely to be a central feature of communications infrastructure mentioned earlier. Initially likely to be introduced by multinational banks, but later indigenous use likely.		Excluded – costs – skills.
Retailing and distribution	Widespread use, especially in stockrooms and warehousing.		As 1 and 2.	Depends on development of consumer-based society —long-term use expected.		Unlikely for some time to come: depends (as 4 and 5) on retailing infrastructure.
Postal services	Widespread, especially in business mail.		As 1 and 2.	Long-term likely involvement as this is one more element of the international communications infrastructure. Likely to involve		Excluded on grounds of costs and skills resources.

The game so far   135

Transporta-tion	Widespread, especially in support functions. Long term may permit highly efficient, highly integrated systems.	As 1 and 2.	multinationals to provide skills and systems in the short-term. Widespread use can be expected in long term—as transport systems are developed, so it is likely that sophisticated technology will be employed. Short-term purchase will be from developed world but long-term possibilities for direct use exist—depends on skill availability.	As above.

Probable, plausible and possible alternatives: weighing the odds

The trend that emerges from the empirical review in Chapter 3 is by no means certain. As we now consider from both an empirical and theoretical point of view, it is reasonable to conceive of a number of distinctive technological 'routes'. Thus, although we believe that the most *probable* path for technological development implies that the technology gap between rich and poor countries will widen, it is also quite *plausible* that a number of developing economies will rapidly catch up, using technologies rather similar to those envisaged for the industrial economies and indeed overtake ailing industrial economies. Both these routes are consistent with present trends (although they imply contrasting behaviour by various actors, especially international firms). But our earlier discussion also suggested that a third kind of technology is *possible*, which would integrate the new information technology with the indigenous and existing technology of the less industrialised countries in a form more suited to their social and economic needs.

We shall explore each of these alternatives. To do this we must assess the changes in comparative advantage between countries as a result of possibilities for technical change at a macro-economic level, and make generalisations about sector-wide and economy-wide processes. In this chapter we also explain the way we transform the data of our empirical study into a form directly applicable to our macro-economic model. As with all generalisations there are a number of problems and limitations, and we shall first consider these in some detail.

Problems with generalisations

There is considerable controversy between economists and others who have studied the question of whether it is useful to attempt to calculate the overall impact of new technologies. To take one example (which we shall refer to again below), Mandeville (*et al.* 1980) describes the attempt by Dixon (*et al.* 1979) to estimate the impact of alternative technology policies on the Australian economy as 'not just worthless, but actually negative'. Another commentator (McGuinness, 1979a) described the same work as 'certainly the most important single contribution to the subject yet to have been published in Australia'. Some exceedingly competent economic modellers believe unambiguous analysis to be 'frankly, beyond the current state of knowledge' (Ayres and Miller, 1983), while others (such as Leontief and Duchin, 1985) have carried out very detailed dynamic input–output calculations for the United States.

Arguments such as these take place at several levels. First, many authors believe that macro-economic models as such, have little or nothing to contribute to our understanding of economic change and its consequences, Schumacher (1973) for example, who has been identified with the concept of 'intermediate' technology was rather emphatic on the subject of people and macro-economic models:

> If it [economic thinking] cannot get beyond its vast abstractions, the national income, the rate of growth, capital/output ratio, input–output analysis, labour mobility, capital accumulation; if it cannot go beyond all this and make contact with the human realities of poverty, frustration, alienation, despair, breakdown, crime, escapism, stress, congestion, ugliness, and spiritual death, then let us scrap economics and start afresh.

Second, many authors do not believe that it makes sense to generalise from the data on choice or impact of new production techniques in particular industries or firms, to the sector or economy-wide level. This is the main thrust of Mandeville's criticisms cited above. This particular debate has a long history, but during the 1970s it was very relevant to an evaluation of so-called 'appropriate technologies' (more rather than less labour intensive technologies for developing countries).

We should learn from the debate surrounding 'appropriate technologies' and the question of capital labour substitution possibilities. A decade or so of debate on the subject led to the publication of a reasonably unifying text (Stewart and James, 1983). But, by the time this empirical and theoretical debate was clarified, at least to the apparent satisfaction of many empirical economists in the field, the topic had become *passé*. Economic planners were no longer concerned with the usefulness of appropriate technology, but were preoccupied increasingly with their national debt problems and the possible impact of the new revolutionary technologies.

With respect to information technology, some authors concerned with empirical studies (for example Rada, 1983) appear not to be against the idea of a macro-economic evaluation, in principle, but believe that the time is 'not yet ready' for a macro-economic evaluation because insufficient empirical data is so far available. Kaplinsky (1983) on the other hand, suggests caution is required in attempting to assess the impact of automation (on overall employment). Yet, he says 'to veer in the other direction and to argue that no attempt can, or should, be made to discuss these crucial issues, is perhaps even more misguided'. In reviewing the considerations needed to make an estimate of the possible impact of new technology (on overall employment) Kaplinsky lists several difficulties with such an evaluation, which we reformulate here.

First, the question must be asked as to what extent automation technology will displace labour in particular sectors (Rada's concern is that at an early stage this is not clear). Even if it is agreed that new technology used in existing processes will displace labour, does the technology have potential for creating new products and processes and hence new employment? *Second*, will this involve changes in patterns of consumption and life styles (for example, a shift to more labour intensive service oriented society, albeit with manufactures produced in fully automated factories)? *Third*, new technology may cut costs and hence cheapen commodities, leading to additional demand—will the consequent increase in output more than compensate for the job loss per unit of output? *Fourth*, how will international trade affect the equation—will international competition destroy jobs or will new technologies increase global sales and hence stimulate further increased production?

Most studies only consider the first question. In the many studies reviewed by Braun and Senker (1981), for example, which attempt to measure the impact of new technologies on the manufacturing industries in the various localities in the United Kingdom, the demand for products from the local region is typically assumed to be unchanged. The studies do not even take account, for example, of the fact that with less labour employed, there might be less demand for the product in the local area itself. Despite this, many authors (especially Ernst, 1983 and Freeman, 1984) would agree that information technology is a truly global phenomenon.

Direct and indirect contributions to employment

The limitations (or approximations) of the various studies can be clarified by a more formal exposition. Following Dell'Mour (1982) we can calculate the total employment from the equation:

$$w = QRy,$$

where w is the demand for labour, Q the productivity (labour/output ratio), R the interaction with other sectors (technically, the 'Leontief inverse') and y is the demand for products. If changes are given by $\mathbf{D}$ and new values characterised by $''$ the partial studies simply take the new level of employment to be given by:

$$w'' = w + \mathbf{D}QRy.$$

Formally this says that the *only* change to be taken into account is the change in labour inputs to production and that these are additive. While this might be reasonable for individual firms in some circumstances, when we want to examine the total experience of a national economy, especially at a time when many industries and economies are undergoing unusually rapid change, such an approach is hardly likely to be sufficient.

Studies of the national impact on employment such as those of Dell'Mour (1982) attempt to go beyond this and attempt to take account of indirect demand changes as well as effects arising directly from changes in productivity. In this case the new level of employment is given by:

$$w'' = Q''R''y''$$

$$= w + \mathbf{D}QRy + Q\mathbf{D}Ry + QR\mathbf{D}y$$

$$+ \text{ second and higher order effects.}$$

The first new term again represents the 'productivity effect'—the changes in employment due to changes in the sectors in which new technology is introduced. The second term measures the interaction effect, especially 'downstream' changes in employment in other sectors brought about because of changes in the output from the changing sectors. The third term describes shifts in final demand from households etc. (i.e. the income effect referred to by Kaplinsky which comes from the changed employment).

Studies such as those described in Chapter 3 estimate the impact of new technologies on employment in particular firms, processes or industries. These studies usually make some rigid assumptions about the total demand for the product. From such data and other assumptions, some economy wide impacts can be estimated. For example, in the Dell'Mour study for Austria the assumptions about GDP determine, through an input–output matrix, the total direct and indirect demand for goods from each sector. Consequently, the study measured only the number of workers displaced but did not take account, either of the possibility that with new technology, products might become more competitive in terms of price or quality and leading to a greater market share, or that other manufacturers in other parts of the world might also adopt the technology so negating the new competitive advantage. In the very detailed Leontief *et al.* (1984) study of the effect of 'automation' on employment in the United States some eighty-nine sectors and fifty-three categories were considered but total demand was simply assumed to grow steadily— a plausible and even conservative approach but also one that somewhat assumes away the problem given the present economic crisis.

So far most macro-economic evaluation of the new technology has been at the national level. The Dixit study above looked at the contrast between a 'Luddite scenario' for Australia (when new technology change does not take place) versus an 'innovative scenario' in which more rapid technical change occurs. The study by Dell'Mour (1982) looked at the impact of information technology on unemployment in Austria, again exploring a number of scenarios. Here scenarios were constructed by assuming different rates of diffusion for the new technology (as well as other assumptions about the length of the working week and overall rate of economic growth). The OECD too have used a macro-economic model to explore the employment effects of new technology on several industrialised countries (OECD, 1982).

All studies have their strengths and weaknesses. Principally, in our opinion, while the national models all explicitly represent a large number of sectors, they do not take account of international effects: either the impact of new technologies in other countries competing with the new technology in the local economy, or changes in the local economy affecting the rest of the world and so affecting the economic environment for the local economy. Just as the micro-economic studies of individual firms or sectors assume that the outside world is not affected by their actions, will not take compensating action or simply does not change, so the national macro-economic studies assume the outside world is fixed, or at best, passive in its response to local change.

Rather than head into greater detail we examine additional first and higher order effects, particularly those arising from the behaviour of international markets. Thus, to the expression given above we add terms such as $DQIy$ and higher order terms to symbolically represent the impact of changing technology on the international economy, I; and terms such as $QDIy$ to represent the impact of the responding international economy on demand and hence on employment; and a second set of terms to take into account shifts in factor prices resulting from changes in their demand and supply. If new technology is really expected to have a dramatic impact on employment, then it must also be expected to affect wage levels. Indeed it will be argued that the introduction of the technology represents in part an effort to shift income distribution between capital and labour, as much as to increase overall competitivness. And this, in turn, implies shifts in relative prices. Hence both factor and commodity price shifts must be included. We consider these terms later.

Ultimately, it is a matter of opinion whether one considers the attempt to evaluate the global economy wide impact of new technology through generalisation of results from micro-economic studies into macro-economic models, is valid. Our reasons for believing the attempt to be useful are briefly stated: first, micro-economic studies by industry often fail to account for shifts in demand, factor prices, etc. They estimate impacts assuming all else is unchanged; nor do they take account of indirect and multiplier effects. Second, the new industrial revolution is clearly already affecting most sectors in the industrial countries and will affect the whole world either directly or indirectly. Studies which look only at a single economy often do not take this into account. Third, although generalisations are dangerous and there are many intersectoral and international differences it is necessary to take broad aggregations in order to establish the 'stylised facts' which ultimately form the basis of theory and of economic policy (see Cole and Nunez-Barigga, 1981).

Gathering empirical data

We should discuss further the judgemental nature of our parameter estimates. We are generalising about the potential of information technology from a sample of firms and activities and diverse studies to a rather highly aggregated category. As the very extensive survey by Vitelli (1980) demonstrated, the choice of definitions and measures used in choice of technique studies by different authors, varies considerably. In our study this matter is compounded by the fact that data is collected from on-site visits and interviews with a great variety of people, so a proper comparison between estimates is bound to be suspect.

When we come later to look at the comparative advantage gained by sectors and economies through the introduction of the technology, it is the total relative factor cost saving which is of paramount importance. The most important feature for us to extract from these data is the 'pattern' of potential change, *first*, between factors for a given activity; *second* between sectors for a given economy; and *third*, for activities between economies, and finally to ensure that changes have been judged consistently across all these.

Our sampling procedure has been described in detail in Chapter 3, but in general it follows that used by other authors in this area. The study of Dell'Mour (1982), for example, estimates shifts in factor use from questionnaires sent to some 200 firms, which were further refined 'in accordance with international figures, especially those derived by trade union institutes'. These authors acknowledge that their estimates are 'very rough' but argue that no other figures were available at that stage. It is possible but not certain that their data would reflect the bias of trade unions in protecting jobs. The study by Dixon *et al.* (1979) selected some twenty-five industries for detailed study (accounting for some 56 per cent of the Austrialian GDP in 1971-2). For all industries, particular types of coefficient were investigated by chosen 'experts' for all industries which, after an initial appraisal, were submitted to a range of industrial, academic and government experts. As with our own study, the authors (see Chapman, 1980) sought the internally consistent set of forecasts of technical change necessary for the general equilibrium analysis to be performed. Compared with these recent studies (such as Dell'Mour and Dixon *et al.*) we rely ultimately more on our own judgement of likely changes, but given the difficulties noted above in interpreting multitudinous data from diverse sources, this seems a proper procedure to use in order to achieve a consistent (if uniformly biased) evaluation.

The use of macro-economic models to evaluate a composite of micro-economic changes is therefore a controversial procedure. The key to our model approach which we describe in Chapter 5 is to ensure that both the categories we adopt in the model and the changes we wish to portray, have a clear and distinctive structure. Thus, we ensure first that the model aggregations give a very sharp contrast in production, technology and consumption. And, second, that there are clear differences in the potential impact of new technologies. If we achieve this, then modest errors or changes in the base year parameters describing technology or economic behaviour should not significantly affect the behaviour characteristics of our model. Nor should modest errors or changes to the estimated shifts in the new technology parameters affect the results of our model experiments.

Trends and alternatives

Rada (1983) insists that

> although it is not possible to generalise from the experience of one sector, one should bear in mind that what is important about electronics is not just changes in the industry itself, but the fact that it is becoming a *convergence* industry. It is indispensable for a growing number of sectors' activities and services, in which the content and format of information flows are changing. The entire industrial and

service structure is thus moving toward a higher technological profile. These in turn will accelerate the process of change.

Although Rada emphasises the increased information content of the new technology, at least as much as the improved productivity performance (which we are primarily dealing with), his emphasis on the ubiquitous nature of the technology is itself critical. As we note in our introduction, improved productivity aspects of the new technologies follow from its informational characteristics.

Although Rada is cautious about making premature evaluation of the new technology, he suggests that in the context of the present slow down in world economic growth and the globalisation of economic competition 'some general features of the current technological development can be tentatively forseen'. He lists the importance of science, the increasing dependence of production on capital and the changing nature of information. With respect to changes in productivity, Rada asserts that the diffusion of technology is dependent on factor saving characteristics whether labour, capital, materials, time, or a combination of all of these. But he says, the labour saving effect is of particular importance, and that there is a consensus that while there is labour saving in unskilled and semi-skilled labour in some manufacturing activities, at this stage in the evolution of the technology, there is an increased demand for skilled labour in design, R & D and knowledge-intensive activities.

On the basis of earlier studies, and those noted here, we might begin to speculate on alternative hypotheses about the new technology to be explored with our model. We leave aside for the moment precisely what form such technical change would take, and look first at the question of the technological 'gap' between different types in the world system.

Rada (1983) suggests that despite the complexity of the interaction between technology and the international division of labour, which makes it difficult to generalise about trends, a 'model' of the international division of labour has evolved. The model assumes that developing countries will develop and industrialise through the transfer of production of relatively simpler and labour intensive products to them, while advanced industrial countries will move 'up-market' through more knowledge-intensive production. Thus, the developing countries will tend to lag behind the industrial countries, with a technology 'gap' remaining between them. As Rada notes, this 'model' is itself a product of competing theories based on different points of view, including the product cycle theory and the comparative advantage theory (based on relative endowments and factor intensity).

Several studies, although rejecting generalisation, nevertheless do reinforce the idea that at least for some time to come, the developing countries are likely to be disadvantaged by the new technology, and that the technology gap is likely to remain or even increase. Boon (1982) for example, concludes that automation induced by micro-electronic technological change will ensure that a few Northern economies will have a lead in the new technology, and so will have a comparative advantage over the rest of the world for 'some time to come'. This, he says, will push the rest of the North and even more the South into a dependency relation. Boon's distinction between different types of industrial countries is supported, for example, by Pavitt (1981) who divides industrial economies into first and second divisions, while other authors (for example, Clarke and Cable, 1983), emphasise differences among the developing economies. With respect to the electronics industry (in Asia) they conclude that early entrants into the industry (i.e. the NICs) have been able to develop a relatively independent industry while remaining pessimistic that the newcomers (i.e. the less industrialised countries) are, by contrast, heavily dependent upon multi-national investment and technology.

Several authors suggest that introduction of the new technology will erode the comparative advantage of developing countries in some traditional 'mature' industries. In the garments industry, for example, Hoffman and Rush (1983) suggest that with the introduction of automated technology, comparative advantage might revert to the developed countries. They argue that the crucial variable in this process is the rate at which new applications are developed and the speed with which they diffuse in advanced industrial countries. Noting that across sub-sectors, change will be irregular and discontinuous but, nevertheless, an inexorable process that is already signposted by current developments. Again, like Clarke and Cable, they believe that this will cause most problems for those 'newcomers' to the industry. (Thus industries which might have been expected to 'trickle-down' to the developing countries, according to the model indicated by Rada (see pp. 142–3), would instead revert to the advanced industrial countries.) Kaplinsky (1983) asks, therefore, whether the new technology is not primarily a 'First World technology'. He prophesises that the coming decades are likely to see the emergence of 'full intersphere automation, leading to a factory of the future', and that only firms in developing economies are conscious of what this entails.

One cautionary point needs to be made, and this is that most studies referred to above examine technological trends in the manufacturing sector. Fewer studies look at trends in agriculture, other industry and services, especially with respect to developing economies. Gershuny and Miles (1983), Barron and Curnow (1979), however, have examined the implication for the service industries in the industrial countries, and conclude that job displacement is unlikely to be compensated for by an expansion of activity in the service sector. Despite this, it is in the service sector, especially, that one might expect to see major innovations through the new technology. It is especially here that the *informational* aspects of the micro-electronics revolution become central to its comprehension.

From a review of the evidence, Kaplinsky (1983) suggests four competing lines of argument about the impact of new technology on the changing pattern of comparative advantage, which we will draw on in part for our analysis. The first three suggest respectively that the new technology will have a negative, positive and negligible impact on the comparative advantage of developing countries. Several of the empirical studies referred to above support this view that new technology could have a negative impact, including those of Boon, Hoffman and Rush, Rada, and Clarke and Cable. The use of the new technology provides significant benefits to innovating firms, located mainly in the industrial countries, and so undermines the comparative advantage of developing countries even with use of their cheap labour in conjunction with the new technology.

The second hypothesis of Kaplinsky is that new technology will have a positive impact on the comparative advantage of developing countries. There is less evidence to support this idea, but the work of Jacobsson (1983) for machine tools, and others, suggests it to be the case in the short run for a number of sectors. Kaplinsky argues that to assume that there will be negligible impact requires that information technology is simply another of a long series of incremental technologies, which essentially leaves the macro-world economy unchanged. The final view is that the impact will vary between developing countries since they are not homogenous. Some newly industrialising countries have established a level of technological 'sophistication' which sets them apart from most other developing economies. The studies of Clarke and Cable, Rada, Hoffman and Rush, and Jacobsson all imply this. And, as noted earlier, Pavitt (1980) and Boon (1982) both argue that divisions in the ability to apply the new technology are evident among the industrial countries also.

For our own empirical evaluation of the available data, we subdivided the industrial economies and the developing economies each into three groups according to their standing in the hierarchy of technological potential, suggested by the above and other studies (see also Cole and Miles, 1984). The data we presented also showed considerable differences in some areas in the ability of the least developed economies to implement

the new technologies in the medium term compared to the newly industrialised economies, but much less contrast between different groups of
industrial economies (including the centrally planned group).

Probable, plausible and possible routes

The empirical evidence we have presented supports the hypothesis that
most 'probable' technological routes will involve a widening technology
gap between the high and low income economies, at least for some time
to come, and is the leading contender for a 'model' of the impact of new
technologies. Thus, certainly we must explore the implications of this
possibility in some detail. This possibility obviously is contingent on the
industrial nations continuing to innovate new products, and also to introduce new processes domestically at a rate at least as fast as that with which
they are transferred to the newly industrialised and developing economies.
It also assumes that less developed countries will not innovate significantly
themselves.

However, the long-wave theory discussed in Chapter 5 suggests that the
pace at which product innovations appear, and the rate at which process
innovations can increase productivity, will decline, so the incentive to push
existing and new technologies to low cost production areas will again be
a dominant consideration. While we concur with Kaplinsky that some
systematic changes (such as 'just on time' techniques) may require the
infrastructure and managerial expertise of the industrial economies and so
give comparative advantage through savings in inventory costs, other
capital saving gains (such as increasing productivity through increased
shifts) are equally feasible in developing countries, and, an international
firm possessing the technology and management skills is equally likely
to locate there. Consequently, while it may be true that in the medium
term some production of mature products will return to the more industrialised countries, in the longer term (beyond 1990) the comparative
advantage could well again pass to the middle or low income economies.
But, since these economies already have very high underemployment, and
since such new technologies are likely to be especially labour saving, this
'plausible' route may do little to solve the employment and social problems of those countries. Certainly this is an issue we must explore with
our model.

Both these routes represent acceptable hypotheses on the basis of
available empirical data, but are likely to have qualitatively different
implications. Less plausible but nevertheless possible, is that micro-
processor devices would be used to create a radically new technology

more directly relevant to the economic and social needs of, especially, the least industrialised low income economies. This new technology can take many forms. As Wad (1984) explains 'the main argument is that micro-electronics offers developing countries a low cost, easy to use technology that is extremely flexible and amenable to small scale applications . . . which if properly exploited will enable these countries to move out of their dependent states and become truly self-reliant.' Bhalla *et al.* (1984) and von Weizsäcker *et al.* (1984) have attempted to clarify this route and provide examples. Above all, they argue the need to integrate 'appropriate' and 'new' technologies. As Bhalla argues, when traditional occupations are swept away by new technology, there is often considerable social loss which does not enter into the calculations of the new enterprise. The value of local knowledge, insights, skills and managerial abilities, as well as physical facilities are rendered wholly obsolete or redundant. He argues for 'technological blending' as follows: 'if traditional production can be upgraded by a marriage with newly emerging technologies, while still retaining much of the substance and form of the older methods, gains in efficiency and competitiveness can be achieved while preserving existing human and physical resources.'

Such an approach is consistent with proposals made by Herrera (1973) that the correct approach towards technology in developing countries is the interpretation of the 'traditional' and 'scientific' approach. Bartsch (1977), for example, has stressed the importance when considering new (agricultural) technologies for developing countries, to distinguish between 'mechanical' inputs and 'science' inputs. An increased level of mechanisation through robotisation is much less important in a labour surplus economy, than the application of extended scientific knowhow based on the use of information technologies. Kaplinsky (1982) indicates the need for 'appropriate' technologies such as irrigation control systems, meteorological forecasting of micro-climates, and rural healthcare systems. We might add here crop scheduling and fertilizer application. While the studies of Bhalla *et al.* (1984) and von Weizsäcker (1984) offer many such examples as yet there is rather little empirical evidence upon which to base a priori estimates about factor inputs and the like. Much more empirical research is needed in this direction.

The problems of innovating such technologies are judged to be less technical than institutional. As Wad (1984) emphasises 'Underdevelopment is not so much a technical problem to be solved by technical means, it is rather the result of complex political, economic and social factors that in turn influence technical conditions.' He cites the green revolution as an example of technology which was supposed to be cheap and easy to use, but which has often been associated with increased inequities in rural areas and displacement of marginal farmers. Obviously then, we must distinguish technical possibilities from the institutional constraints.

Even if we consider this third 'possible' technological route to be the least likely, we can, nevertheless, speculate about it, and use our model to estimate the magnitude of technological change needed to make this route a viable enterprise. Thus, instead of using empirical data to provide inputs to the global economic model, we use the model to provide estimates of needed changes and then consider whether such change is inconsistent with what we believe to be the possibilities for the new technologies.

The three kinds of technical change which we consider are shown schematically in Figure 4.1. The 'probable' technical change route shows an increasing technological gap emerging between the industrial and less developed countries. The 'plausible' technical change shows a catching up by the less developed economies, but using technologies similar to those of the industrial economies. Finally, the 'possible' technical change hypothesises a variant in which a contrasting style of technological development takes place in developing countries.

Empirical inputs for the model

We return now to the empirical evidence presented in Chapter 3 and process that data into a form compatible with our general equilibrium model. Here we describe principally the processing of data for the 'probable' technology route. We adopt a similar approach for dealing with the 'plausible' technology route. But for our possible technology route we reverse the procedure. Rather than examine the impact of an assumed technology, we instead shall ask the question 'What technology is required in order that specific social and economic objectives are achieved?'

In Chapter 3 data collected from many economies and countries were combined first into some 28 production sectors, and then subsequently into eight sectors. The detailed sectors corresponded to the conventional two- and three-digit classifications. The second subdivided these sectors into categories based on how sophisticated the activity was deemed to be. 'Industry' was grouped into the basic, intermediate and advanced categories shown in Table 4.1. Thus, basic industry comprises activities such as food processing, textiles and footwear; intermediate industry includes machinery, metal and plastic products; and advanced industry includes drugs, medicines, office equipment and computers. The categorisation is useful for two reasons. First, while basic production takes

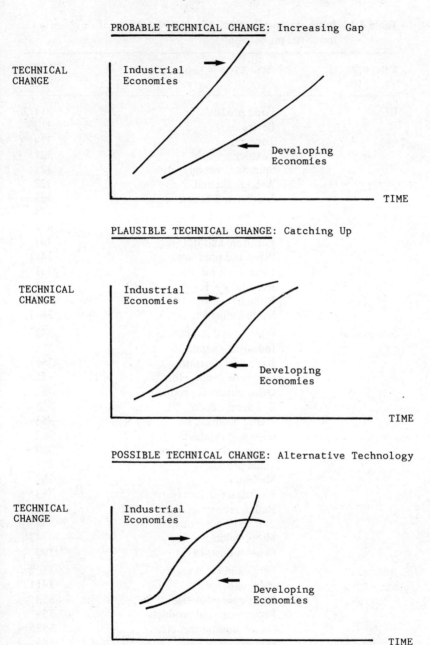

Figure 4.1 Alternative technology routes.

Table 4.1   Basic, intermediate and advanced categories of industrial production

Category	Activity	ISIC code
Basic	Food products	311/2
	Beverages	313
	Tobacco	314
	Textiles	321
	Spinning, weaving, etc.	3211
	Wearing apparel	322
	Leather and products	323
	Footwear	324
	Wood products	331
	Furniture and fixtures	332
	Paper and products	341
	Pottery, china, etc.	361
	Iron and steel	371
	Non-ferrous metal	372
	Shipbuilding and repair	3841
Intermediate	Printing and publishing	342
	Industrial chemicals	351
	Basic excl. fertilisers	3511
	Synthetic resins, etc.	3513
	Other chemical products	352
	Rubber products	355
	Plastic products nec	356
	Glass and products	362
	Non-metal products nec	369
	Metal products	381
	Machinery nec	382
	Electrical machinery	383
	Radio, television, etc.	3832
	Transport equipment	384
	Motor vehicles	3843
	Other industries	390
Advanced	Drugs and medicine	3522
	Pulp, paper, etc.	3411
	Petroleum refineries	353
	Petroleum, coal products	354
	Office, computing, etc.	3825
	Professional goods	385

nec = not elsewhere classified.

place in all types of economy, the most advanced activities are expected
to be found predominantly in the most industrialised economies. Second,
according to our empirical data the basic industries appear to be most
easily adapted to micro-processor related production techniques. Service
sector activities have been similarly divided into basic services and advanced
activities, the latter comprising trade and finance. Agriculture, extraction,
and utilities are not subdivided.

Table 4.2 shows the composition of these activities in each of the six
kinds of economy identified in Chapter 3. The proportions here are estimated on the basis of data for sample countries given in the *Year Book of
National Account Statistics* (UN 1975–77), and the World Bank Tables for
c. 1975. The table shows that in the advanced industrial economies,
advanced industry forms around 10 per cent of all extraction, industry and
utilities combined, but only about 2 per cent in the developing economies.
By contrast, basic industry forms some 44 per cent of this combined
industry sector in the least industrialised economies, but only 11 per
cent in the most advanced economies. Generally, the table supports the
contention that advanced activities are to be found in the more industrialised countries, while basic activities dominate in the least industrialised
economies.

The impact of information technology by detailed sectors for the six
economy types was shown in Chapter 3 Table 3.2. Table 4.3 summarises
these data for the eight sectors identified above. For each activity the

Table 4.2 Composition of production by economic group and sector

	Group 1	Group 2	Group 3	Group 4	Group 5	Group 6
Agriculture	100	100	100	100	100	100
Extraction	5.1	3.6	3.0	2.5	72.3	16.8
Basic industry	10.9	14.5	29.0	37.9	13.0	44.0
Intermediate industry	66.9	65.9	55.0	49.5	12.2	34.9
Advanced industry	9.6	5.9	4.0	2.2	0.4	2.3
Utilities	7.5	10.0	9.0	7.9	2.0	2.0
Basic services	54	57	59	62	65	68
Advanced services	46	43	41	38	35	32

Source: United Nations Yearbook of Industrial Production.

Table 4.3 Impact of probable micro-processor related techniques on factor productivity in various types of economy

	Group 1	Group 2	Group 3	Group 4	Group 5	Group 6
Agriculture						
Systemic	−LL	−LL	−LL	−VL	−VL	−N
Skilled	+VL	+VL	+NL	+NL	+NL	+N
Unskilled	−LL	−LL	−LL	−NL	−NL	−N
Capital	+NL	+NL	+NL	+NL	+NL	+N
Extraction						
Systemic	−LM	−LM	−LM	−LM	−LM	−LM
Skilled	+VL	+VL	+NL	+NL	+VL	+NL
Unskilled	−VL	−VL	−NL	−NL	−LL	−NL
Capital	+NL	+NL	+NL	+NL	+VL	+NL
Basic industry						
Systemic	−L	−L	−L	−LL	−LL	−LL
Skilled	+LL	+LL	+LL	+VL	+VL	+VL
Unskilled	−MH	−MH	−MH	−M	−M	−LM
Capital	+VL	+VL	+VL	+VL	+VL	+VL
Intermediate industry						
Systemic	−M	−M	−M	−L	−L	−L
Skilled	+VL	+VL	+VL	+VL	+NL	+N
Unskilled	−LM	−LM	−L	−LL	−NL	−N
Capital	+LL	+LL	+VL	+VL	+NL	+N
Advanced industry						
Systemic	−LL	−LL	−LL	−VL	−VL	−N
Skilled	+VL	+VL	+VL	+NL	+NL	+N
Unskilled	−VL	−VL	−VL	−NL	−NL	−N
Capital	+NL	+NL	+NL	+NL	+NL	+N
Utilities						
Systemic	−LL	−LL	−LL	−LL	−LL	−VL
Skilled	+VL	+VL	+VL	+VL	+VL	+VL
Unskilled	−VL	−VL	−VL	−L	−L	−VL
Capital	+NL	+NL	+NL	+LL	+LL	+NL
Basic services						
Systemic	−L	−L	−L	−LL	−LL	−N
Skilled	−NL	−NL	−NL	−NL	−NL	−N

	Group 1	Group 2	Group 3	Group 4	Group 5	Group 6
Unskilled	−NL	−NL	−NL	−NL	−NL	−N
Capital	+NL	+NL	+N	+NL	+NL	+N
Advanced services						
Systemic	−M	−M	−M	−LM	−LM	−L
Skilled	−LL	−VL	−VL	−VL	−NL	−NL
Unskilled	−LM	−LM	−L	−L	−L	−NL
Capital	+LM	+LM	+L	+L	+L	+NL

Key to scale (percentage change)

N	NL	VL	LL	L	LM	M	MH	H	HH	VH
0	0.5	2.0	4.5	8.0	12.5	18.0	24.5	32.0	40.5	50.0

table shows the expected change in the amount of skilled labour, unskilled labour and capital. The table also shows the expected change from 'systemic effects'. Following the discussion in Chapter 3 we distinguish changes in factor productivity which arise from introducing the new technology into more or less the present organisational structure of production, from those changes which arise if new systems of production emerge. (The consideration here typically is that initially a new piece of equipment may save unskilled labour costs at a cost of increased capital and skilled labour but subsequently capital savings will be achieved through the greater reliability, reduced 'down' time and increase in the number of shifts operated.) The entries in the table reflect judgements about changes in factor use (per unit output), for example, +VL indicates that the expected increase in factor intensity (i.e. a *decrease* in productivity) is 'very low' while −MH indicates that a 'medium to high' saving (i.e. an increase in productivity) is expected. Systemic effects are primarily expected to be capital saving and to take rather longer to implement than the earlier labour saving change. Consequently in the experiments with the model in later chapters we shall explore the two effects sequentially in order to judge their relative importance. As already noted we should expect differences to arise in both international trade and economic growth.

Referring to our discussion of the likely success of different economies in implementing the new technology, we see that for most sectors the estimated impact on factor inputs varies systematically as we move from the most industrialised to the least industrialised economies. This seems to support the first technology route we have hypothesised (following Kaplinsky and others). In basic industry, for example, unskilled labour saving is considerably greater in the industrial economies than the developing economies, but the capital requirements are correspondingly higher. From this data alone, we cannot say what the total factor *cost* savings are—that depends on individual factor prices (wages, interest rates) in each economy—a small saving on an expensive factor may be more significant than a large saving on an inexpensive factor. However, we can see that the fractional changes implied in most sectors are higher in the industrial economies. Nor does the data tell us anything about the overall impact, since that depends on how changes in comparative advantage affect overall shifts in production structures and incomes. This, we will calculate through our macro-economic model.

However have we *quantified* the entries in Table 4.3? As the key to the table shows, an entry +VL, showing that we expect a very small increase in the use of a factor is taken to mean a 2 per cent increase on existing levels. An entry −MH assumes that about one quarter of existing labour will be displaced (per unit of output). Although these estimates were themselves compiled as far as possible from quantified studies, described in Chapter 3, the precise estimates themselves obviously remain a matter of judgement and the conversion of the qualitative estimates to a numerical form may bias the results (see Cole and Metcalf, 1970). However, tests with our data showed that the final rank ordering of factor cost comparative advantage arising from the new technology and the model results were not overly sensitive to different coding procedures (for example, a linear versus exponential scaling). The reason for this lack of sensitivity was that economies and sectors had a priori been grouped to display structural differences as far as possible, and wherever differences in the impact on economies were not as large as our intial categorisation of economies implied, economic groups were amalgamated together; this was the case for all three industrial economies and for two groups of developing economies.

High, middle and low income countries

For reasons given below, the economic model we shall use describes only three sectors of production, agriculture, industry and services, and so we must aggregate yet further the data for the eight sectors shown in Table 4.3. The estimated shifts in factor inputs at the three-sector level are obtained by combining the shifts of this table with the sub-sector weights given in Table 4.2. At this level of aggregation we find again clear trends across economies for each sector and factor and also marked differences in the expected impact on agriculture, industry and services. The impact in the combined industry sector is greatest, followed by services and then agriculture.

We see here again that with the rather few exceptions noted in Chapter 3 that there are no large differences between our estimates for the three groups of industrial economy. The principal difference arises for the centrally planned economies in the industry sector (because the rate of automation in the intermediate industry sector is assumed to be slower than in the market economies), and in the service sector (where both basic and advanced services are configured to maintain overall 'full employment').

Apart from these differences between the industrial groups, there is no reason to differentiate these economies simply on the basis of their potential for changes in factor inputs (as suggested in Chapter 3). The same applies also to the situation between the newly industrialised economies and the oil exporting economies. Barring the preponderence of the oil extraction sector in the latter economies and the different expectations for technical change for oil compared to other mineral exploitation, the estimated changes are again small, but both are distinctively different from the situation of the least industrial economies.

This suggests that in our model we should work with three rather than six groups of economies, in the following combinations:

High income industrial economies (*Groups 1 to 3*)
    Dynamic industrial economies
    Lagging industrial economies
    Centrally planned industrial economies
Middle income developing economies (*Groups 4 and 5*)
    Newly industrialised economies
    Oil exporting economies
Low income developing economies (*Group 6*)
    Least industrial economies.

By weighting the estimated shifts in Table 4.3 with the levels of output by sector and economy we obtain aggregate impacts for the three new groups. As shown in Table 4.4 there are clear trends across these economies. We should observe that this aggregation procedure obliterates the 'anomalies' for the centrally planned and oil exporting regions. This prevents us from exploring further the hypothesis that there may be quite different consequences for the advanced and lagging industrial economies (first and second division in Pavitt's (1980) terminology). But,

Table 4.4   Impact of probable technology on factor inputs
(percentages—no systemic change)

	Economy group		
	High	Middle	Low
Agriculture			
Skilled	1.15	0.50	0.00
Unskilled	−4.50	−0.50	0.00
Capital	0.50	0.50	0.00
Industry			
Skilled	2.51	1.12	1.00
Unskilled	−11.60	−8.20	−5.60
Capital	3.17	2.05	0.97
Services			
Skilled	−1.40	−0.91	−0.16
Unskilled	−5.00	−3.20	−0.16
Capital	5.62	3.29	0.16

while we lose the opportunity of examining these particular possibilities, we hope to gain much more stable results in relation to the categories that remain. Thus, we may be more confident in the final results we obtain.

Expected comparative advantage

As mentioned above, the impact on comparative advantage of factor intensity changes depends both on the size of those changes and on existing factor prices (wages and rates of interest). It also depends upon changes in commodity and factor prices which may be induced as a result of the new technology or for other reasons. For example, if the new technology is really as labour saving overall as Table 4.4 suggests, and if unemployment rises then real wages are likely to fall. In fact in estimating changes in comparative advantage, few authors (and especially the enterprises implementing the technology) take account of these reactive effects. Rather, in calculating their new production costs, they assume that factor process will remain at present level over the lifetime of the technology. In our economic model we shall calculate changes in factor and commodity prices.

It is, nevertheless, informative to look at the new 'expected' production costs, since these give us our *prior* expectations about what may happen when the new technology is introduced. Certainly, in a market economy we should expect net production costs to *decrease* if entrepreneurs are to implement the new technology. Thus, savings from the displacement of unskilled labour should exceed any additional skilled labour or capital costs.

We take the costs of production to be given by:

$$\mathbf{P} = A\mathbf{W} + I\mathbf{P},$$

where **P** and **W** are the vectors of commodity and factor prices and A and I are matrices describing unit factor and intermediate goods inputs. Simplifying this to the case of a single commodity economy and single labour type for the sake of exposition we have (with no excess profits):

$$P = aw + kr + ip,$$

where p is the commodity price, w the wage rate, r the rate of interest, a, k and i the labour, capital and intermediate goods inputs (per unit of output).

Denoting the new factor inputs as estimated from our empirical data by $''$ we have for the new commodity price:

$$p'' = a''w + k''r + i''p$$

or using the notion of Dell'Mour (1982) earlier:

$$Ap = p + \mathbf{D}aw + \mathbf{D}kr,$$

if we do not assume here changes in intermediate goods inputs.

The new 'expected' prices by sector and economy are given in Table 4.5. Because of variations (in estimated factor savings) and differences in the existing factor inputs and prices also vary. Looking first at our original economic groups we note that with three exceptions new production costs have declined. For the agriculture in the least industrial economies, no significant involvement of the new technology was assumed.

For all economies the most significant gains appear in the manufacturing sector, followed generally by services. Generally, the gains appear greater in the industrial economies than in the less developed economies. One deviation from our first hypothesis here is that production cost savings in the industry sector of the least industrialised economies are in fact little different from the newly industrialised economies. This is despite the lower impact on factor inputs. Looking back to the table, we see that this is because of the predominance of the basic industry

Table 4.5a   New commodity prices with base year input prices
(percentages—no systemic change)

	Economy group		
	High	Middle	Low
Agriculture	0.998	0.999	1.000
Industry	0.989	0.995	0.997
Services	0.994	0.998	0.999

Table 4.5b   New commodity prices with base year input prices
(percentages—systemic change)

	Economy group		
	High	Middle	Low
Agriculture	0.974	0.991	1.000
Industry	0.952	0.958	0.972
Services	0.961	0.968	0.991

sector in the least industrialised economies (and the propensity of that
sector for introduction of the new technologies).

Concentrating on the new production costs for the economies regrouped
as high, medium and low income countries we see a corresponding change.
In all sectors the high income industrial countries gain greater comparative
advantage than other economies, and with the marginal exception in the
industry sector, the middle income economies gain more than the low
income economies. From this we might begin to speculate immediately
about the implications for the international division of labour between
these economic groups. The most competitive sector now appears to be
industry in the high income countries. Given this we should expect our
model analysis to show this economy expanding production and exports
to the relative detriment of other economies. But since both the agriculture and service sectors in this economy also gain relatively, there are
reasons for entrepreneurs to expand production in these sectors also.
Thus, there will be competition for factors of production in the high
income countries, and production structures will change. This in turn will
affect production costs between sectors and relative to other economies.
Levels and patterns of consumption will also change as household (and

government) incomes adjust to the new situation. Corresponding changes will take place in these economies too.

As a result of this interrelated set of events, the pattern of comparative advantage shown in Table 4.5 will change, so the final result for shifts in economic fortunes may be very different from our prior expectations. Obviously we must soon lose track of this global bargaining process since it depends on precise parameter values changes, and chains of processes which continue until some new global equilibrium is reached, or at least until new 'shocks' to the system stimulate further adjustment. A general equilibrium model such as we describe in the next chapter provides us with one way of seeking greater understanding of these processes.

This chapter has concentrated on preparing the ground for such an exercise by explaining some of the pitfalls in using the available data in a macro-economic context, clarifying the alternative hypotheses which emerge from this data, theory and the literature, and finally transforming the data into a format that can be used directly in our model.

5 Technology, trade and distribution: the rules of the game

Market mechanisms: the hidden hand or the hidden boot?

Technological change introduces tendencies in the world economy from which some actors in the world economy may gain, and others lose. These effects are not straightforward. For example, within any economy, specific actors may gain even though, overall, the economy may suffer little or no gain in real income. Alternatively, a country may experience a substantial increase in its exports and also its total income but the situation of particular groups may worsen. This is because the introduction of the new technology will induce changes in the pattern of specialisations within and across countries, so that, for example, levels of employment of resources will change as will the relative prices of commodities and labour.

In this chapter we review the relevant economic theory and describe the empirical model which we shall use to examine these processes. Again we shall adopt a rather straightforward approach which enables us to bridge the gap between available empirical data and theory. Because so much of the discussion of information technology is couched in terms of international and intersectoral competitiveness, our model emphasises the principal medium through which this competitiveness is conducted—international and domestic markets.

Despite this stress on the importance of markets, we are not subscribing blindly to the increasingly popular notion (among conservative politicians at least) that the market alone provides solutions to the social problems presented by changing technology. What we do argue however is that the market cannot be ignored: it *helps* to explain why new technology is being introduced at this time, and what its impact may be. While we do not adopt a particular theory of technical change in this book, we accept that the movement of international capital (to Europe from the United States immediately after the Second World War and from all industrial countries to the developing economies subsequently) and the search for a new labour displacing technology are a consequence of desire by producers to maximise profits in the face of domestic and international competition. With rising real wages in the industrial economies, and the failure to introduce or appropriate a technology which brought production costs down to the level of those in the low wage economies such a move was inevitable. Even the most protectionist governments would be hard-pressed to subsidise firms at the level required to compensate them for not relocating production abroad, especially when overseas incentives (tax free zones and the like) are equally generous. This introduction implies that technical change is in part a result of changing income distribution.

What do we mean by a technological revolution in this context? Most theories of economic growth (whether neoclassical, Keynesian or Marxist) have been concerned to identify the conditions under which 'balanced growth' could be achieved and the implications for technical change. Generally such theories look for a smoothly changing technology in which factor intensities shift in tune with changing factor availability as a result of population growth or capital accumulation. Here we are not so much concerned with changes in these variables but with the situation when technology, for a time, changes very rapidly in relation to them, and to other less tangible variables such as the institutional structures and the social organisation of production. For our purposes this defines what we mean by a 'technological revolution'.

In this book we adopt a somewhat bipartisan attitude to the treatment of international and domestic markets, and of technical change. We must analyse their effects, but we do not accept that they are always desirable. The model we adopt is a general equilibrium model: thus it emphasises the importance of competitive markets in determining factor and commodity prices and ensuring the 'efficient' use of economic resources through a search for maximum profit. The impact of technical change depends very much on international and domestic markets function. For example, 'robotised' industrial production in the rich countries of North America, Japan or Europe may make production of everyday products in those countries less expensive, but it also will affect the way even informal production in South Asia or Latin America operates. Conversely, if these new technologies were introduced into those developing nations it would have an impact on diverse sectors across the industrial economy. Even though we might not believe that markets function perfectly anywhere in the world, we can recognise that such processes play a dominant role in the global economy. To examine these mechanisms a general equilibrium model is a valuable device.

The medium whereby these processes are transmitted are international markets for goods, technology and finance, carried for example, by transnational firms. Both conservative and radical economists would agree on this. Murray (1972) sees transnational firms as 'the carriers of market signals', and other Marxist contributers to the New International Division of Labour theory, such as Frobel *et al.* (1980), consider the 'new

international division of labour' to be one result of the inexorable spread
of capitalism with capital pursuing, effectively unhindered, the maximisation of profit. As Kaplinsky (1984) points out,

> Curiously in some important respects this analysis parallels contempor-
> ary neoclassical theory in that it assumes (a) the mobility of capital,
> (b) that the maximisation of profit is the main determinant of resource
> allocation and hence that comparative cost advantage is the principal
> underlying international exchange.

To put this succinctly, one does not need to reject neoclassical theory or
the idea of general equilibrium to demonstrate that market mechanisms
can lead to very great and untenable economic divisions and the potential
for social disruption.

At the other points in the ideological spectrum an adherence to the
pre-eminence of markets is less curious—indeed, some international
agencies maintain that the world economy is becoming more market
oriented. The World Bank (IBRD, 1983), for example, reports that 'in
the industrial market economies prices play a pivotal role in the allocation
of resources. The centrally planned economies have also started to move
in that direction, and in developing countries there is a growing body of
evidence on the use of prices to reflect scarcities and to encourage growth'.
Elsewhere the World Bank (IBRD, 1982) reports a somewhat more salu-
tary experience. 'For much of the past thirty years, growing interdepend-
ence through trade, capital and migrations—strengthened the forces of
economic expansion and spread them around the world. But as recent
events have illustrated, these links can transmit problems from country
to country, just as surely as the benefits'. Embedded in the idea of 'gains
from trade' to which these agencies subscribe is the idea of 'trickle down',
i.e. as one group or nation increases its wealth through increased economic
activity so some of this wealth will pass down to other less wealthy actors.
But as the above experience suggests, losses as well as gains are passed on,
and in *both* directions. Thus 'trickle up' as well as 'trickle down' may be
equally powerful forces in the world economy. Markets tend to dissipate
and distribute growth from wherever it is generated so they can act for
or against distribution.

The World Bank (IBRD, 1984) focuses more directly on the issue of
growth than on distribution but while their empirical data are impressive
(see below), and their 'statistical analyses clearly suggest that prices do
matter for growth, price distortions alone can explain less than half
the variation in growth among developing countries, the rest is the result

of other economic, social, political and institutional factors'. They argue, however, that a country well endowed with natural resources (like Nigeria) or with an 'active and mobilised' labour force (like China) would experience 'significantly faster' growth if its price structure was 'less distorted'. This is partly the result of the way even the most ideal markets operate, but in addition there are institutional factors at international level also. Pressures from international agencies and aid-granting governments promote and facilitate the market. The United States as a major donor has been most explicit in recent years, in stating that aid will be granted only to developing countries adopting free market policies. At the same time industrial economies set up tariff barriers between themselves and especially the developing economies. These obviously can have a very great impact on the location decisions of individual economies and the world at large, but are in themselves a response to market conditions (for example, a social policy to adjust the functional distribution of income, or a subsidy to an otherwise non-sustainable decaying, infant or strategic industry). In the opinion of the United Nations, international markets are biased against developing countries: 'The international trading system is neither open nor liberal. It is becoming increasingly regulated in an *ad hoc* manner, which serves the interests of very few countries' (UNCTAD, 1983). Given these caveats, the general equilibrium approach we adopt must be seen as a starting-point from which more subtle considerations may be ventured.

Technology and trade

The central issue dealt with in the model, then, is the interrelationship between international and domestic income distribution and changing technology. Thus international trade is a dominant consideration.

Formal theory contains some very powerful ideas which provide the conventional wisdoms of the subject. With respect to the direction of trade, the most important of these is the Hecksher–Ohlin (gains from trade) model of comparative advantage which suggests that trade between two economies is determined by differences in factor endowments between countries. A country that is rich in capital will export capital intensive goods, while a country with abundant labour will export labour intensive goods.

The theory demonstrates that countries would gain by specialising and trading according to their comparative advantage. Thus both partners gain from trade. There are several important caveats necessary for this result, most pertinently for us is that international and domestic markets are perfectly competitive; both economies use the same technological opportunities for production of equivalent goods, but each economy uses different technologies for different goods. With respect to gains from trade, the second important theorem is that of Stolper–Samuelson which demonstrates that under certain restricted conditions trade leads to complete equalisation of factor prices. Thus provided there is not complete specialisation (for example, one partner producing only industrial goods and the other only producing agricultural goods) the theory predicts that there will be a tendency for factor prices in trading nations to converge.

This result has provided a very powerful direct and implicit underpinning for agencies such as the World Bank, cited above, which deal with the economic relations between industrial and developing countries, or those such as the European Commission or GATT (General Agreement on Tariffs and Trade) which deal with relations between industrial economies. Are these theories verified in practice? Are even the underlying assumptions reasonable? Empirical demonstrations for either comparative advantage or factor equalisation are certainly ambiguous and disputed (see Sodersten (1980) for a review). But as Sodersten points out

> We have to keep in mind that the factor equalisation theorem, and static theorising in general, should not be viewed as directly amenable or geared towards empirical testing. It gives us however, indispensable tools and insights into the general equilibrium nature of economics. It is the necessary background for all further theorising.

But when the crucial assumptions of these theories are relaxed, as they must be if we are to evaluate with any degree of realism a situation in which technology worldwide is changing, and countries with very different technologies and wealth are trading, a number of important and acknowledged 'paradoxes' are observed. These concern the effects on overall welfare and its distribution of policies which constrain free trade (such as tariffs) or economic transfers (such as development aid) or situations where trading partners are of very different size or have different production structures and technology. For a review of such 'paradoxes' readers are referred to Sodersten (1980), Graham (1982) and, especially, to Jones (1982). We identify a number of these here as they are relevant to the results of our own model, with its highly diverse technology, production, income distribution and patterns of consumption.

First, although it is a clarification, rather than a paradox, we should note, the theory does not say that incomes will equalise, in particular, the more capital a country has for a given amount of labour the higher will be the average income. With respect to distribution between labour and capital within an economy the theory suggests that the intensive factor of production will always suffer in moving from autarky to free trade (see Sodersten 1980).

Second, is the paradox of 'immiserizing growth' (for example, Bhagwati 1958) whereby in a closed economy growth of production possibilities, such as capital, is usally associated with an increase in welfare, but in any open economy domestic growth can lead to a worsening of terms of trade so that the welfare gains from growth are transferred to the trading partners elsewhere in the world.

Third, the standard model assumes two countries in perfect competition, with perfect domestic markets producing two goods and with equal technologies. The last assumption implies that technology itself is a 'free good' and available equally worldwide. Technology transfer is therefore an 'instantaneous' process, a point we consider further below.

Fourth, is the situation when trading partners are very different in size. Rather than both partners gaining from trade one may gain and the other lose. As Graham (1982) observes in the special case in which one nation is very much smaller than its partner, the small nation will register gains from trade—but the larger will not. This 'special' case is the norm for trade between most industrial and developing nations.

Fifth, with respect to economic transfers Leontieff (1936) and more recently Gale (1974), Chichilnisky (1980) and de Meza (1983) have pointed out that while, in general a gift from rich to poor countries might be expected to be to the relative benefit of the latter, this is not necessarily the case. Gale demonstrates how when three actors are taken into account, both donor and recipient may gain at the expense of a third party. Chichilnisky shows how even the recipient of an economic transfer may suffer an overall loss.

The introduction of multiple countries into the picture as well as multiple actors introduces further complications. As Dixit (1983) and de Meza (1983) demonstrate in a more general theory of multi-country transfers (many countries/two goods) there are several 'paradoxical possibilities in relation to the number of countries and the composition of income and substitution effects'; for example when recipient and donor countries have a different pattern of trade and aid with third parties.

With respect to the application of tariffs and protection too there are also paradoxes. Lerner (1936), for example, showed how a tariff may worsen a country's terms of trade. Metzler (1949) demonstrated that a country might levy a tariff on imports to maintain domestic prices, but that even after the exercise the domestic price of imports falls. Such results depend on the relative price elasticities of imports and exports, which in turn depend on the fact that different income households and industries in different parts of the world have different propensities for final and intermediate consumption.

As Jones (1982) emphasises, in the explanation of these paradoxes 'income effects' are crucial. Perhaps instead we should assume the converse, that as a rule income distribution effects are likely to be observed in any model which contains the detail necessary for them to be observed. And in such a model we might even expect 'paradoxes' to be the norm.

The above paradoxes often depend on differences in the economic structures of trading partners. Thus we are especially concerned with the consequences of differences in technology. As Graham (1983) points out such limited assumptions as to the nature of comparative advantage do not invalidate the idea of 'gains from trade'. 'All that is invalidated by disproving the assumptions is the argument that relative factor endowments are the primary determinants of comparative advantage among trading nations.' Thus the factor proportions model can be adapted to deal with the case of differing technologies among trading nations.

The effect of changes in technology, whether through innovation or transfer, is especially complicated. As several authors have shown (for example Johnson (1955), Findlay and Grubert (1959), and Jones (1970)). to assume transfer of a disembodied technology from advanced to developing economies leads to inconclusive results. Total world income invariably increases as a result of the transfer, but the income of the advanced nation may increase or decrease depending on the specific circumstances. This implies that the less advanced nation should gain from the transfer although, given the discussion above of transfers in a multi-country theory, this is not automatically the case. Furthermore, if the amount of technical change is sufficient to bring about factor reversals (i.e. the relative intensity of use of capital and labour is reversed) then again the Hecksher–Ohlin model does not apply (see Sodersten, 1980).

With respect to innovation, Sodersten (1980) observes that 'the effects on real national income are closely linked to those on the terms of trade. Technical progress which improves the terms of trade has a strongly positive effect on the growth of real income. With innovations that lead to deteriorating terms of trade, the situation becomes more complex. If the losses in terms of trade are large, they might cancel out most of the prospective gains in income'. As a result, he observes: 'labour saving innovation in the capital intensive sector can have any effect on relative prices. Contrary to the case of neutral and capital saving technical progress in this sector, the effects on terms of trade are *indeterminate*'.

We have emphasised the ambiguity here for two reasons. First, the technical change with which we are concerned may be on balance labour saving. Second, because even in the simple two country/two good cases the results are ambiguous and non-generalisable, and therefore depend on the details of the productions system, trade arrangements, domestic distribution and consumption and so on. This obviously means that to reduce ambiguity as far as possible we must have a reliable estimation of the characteristics for each of the economies and technologies we are concerned with.

The theory of comparative advantage is static and compares only two countries in a given setting, saying nothing about their economic *development*. As changes take place (e.g. technical progress, population growth or capital accumulation) so will the pattern of specialisation predicted by a model. The model strictly allows us only to *compare* the impact of different sets of assumptions, for example, to ask how a different set of choices about technology would affect other economic variables. But although the general equilibrium model we employ is comparatively static we shall use it to build up a picture of the way in which different dynamic forces act. For example, we shall explore the response of different public and private sector institutions (i.e. government and entrepreneurs) to the pressures experienced through changing technology.

What this brief discussion clearly shows is that whether markets act for or against the interests of particular targets for distribution (e.g. low income countries) depends on their domestic situation and location in the world economy. Similarly the theory of growth and trade shows that technical and other change can have quite perverse effects on the real national income of a trading economy. In particular, certain types of technical change lead to strongly positive growth of national income, others lead to rapidly deteriorating terms of trade and little, if any, positive gain to national income.

Alternative explanations of technical change

The general equilibrium theory discussed above may tell us much about the tendencies induced in the world economic system as a result of technical change, but less about the change itself. Now we look at some alternative models of technical change, and in so doing clarify our treatment of this variable, for the technology routes suggested in Chapter 4.

The invention possibility function

One of the more sophisticated theoretical formulations of technical change in the (two factor) neoclassical model of economic growth originated with

Kennedy (1964) and von Weizsäcker (1966). In his theory Kennedy assumes that present technology, present factor costs and future engineering possibilities determine the direction of technical change. In this treatment the idea of an 'invention possibility function' is introduced to represent the trade-offs between labour and capital saving innovations. This is distinct from a production function (with substitution possibilities) which allows entrepreneurs to change technology by selecting among a given set of *existing* techniques but does not provide the continuous change required to sustain economic growth. The model has been used by some economists (for example Samuelson 1976) to provide an endogenised description of 'induced' technical change.

The situation described in the theory is shown in Figure 5.1. The invention possibility function is described by the curve TT'. A possible 'optimal' direction of technical change corresponding to a particular existing technology is indicated by the line CC'. When the existing technology involves a relatively high capital component in total production costs the tendency implies a high rate of capital augmentation and a low rate of labour augmentation. Since the direction of induced change depends on factor prices as well as relative physical factor inputs, induced direction of change may be very different between the different types of economy described in Chapter 3.

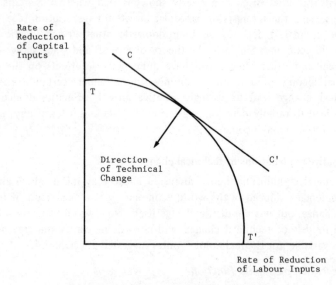

Figure 5.1   The invention possibility function
Source: Based on Jones (1976).

However, as Urquidi and Nadal (1980) point out there is a common misconception that technical change in economies where labour is the less abundant factor of production necessarily means that labour saving is the order of the day, but the theory of Kennedy shows otherwise. In general, the model demonstrates that firms will attempt to save both capital as well as labour and that increasing the savings of one factor will reduce the possibilities for saving the other. Entrepreneurs operating in perfect markets must seek a balanced net improvement in their combined productivity. As we have noted the Kennedy model considers only two factors of production and considers also that cost reduction is the only motivating force behind technical change—for these reasons it is not of direct application to our present study. The idea of an innovation possibility function remains, however, rather useful for our purpose, especially when in Chapter 8 it is extended to cover other inputs, including intermediate goods and specialised production skills.

Product cycle theory

Product cycle theory originating with the work of Vernon (1966) provides one possible construct for reviewing the impact of new technology. Essentially this underpins the hypothesis of Rada (1983) cited in the last chapter. In contrast to contemporary general equilibrium theory product cycle theory assumes distinct stages in the evolution of technology and its impact on patterns of trade and foreign investment. In other words there is a delay in the transfer and diffusion of new technologies. In the initial stages of the development of a new product, technological and market uncertainty is considerable, with rival designs and producers competing for survival. During this stage both inputs and outputs from production are concentrated in the local market, but in the second stage, as a dominant product design emerges, greater emphasis is placed on the rapid development of process technology (to reduce production costs). Generally this requires larger scale production and the opening up of foreign markets. In the last stage the technology 'matures' with standardised products and processes for which competitive advantage is determined by conventional comparative cost consideration (principally labour costs). According to the theory, market size and greater resources of skilled labour favour the evolution of a new product and production processes in the larger industrial economies, but this advantage declines as the technology matures and production passes to the developing countries. Thus, trade patterns are the result of a repeated process of technological divergence and convergence.

Some authors (such as Krugman (1979), Cole (1978)) have attempted to incorporate this innovation and diffusion of new products and technology into a simple dynamic general equilibrium theory. In both theories, the advanced economies are assumed to create new product innovations at an exponential rate, leading to a technology gap. This gap gives the advanced countries a temporary monopoly of certain products (and hence a rent which keeps incomes in the industrial economies above those of the developing economies). But once the technology is transferred, the industrial country can no longer produce the goods in the face of lower wage costs in the developing economies.

Although in broad terms, such theory may well help us to place new micro-processor related technologies into context, it clearly requires some modifications. For example, it is obvious that many areas to which the technology is to be applied such as textiles or shoes (see Hoffman and Rush 1983) are mature industries, which, to a great extent, have already migrated to developing economies. Thus, another round of process innovation would (if we believe the studies of Rush (1983), Boon (1982), Clarke and Cable (1982), etc.) determine that the production of some mature products would return to the advanced countries, in addition to new products which evolve from the new technology, as we indicated in the last chapter.

In complete contrast to this critique, Vernon (1981) the originator of this theory, has expressed doubts about the theory on the grounds that the technological capabilities of several nations have advanced very rapidly in the past decade or so, and additionally the ability of local firms in these nations and the tendency for multinational firms to utilise new technologies to abroad has, according to Graham (1982) very much reduced the relevance of product life cycle theory as an explanation of international trade and investment in new technology intensive goods. As we suggest below the empirical evidence is not clear on this point, at least with respect to information technology.

Long wave theories

We mention one further theory of technological change which further influences our alternative technology routes described in Chapter 4, and also ironically lends some additional support to our general equilibrium approach. This is 'long wave' theory, which asserts that the world economy undergoes cycles of some 50-60 years—possibly associated with the introduction of 'bunches' of innovations or 'heartland' technologies. Some authors (for example Freeman (1977), Mensch (1977)), following Schumpeter, observe that in the past, successive cycles have accompanied the introduction of textile innovations and steampower in manufacturing, then railways and steel production, and last electricity, the internal combustion engine and the chemical industry. Each of these three cycles is argued to have an expansionary upswing in which the new 'heartland' technology is used, principally for the production of new commodities followed by a 'rationalising' downswing in which the new technology is used to enhance competitiveness in the context of growing competition. Thus, the theory is not inconsistent with the product cycle theory but operates on a much grander scale and is, therefore, possibly more appropriate to the analysis of a widespread micro-processor 'revolution' as a basis for the fourth, and latest, long wave.

As we observed in Chapter 2 a significant feature of the last 35 years has indeed been the swarm of new high-technology industries, notably electronics, semi-conductors, synthetic and composite materials, aerospace and petroleum and agricultural chemicals, each generating further new technologies and new markets, and additional demand for old consumer and industrial products. The dynamic growth phase (1945–64) saw the introduction of radically new products, and the 1960s a consolidation phase with increasing productivity and attention to process rather than product innovations. Although productivity reached historically high levels, markets now began to saturate, and increasing emphasis was placed on price competition with the result that firms began to relocate the production of mature products in low cost areas and developing economies. This further reduced employment (and hence demand) in the industrial countries, contributing to a situation of overcapacity and stagnation.

In terms of the long-wave theory, therefore, the years 1950 to 1975 saw the expansionary up-swing of a micro-electronics based cycle, with full employment and a growing international division of labour as the technology diffused. But now the world is in a rationalising down-swing with a concentration of production and with a growing unemployment (in part as a result of the new labour saving micro-electronics technologies). According to Rothwell and Soete (1983), many of the industries noted above (synthetic fibres, consumer electronics, electrical goods, automobiles and petro-chemicals) have all reached maturity. Studies by Rothwell (1984) of the semi-conductor industry, and Freeman *et al.* (1982) of electronics suggest this is also the case for these industries. As Soete and Metcalfe (1983) point out, uncertainty is far more critical in the earliest stages of innovation. But they say for the diffusion of more mature technologies, availability of necessary skills and factor costs are more important.

Schumpeter referred to the process of constant social and economic re-organisation as one of 'creative capital destruction' and technical innovation itself as 'more like a series of explosions than a gentle though incessant transformation'. As Rothwell and Soete (1983) observe 'structural adjustment disequilibria' are a logical outcome of economic development in such a system. But, if it is also true, as they suggest, that information technology already has entered the rationalising maturation stage then it is certainly relevant and reasonable to assume that the different producers ability to compete is on the basis of comparative production costs. Furthermore, since monopoly rents are generally lower in the rationalisation phase, we may assume as an approximation that producers make negligible excess profits—but that this is the final result of a domestic and international profit maximising behavior of firms. In Schumpeter's view, the competitive process set in motion by the bunching of innovations gradually erodes the margin of innovative (excess) profits, but before the system settles into an equilibrium, the process starts again through the destabilising effects of the next wave of innovations. But, despite the existence of disequilibrium, there are periods when this phenomenon is less marked and so more amenable to a general equilibrium approach. If the evidence we have just cited is correct, then the present may be such an era.

Before closing this topic we add some final caveats. A principal assumption of general equilibrium theory is that markets, whether they be for factors of production, or commodities rapidly find a 'market clearing' price which ensures that supply equals demand in each market. Thus unnecessary stocks of goods or involuntary unemployment is eliminated. This is of course an approximation, and one we should be aware of. Malinvaud (1977) and other disequilibrium theorists have pointed to the deficiencies of the system for the analysis of short-run phenomena where the fact that different markets clear over different time spans can create serious departures from the 'efficient' market solution. Others (for example Clower, 1965), have argued that disequilibrium effects increase the perception of risk, and hence affect the rate of investment, even leading to a downward spiral in an economy. In this sense therefore a general equilibrium model tends to paint a rosy picture of the world—actual events will always be worse and, of course, if the conclusions of a general equilibrium analysis are undesirable, so certainly will be the results of the equivalent disequilibrium analsysis.

Amin (1974) has discussed the extent to which the concept of the 'multiplier' resulting from the working through of general equilibrium mechanisms is valid in developing countries and their interaction with the international economy. He accepts the possibility of disequilibrium mechanisms in which the *order* of interventions in the economy by different actors can lead to a situation which exacerbates an initial change and so causes a spiral away from equilibrium. On the other hand he argues that there are situations in which the successive deployment of economic mechanisms results in a new equilibrium. He observes that here 'simple mathematical procedures enable us to reveal the "multipliers" which "summarise" the way in which the situation has evolved'. Amin is concerned especially with the indirect cumulative effects of new investment rather than new technology, but he gives reasons as to why the multiplier effect in developing countries is not as great as conventional wisdoms might suggest. In our study, working largely within the confines of a general equilibrium analysis, we shall see that often multiplier effects simply 'trickle away'.

The idea of a 'perfect' market rests on the assumption of full access to data and analysis by all actors. In Chapter 4 we noted the synergism between the information and productivity enhancing characteristics of new technology. It is evident that the former are also related to the speed with which markets clear. In particular, the speed and comprehensiveness of modern communications technology should mean that market signals are more rapidly and ubiquitously transmitted between actors and around the world, in principle leading to better informed, more rapid decisions and so on. The extent to which this is indeed the case, depends on who has primary access to the additional information just as it depends on who uses the new technology.

As we detailed in Chapter 3, access to the new technologies is most likely to be uneven. But in addition to this, we should take account of the way different institutions react to new information. Olson (1982) has argued that the lags in market clearing come from the slowness with which institutional actors (such as governments, trade unions or enterprises) react to market signals. In particular special interests and distributional coalitions are, for a time, able to buck the market. His argument fits well with the institutional theories of the long wave of Perez (1983) and Gordon (1983), and also with some theories of regional development (for example Perry and Watkins, 1977). Obviously these barriers can lead to a situation whereby the general equilibrium calculations no longer indicate well even the *tendencies* in the world economy as we are tacitly asserting in this book, and need to be examined further. For the moment we endeavour only to clarify market phenomena—since so much emphasis is placed on this system today as an ideal, we should at the very least attempt to determine its likely behaviour.

A pragmatic alternative

How then should we represent changing technology? As Cooper and Clark (1982) point out attempts to encompass technological change in growth theory, while logically elegant, involve a degree of abstraction which is apt to induce considerable scepticism in the light of available empirical research on innovation. In spite of its limitations Cooper and Clark argue that neo-classical theory of technical change contains some concepts which are potentially useful in any framework. (We see that this conclusion parallels precisely that of Sodersten with respect to the usefulness of neo-classical theories of international trade.) They argue that the way in which technological change is modelled embodies assumptions; in particular, substitution possibilities between capital and labour and the smoothness of change are hard to reconcile with micro-economic understanding of innovation. Further, while the idea of a production function reflecting a 'state of knowledge' in which a range of possible techniques can be realised, involving substitution of factors of production for one another is appealing, it is hard to conceive in empirical terms. Although these more 'realistic' ideas due to Schumpeter and others are embodied in product cycle theories of trade, they are difficult to formalise.

Soete and Metcalfe (1983) suggest that the size of an economy (as a variable determining the degree of uncertainty and risk taking during the process of innovation), the skilled population (as a necessary ingredient for innovation or adopting of new technology) or wage and other factor costs (as critical determinants of comparative advantage for production of mature goods) are the key variables needed to set up an endogeneous model of technological change. Certainly we are sympathetic to such an approach. However, we do not attempt to do this in this book but follow other authors (such as Dell'Mour (1982), or Dixon (1979)), who have made exogenous assumptions about technical change based on empirical case studies. The reason for this less ambitious approach is partly that we wish to test several alternative hypotheses which we consider to be consistent with the empirical evidence. Furthermore, we wish to speculate about alternative technological routes which are less pre-determined than present data would allow, but which might permit us to suggest directions which technology ought to take if certain social objectives are to be met (rather than simply asking what are the implications of alternative assumed trends).

Nevertheless, this approach certainly does not resolve all our problems. As we have seen, the effects of technical change, propagated around the world by national and international market forces, can give rise to a

number of ambiguities which may themselves determine the subsequent
location of new investment and the new direction of technical change. It
is not possible to say that technical change will automatically be to the
advantage of the economy introducing the technology. More important
yet is the fact that we shall consider technical change as a set of fixed
changes in productivity, and not as a continuous and indefinitely proceeding process. The reason for this is that we are examining the implications of a relative speeding up of technical change, but we point out here
that simple growth theory shows that, for long run growth (above the
growth in labour force) to be maintained, productivity improvements
must not stop (see for example Jones, 1979). For this reasons, our calculations should not be taken to provide a long term view.

From our discussion, then, it will be evident that our formal description of technical change is very simplified compared to the serendipity
of the process of innovation (see e.g. Rosenberg, 1983). Our treatment
of technology is the response of pragmatism to the intractability and
complexity of the concepts involved. To quote Nordhaus (1973), 'although
in most modern price and growth theory technological change is treated
as exogenous this must be interpreted as analytical convenience rather
than a serious statement about the economic system.'

Long versus short term

One of the central questions is how rapidly the processes of technical
innovation and transfer proceed relative to other equilibrating mechanisms
in the world economy. The model of comparative advantage implies the
process of transfer to be very rapid and the process of innovation to be
relatively slow. Hence, the pattern of natural and other endowments
between nations to changes only slowly. But, with respect to the issue
of specialisation and gains from trade Sodersten (1980) observes:

> It may be that during the nineteenth century most economies had
> durable, stable characteristics, such as the possession of specific raw
> materials and primary products or skills, the knowledge of which spread
> only to other countries. Therefore trade was grounded in typical and
> only slowly changing characteristics, which gave rise to a situation of
> durable comparative advantage. A great deal of trade is of this nature
> today. But it seems that comparative advantage is increasingly founded
> in superior technology, the possession of which can only be kept secret
> for a very limited time.

Data on the time scale relevant to new technology are implicit in our alternative technology routes. The discussion in Chapter 3 suggests that the 'lead time' between initial investment and actual implementation for production is rather longer than in the past, but that product life cycles are somewhat shorter, and the relationship between product and process innovations is less sharp, so diffusion and transfer may be speeded up.

Thus the issue of technology and changing technology focused on in this book becomes central to development at the international level. Certainly our model shows that technical change (both innovation and transfer) can induce quite large shifts in worldwide patterns of specialisation. But an almost opposite analysis to that just cited may be made for the internal growth process of individual countries. For example, Felix (1977) has argued that by contrast to the nineteenth-century growth of the now industrialised countries in which differences in technology, skills and social distribution (i.e. 'dualism') were self-liquidating, in the twentieth-century developing economies 'normal market forces tend to atrophy the artisan leg well before the modern sector can provide adequately offsetting employment'. Thus there are structural and distributional issues concerned with the use and transfer of technologies within economies as well as across them. Even if we must conclude ultimately that we have only begun to scratch the surface of these issues, and our model does not address certain key questions, it certainly incorporates some critical features of the contemporary world economy.

In our model experiments we shall assume the possibility of differing degrees of appropriation of technology (i.e. the ability to prevent the equalisation of technology). Cooper and Clark (1982) question whether, since innovation monopolies are eventually eroded anyway, the perfect information assumption may be good enough for discussion of long term growth? They conclude that 'There are at present no clear answers, although those who concern themselves with the economics of innovation in an oligopolistic market might have their doubts'. Our answer to this question must be 'no' for our present practical purposes, since it is evident that rather large differences in technology do exist between countries and are sustained for indefinite and extended periods of decades and the consequent distributional impact experienced from generation to generation. Further, even if there is evidence that the relative technological capability of economies changes, there is certainly conflicting evidence about the possibility that in the very long-term technological change is slowing down. Long-wave theories (such as those referred to above) suggest that the pace of technical change fluctuates, and with this so do the technological capabilities of industrial centres and nations.

An empirical model

The empirical model we use was initiated at the Science Policy Research Unit by one of the authors with his colleagues (John Clark, Tony Meagher and Henry Lucas). The equations of the model derive largely from a theoretical specification by Graciella Chichilnisky (see Chichilnisky and Cole, 1978a) and its theoretical properties have been presented in a number of papers (for example Chichilnisky (1978), Chichilnisky and Cole (1978b), Chichilnisky (1981)), and received some attention from other economists (for example Taylor (1979), Jones (1982), Bhagwati, Brechter and Hatta (1982), de Meza (1983), Sadulet (1983) and Cohen *et al.* (1984), especially those results which deal with the perverse effects of development aid and reversals in the terms of trade. We are not concerned directly with these topics here—since concepts such as the terms of trade are not unambiguously defined in a multi-sector, multi-region model. Several of these authors revise the model, but as Lysy (1981) concludes:

> Chichilnisky's model is interesting because it makes explicit the con-
> sequences of income effects in a general equilibrium model of world
> trade. Although it has been known for a long time that such income
> effects do exist and that they may upset traditional conclusions, they
> have not, as far as I know, been incorporated into a specific model

but he emphasises, with reference to the theoretical anomalies noted earlier, 'this will have to be answered by more careful empirical calcula-tions'. Some further research has been conducted in this direction (see Chichilnisky and McLeod, 1984).

This need for more intensive empirical research also applies if we wish simply to explore the income distribution effects, anomalous or not, and for this reason we have put some effort into obtaining adequate data for the model. The equations and method of estimation of the model have been published elsewhere (Meagher and Cole (1984), Cole and Miles (1984)) so we will concentrate here only on the relevent model structure and parameter values.

First, we consider the question of the level of detail to be employed. If a model is too aggregated it may give no practical insights beyond those of the simplest theoretical models. If it is too complicated it may be impossibly demanding of data and be too unwieldy in its use for many alternative hypotheses to be tested. We would describe our model as a semi-empirical or stylised model. It is sufficiently simple (in terms of the number of sectors and economic actors), that its results can be compared with the 'parables' and predicted anomalies of trade theory. But it is also sufficiently detailed that the economies and sectors included are sufficiently representative of the real world, and that the results of the model do indeed depend upon these data as well as its algebraic specification.

The earlier theoretical and empirical discussions suggest that at the very least, we must employ a multi-country model (i.e. at least three countries), and that within countries too we must identify at least two types of actor and sectors of production; and that while market mechanisms should be prominent, we must leave open the possibility of testing governmental as well as private sector behaviour. But the discussion (in Chapter 3) also suggests that there may be no level at which one can be totally confident about the conclusions drawn for particular actors, countries or sectors. This is because technologies and behaviour are sufficiently diverse within categories drawn up at any arbitrary level, that ambiguities about sub-categories will still remain! For example, the complexity of change within the manufacturing sector in the world economy is very diverse. But even if we subdivide, to examine, say, machine tool production, we still see that certain categories of machine tool production are migrating to newly industrialised developing countries, while other (especially 'high' technology machine tool) production is strengthening in the declining manufacturing centres in the older industrial nations.

Thus to examine the process in full detail we may need to separately identify all countries in the world and a very great number of sectors, subdivided according to conventional characteristics (such as SITC classification) as well as into less conventional sub-groups (such as 'high' and 'low' technology). In addition we should distinguish between many types of economic actor, different levels of management and operative skill, different resource bases, access to transport and public utilities, locations whether rural, urban or metropolitan, style of government and indeed cultural and ethnic heritage. Within any nation, all of these are important. We might subdivide further within nations, since for example, the regional economic diversity within a nation such as the United States is as great as that across the European nations. In this sense, the United States is as much a collection of interacting economies as is continental Europe (Cole 1984). The same applies to developing nations such as India, Mexico or Nigeria. As Jacobs (1984) has pointed out 'nations' are often little more than the sum of their cities.

In our model therefore we try to capture some limited characteristics of distribution and technology. As explained in Chapter 4 we identify countries as 'high income', 'medium income' and 'low income'. In practical terms, the first category includes all the OECD industrial nations and the CMEA industrial economies. Together they represent about some 81 per cent of total world income and 25 per cent of world population (see Table 5.1). For purposes of preparing data and considering the rate of adopting new technology, this group was further subdivided into leading and lagging industrial market economies (following Pavitt 1980). The 'middle income' group combines both newly industrialised countries such as Brazil, South Korea and the Philippines, and oil rich exporting and industrialising economies such as Nigeria and Mexico. These economies are responsible for about 14 per cent of world income and 14 per cent population. The third 'low income' group comprising all other countries in the world including the major economies India and China contains only 5 per cent of income and 61 per cent of population. Thus the group wide percapita incomes are in the ratio 40:13:1.

There are obviously great variations across countries within each group so a great deal of information is lost. Yet nevertheless there are very significant differences between the groups, sufficient to suggest that in the adopting of new technology the kind of 'paradoxes' discussed earlier indeed may be the norm in their mutual patterns of behaviour.

Within all economies, three sectors of production are identified: agriculture, industry and services. The levels of production (in terms of US\$ 1975 billion value added) are shown in Table 5.2. These three sectors are conventionally highlighted in international statistics—indeed (Mozak 1978) has suggested that it is only at this highly aggregated level that there is good comparability between data for different countries. Despite the very different production structures no economic group specialised in

Table 5.1 Population and average per capita income of economic groups

	Economy Group		
	High	Middle	Low
Domestic product US\$ bn 1975	4,482	786	284
Population (m)	1,018	548	2,468
Regional per capita Income US\$ '000s 1975	4.4	1.4	0.11

Table 5.2 Value added by economy and sector (US$bn, 1975)

	Economy Group		
	High	Middle	Low
Agriculture	308	107	85
Industry	1,933	308	77
Services	2,239	369	121

production of any commodity so the limitations on factor equalisation are not relevant to our analysis.

Although we have chosen to remain with conventional production categories, for the purpose in hand it may well be more advantageous to forego comparability for greater theoretical relevance, for example, to aggregate explicitly high and low technology sectors or innovating and non-innovating sectors. Apart from being difficult empirically (see Cole and Miles, 1984) it has both positive and negative attributes. Our model shows, as the earlier theories suggest, that existing production structures as well as technical change are very important to how economies behave. Thus, categorising by 'innovating' and 'non-innovating' sectors, for example, may entail combining sectors with very different technologies (i.e. very different inputs of capital and labour), so that in gaining clarity with respect to technical change one loses it with respect to the underlying contemporary situation. The difficulties of dealing with aggregation 'bias' are far from resolved (see for example Thirsk, 1980). On balance therefore we retain more conventional sectors but attempt to elaborate somewhat on the description of technology and technical change (at least as they impact on income distribution) by classifying technology and technical change according to its skill content as well as its capital and labour content. This is obviously vital in considering new technology as Chapter 3 makes clear.

We have prepared a 'base year' set of data for the model against which all experiments testing the impact of new technology will be compared. Tables 5.3 and 5.4 give details of capital/labour and skill/labour ratios for our three economies and sectors. This demonstrates very large differences both across countries within sectors and within countries across sectors. Worldwide agriculture capital labour ratios differ by nearly 1,000.

Table 5.3 Labour/capital ratio by sector (workers per US$m, 1975)

	Economy Group		
	High	Middle	Low
Agriculture	8	554	5,460
Industry	38	193	589
Services	65	397	1,238

Table 5.4 Skilled/unskilled ratios by sector*

	Economy Group		
	High	Middle	Low
Agriculture	0.067	0.009	0.003
Industry	0.16	0.10	0.04
Services	0.27	0.12	0.1

* Units are skilled labour years/unskilled labour years per unit output.

Between agriculture and industry in the low income countries this ratio differs by nearly a factor of ten and by a factor of five (in the reverse direction) in the high income economies. The skill content of production shows similar diversity, roughly a factor of twenty in agriculture and from four to thirty-fold between agriculture and services. Such wide variations are widely recognised in the literature (see for example Parker (1984), Diwan *et al.* (1979)). Thus despite the high level of aggregation a high degree of heterogeneity remains which obviously means that generalisations about the advantages of technical change and international trade based on the idea of equal technology worldwide must be suspect at best.

What then is the relationship of these data to the overall structure of the three economies? This is shown in Tables 5.5 to 5.8 where the

Table 5.5 Key to social accounts for all economic groups

	Production sectors			Factors of production			Final demand					Total
	Agricul.	Industr.	Service	Skilled	Unskill.	Capital	Rich HH.	Poor HH.	Governm.	Investm.	Foreign	
Agriculture		Intermediate					Institutions			Investment	Trade	Total income
Industry		Consumption					Consumption					
Services												
Skilled		Factor										
Unskilled		Payments										
Capital												
Rich households				Transfers to								
Poor households				institutions								
Government		Indirect taxes					Direct taxes				Overseas	
Investment							Savings				transfers	
Total						Total expenditures						

Table 5.6 Social accounts for high income industrial countries (US$bn, 1975)

	Production sectors			Factors of production			Final demand					Total
	Agricul.	Industr.	Service	Skilled	Unskill.	Capital	Rich HH.	Poor HH.	Governm.	Investm.	Foreign	
Agriculture	122.5	285.5	15	0	0	0	40.8	110.9	0	1.3	−9.4	566.6
Industry	96.2	1,690.4	532.1	0	0	0	339.8	712.9	109.4	1,014.1	55.1	4,550
Services	39.5	640.5	953.1	0	0	0	485	866.3	699.7	42.9	13.1	3,740.2
Skilled	11.3	308.4	694.8	0	0	0	0	0	0	0	0	1,014.5
Unskilled	56.6	655.3	875.8	0	0	0	0	0	0	0	0	1,587.7
Capital	245.1	642.6	551	0	0	0	0	0	0	0	0	1,438.7
Rich households	0	0	0	1,014.5	0	637.5	0	0	0	0	−36.6	1,615.3
Poor households	0	0	0	0	1,587.7	324.9	0	0	0	0	−10.1	1,902.5
Government	−4.5	327.2	0	0	0	476.3	178	43.7	177.9	0	−12	1,305
Investment	0	0	118.3	0	0	0	571.7	168.6	318.0	0	0	1,058.3
Total	566.6	4,549.9	3,740.2	1,014.5	1,587.7	1,438.7	1,615.3	1,902.5	1,305	1,058.3	0	0

Table 5.7 Social accounts for middle income developing countries (US$bn, 1975)

	Production sectors			Factors of production			Final demand					Total
	Agricul.	Industr.	Service	Skilled	Unskill.	Capital	Rich HH.	Poor HH.	Governm.	Investm.	Foreign	
Agriculture	12.1	35.7	3.5	0	0	0	8.2	78.8	2.8	13.6	3.6	158.2
Industry	23.9	191.3	29.1	0	0	0	58.5	102	29	181.8	-27	588.6
Services	14.3	53.6	29.5	0	0	0	77.2	151.5	104.3	12.4	-10.6	432.2
Skilled	2.5	34.6	75	0	0	0	0	0	0	0	0	112.1
Unskilled	64.4	76.2	146.8	0	0	0	0	0	0	0	0	287.3
Capital	39.4	146.7	138.9	0	0	0	0	0	0	0	0	325.1
Rich households	0	0	0	112.1	0	120.7	0	0	0	0	17.2	250.0
Poor households	0	0	0	0	287.3	82.5	0	0	0	0	9.3	379.1
Government	1.6	50.6	9.3	0	0	121.9	1.3	-9.6	83.5	0	7.5	266.0
Investment	0	0	0	0	0	0	104.9	56.5	46.4	0	0	207.7
Total	158.2	588.6	432.2	112.1	287.3	325.1	250.1	379.1	266.0	207.7	0	0

Table 5.8 Social accounts for low income developing countries (US$bn, 1975)

	Production sectors			Factors of production			Final demand					Total
	Agricul.	Industr.	Service	Skilled	Unskill.	Capital	Rich HH.	Poor HH.	Governm.	Investm.	Foreign	
Agriculture	16.2	12	1.3	0	0	0	18.0	74.2	1.1	0.9	5.8	129.5
Industry	14.5	71.5	22.2	0	0	0	15.4	37.1	8.4	56.9	−28.1	197.9
Services	13.6	37.1	19.5	0	0	0	18.0	43.3	34.5	1.1	−2.5	164.5
Skilled	0.9	4.1	22.2	0	0	0	0	0	0	0	0	27.2
Unskilled	67.9	20.1	45.4	0	0	0	0	0	0	0	0	133.4
Capital	14.8	42.2	47.8	0	0	0	0	0	0	0	0	104.8
Rich households	0	0	0	27.2	0	42.0	0	0	0	0	13.4	82.5
Poor households	0	0	0	0	133.4	28.0	0	0	0	0	5.7	167.1
Government	1.7	10.8	6.1	0	0	34.8	−0.5	−1.1	19.4	0	5.7	76.9
Investment	0	0	0	0	0	0	31.7	13.6	13.5	0	0	58.9
Total	129.5	197.9	164.5	27.2	133.4	104.8	82.5	167.1	76.9	58.9	0	0

data is presented most conveniently in the form of a 'social accounting matrix' (see for example Pyatt and Roe, 1979). For each economy these display how sectors of production and actors in the economy mutually balance their accounts. The first column, for instance, shows how much the agriculture sector spends on inputs of intermediate goods (from agriculture, industry and services), how much is paid (in US$ billions 1975) to factors of production (labour, skills and capital) and paid to or received from government (as indirect taxes or subsidies). The first row in the table shows how agricultural output is consumed by other sectors, by households and government, how much is reinvested and the net export of the economy. 'Technology' in the model is described by the ratio of the data in the top left hand block of the table (which shows intermediate consumption and payments to labour and capital) and the total output by sector.

Other blocks of the table describe corresponding features of the economy (see Table 5.5); in particular, the allocation of income by households government and investors to different goods, the level of net taxes and overseas payments, and investment. Note that total net exports balance total net overseas income. Details of the preparation of such data are given in Meagher (1980) and Cole and Miles (1984).

Since we are concerned with the issue of overall income distribution as well as different kinds of employment we sub-divide households in each economy into 'rich' and 'poor'. Obviously there is a great deal of difference between the per capita income and consumption of corresponding groups across countries. As Table 5.9 shows, the per capita income of rich households in the low income countries is far less than that of poor households in high income countries. Even when these data are adjusted to take account of differences in purchasing power of money across countries (for example Kravis *et al.*, 1982), the relative consumption levels differ greatly.

Households are distinguished principally on the basis of whether they receive income from skilled or unskilled labour. The definition of skill is based on formal and vocational qualifications, and as far as possible these have been matched across countries on the basis of ILO and UNESCO data (see Cole and Miles 1980). To some extent this avoids the tautology that wage levels are a measure of skill since they measure the marginal productivity of different types of labour.

The number of workers in each category depends on how much of the total available labour force is to be employed. If most labour is already utilised then wages and supply elasticities will be relatively high. If only a small amount of the labour potential is employed then wages will be

Table 5.9 Per capita consumption of rich households relative to poorest groups

	Economy Group		
	High	Middle	Low
Rich	80	12	8
Poor	33	6	1

much lower. This situation is shown in Figure 5.2. We retain separate curves for high and low income labour to reflect the fact that mobility between categories is a relatively slow process, and requires explicit policies with respect to education and training. For example, in the United States, new labour force entrants rather than workers displaced by restructuring of old manufacturing industries find employment in service and new technology industries (Yago and McGahey, 1984). In low income economies we estimate that only about 40 per cent of unskilled labour is employed. This is in agreement with International Labour Organisation data. Thus as the total demand (from all sectors) for a certain category of labour increases—so will wage rates. Wages income therefore will increase both because of increased employment and increased wage rates. This assumption is built into the model, although we shall consider also situations where the assumed fixed relationship is changed (through a more active wage policy). In the limiting case when labour is very abundant this approximates to the situation described by Lewis (1954) and others when wages remain at the subsistent level. By contrast about 80 per cent in our 'skilled' category are reckoned to be employed worldwide. These data are given in Table 5.10.

Households receive income from their capital investments as well as from their labours. After taxes a certain amount is saved, the rest is allocated to consumption and saving as shown in Table 5.11. As disposable household income changes so will saving and patterns of consumption. We assume that as per capita income and profitability increase, so will saving (and also investment), and that, in general, agricultural expenditures fall and expenditure on services rises as households become richer. In practice, there are deviations from this simple assumption (for example Lluch and Powell, 1977) and also a number of other complication issues. In particular, the real purchasing power of income varies across countries (for example Kravis *et al.* 1982).

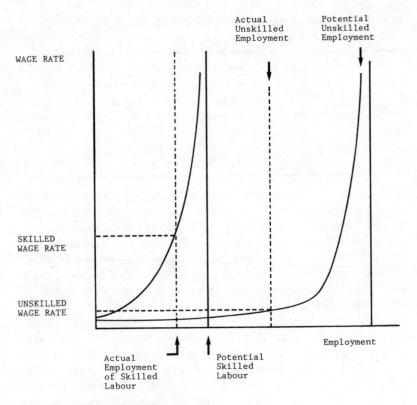

Figure 5.2   Labour supply elasticities.
Source: Based on Cole and Miles (1984)

Government behaves as a consumer, as an agent for redistribution between households, and as an active agent in supporting or taxing producers. Government expenditure is assumed to rise with national income and also to be mildly redistributive in all economies in that if the income of rich households rises relative to poor households then transfers between them will increase. This may be a reasonable assumption for high income countries, but more suspect for medium and low income countries since several studies (for example Foxley, 1976) show that overall taxes in developing countries have rather little impact on income distribution.

Reviewing these assumptions we see that some behaviours are treated as passive and 'endogenous' to the model, while others will be taken to be

Table 5.10 Utilisation of skilled and unskilled labour by economy

	Economy Group		
	High	Middle	Low
Skilled labour	82	73	83
Unskilled labour	70	41	44

Table 5.11 Percentage of consumption by rich/poor households

	Economy Group		
	High	Middle	Low
Agriculture	5/7	6/24	35/48
Industry	39/42	41/31	30/24
Services	56/51	53/46	35/28

active in that in our experiments a deliberate 'exogenous' change will be made. The behaviour of households (and labour) in particular is taken to be passive. There is a certain pattern of preferences with respect to the trade-offs between consumption of different goods, saving and leisure.

Obviously we shall treat technology as an active variable—that is we will assume a particular shift in technology and measure its outcome. This does not mean that in the real world we assume that technology is any more or less a determinant of change than any other; but to treat technical change as induced by allowing it to respond to changing factor prices as in the neo-classical model, would to some extent defeat the purpose of our exercise (as in a Cobb–Douglas or CES production function, see, for example, Nordhaus, 1969).

Our treatment of capital use and depreciation also requires some explanation. In general we assume a fixed stock of capital in each economy which is used in the most efficient (profit–maximising) way. As changes in technology or other variables (e.g. government subsidies) occur—the pattern of allocation within each economy changes. Beyond this we argue that as restructuring takes place unused capital will be brought back into production, while other capital is discarded or temporarily taken out of production. The world-wide location of capital too is taken to depend on changing rates of profit internationally, and this process is simulated in the model.

While this has been a very brief summary of our model and a relevant body of economic theory, it has provided the detail and context which is needed for an understanding of the experiments described in the following chapters. With these experiments we shall build up a picture of how different types of new technology could affect the economic situation of the various actors in the model, and what might be the consequences of their different responses. Thus we shall not present only a single technology or (alternative set of policies) as the definitive future, but try to clarify some of the processes and issues underlying the introduction of new technology and its world-wide impact.

6 Winner takes all? Labour saving versus capital saving technology

Experiments with the model

In this chapter, we shall examine the impact of the widening gap 'probable' technology route. This will be done in two stages: first we explore the effects of changes which are principally oriented towards improvements in labour productivity; second, we shall consider the effects of changes more especially aimed at improvements in capital productivity.

The income and employment effects of the new technology are found to be by no means uniform and so, in Chapter 7 we shall explore in addition the responses of major actors to the initial impact of the technology. This includes both governmental and private sector responses. In particular we look at the way that entrepreneurs may shift resources from sector to sector, and international capital relocates production worldwide in order to take advantage of new overseas opportunities. In the public sector, governments may attempt to protect employment, or particular sectors or regional interests or to offset hardship, or stimulate markets abroad (through development aid). Thus, we attempt to demonstrate how effective these various responses might be and indeed whether or to whom the new technology is likely to be of primary benefit, and which policy measures may be ultimately damaging.

In Chapter 8 we shall look at the two other alternatives for technology —the plausible 'catching up' route for the developing economies and also 'possible' technologies, yet to be well conceived, but which may have much more positive consequences for the development of low income economies.

We emphasise also that we do not attempt here to set up a fully fledged 'scenario' of what the future world economy would look like when, or if, new technology is finally implemented on a worldwide basis. (We have attempted to do this in a wider context elsewhere; Cole and Miles, 1984.) We do not, therefore, take into account population growth, educational policy, the growth of capital, other changes in technology, shifts in the price of energy, climatic change—all of which are likely to affect our future—except where we say so explicitly. (This is because we take a technological 'revolution' to imply a rapid shift in technology compared to other variables.) Rather we look at the possible pattern of action and reaction as different agents begin to 'stack the chips' and to understand some of the underlying processes. Thus, we confine ourselves here to an investigation of how new technology will affect levels of production (by sector), income and consumption (by economic actor), patterns of import dependence (by economy type) and policy action (by government). Our model will show us, as we employ the data of previous chapters, how these levels might change, and thus how various actors will be affected.

We have stressed the importance of obtaining a well-defined structure for the model and the data on new technology if clear and unambiguous results are to be obtained. As far as possible we have attempted to assure this. Even so we do not always arrive at unambiguous conclusions about the impact of new technology! Despite this, one advantage of our simple model is that we are able to perform a great many experiments with the model to test how robust or how ambiguous particular results are. Although we have carried out several dozen experiments we shall not describe them all here but rather give some appreciation of the stability of key results. Uncertainty in results comes principally from three directions. These are:

(i)   the equations of the model in terms of sectoral definitions and behavioural relationships (i.e. the accounting categories and equations);

(ii) the numerical parameter values used to specify the base year of the model (such as current capital labour ratios);

(iii) the data used to describe new technology (such as hypothesised future capital labour ratios);

(iv) the precise experiments we choose.

With individual experiments we have sought to clarify certain processes and together to follow the initial impact of successive responses to changing technology. To examine the impact in our 'probable' technology scenario we carry out the succession of experiments shown in Figure 6.1. First, we describe the impact of technical change alone, including a sensitivity test on the base year data. Obviously although we are assuming this pattern of technical change to be most probable, we do not necessarily have to accept the result since other forces come into play, in particular, the response of private sector and public sector agents. Thus our second experiments examine changes in the location and use of capital, and attempts to support threatened sectors or income groups. Finally we attempt an overall evaluation of probable technology. For our 'plausible' and 'possible' technology we follow a similar scheme.

For each experiment we shall compare results with data for the base year economy. For convenience we shall show percentage deviations from

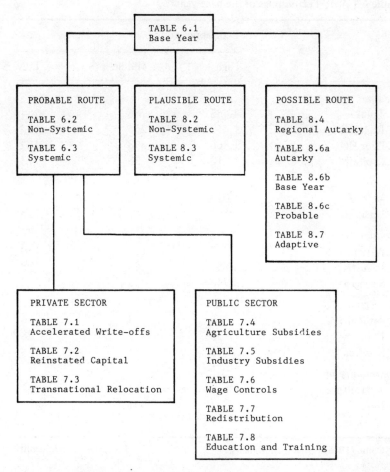

Figure 6.1 Guide to experiments for the probable, plausible and possible technology routes

the summary data in Table 6.1 based on Tables 5.6 to 5.8. This shows 'real' consumption nationally and by high and low income households, levels of employment of skilled and unskilled labour and the rate of profit, 'physical' production levels and net exports by sector and economy group. Because relative prices between commodities changes in the experiments, the 'GDP' (gross domestic product) of each economy is adjusted by a price index weighted by the composition of the national consumption basket (i.e. the total bundle of goods of high and low income

Table 6.1 World economies in the base year*

| | Economy Group | | |
	High	Middle	Low
Income			
Total	4,482	786	284
Rich HH	1,452	255	83
Poor HH	1,866	393	169
Capital†	12	38	13
Employment			
Skilled	1,014	112	27
Unskilled	1,588	287	133
Production			
Agriculture	567	158	130
Industry	4,550	589	198
Services	3,740	432	165
Net Exports			
Agriculture	−9	4	6
Industry	55	−27	−28
Services	13	−11	−3
Commodity prices			
Agriculture	1	1	1
Industry	1	1	1
Services	1	1	1

* $USbn. (1975) physical equivalents.   † Percentage rate of profit.

households, government and investors). The 'real' income of high and low income households is similarly adjusted by a price index based on their particular patterns of consumption. This enables us to compare actual consumption of goods and services directly with the base year data.

The procedure is important because an increase in the price index could easily offset an apparent increase in monetary income (when all prices are measured against the nominal price of a single commodity). The relative price of agricultural goods changes markedly, so for low income households in the least developed countries (whose consumption includes a large proportion of foodstuffs) the effect is especially crucial. Levels of employment are also measured in physical terms (albeit in billions of dollars worth of labour at 1975 prices) as are levels of production and net exports (again measured in 1975 units). The actual value of each of these items is obtained by multiplying the physical output by the new price (for example the sales of industrial goods equals the output multiplied by the world price of industrial goods).

Route one: 'probable' technologies

World-wide technological change—the gap widens

We introduce first only the labour saving component of technical change using data for the 'probable' technology route given in Table 4.3. This first experiment may assure us that the results of the model are not out of line with common sense (or at least our expectations) or even the economic theories reviewed in Chapter 5.

The results are shown in Table 6.2. Looking first at the 'real' gross domestic product of each economy, we see that the GDP of the high income countries increases only marginally, the middle income countries by 1 per cent while the low income countries' income rises by more than 2 per cent. Thus it appears that much of the benefit of the technical change is initially exported. Nominal worldwide GDP (measured relative to the price of industrial goods) also rises as orthodox theory would predict as average worldwide technology has risen in every sector. The new pattern of world prices reflects the differential factor saving of the new technology. Thus prices of agricultural goods rise by nearly 5 per cent relative to industrial goods, while the cost of services shifts only slightly.

Changes in rates of profit, employment, wage levels and household income are more varied. In the high income countries the rate of profit increases substantially but income distribution worsens. In the middle income countries income distribution improves (with wage levels moving in opposite directions), but the rate of profit increases only slightly. In the low income countries also income distribution improves but the rate of profit falls. In all cases the overall gains to each economy are certainly not evenly distributed.

Levels of net international trade increase generally; in particular, the high income countries become more dependent on imports of agricultural goods from the developing countries, which in turn become more dependent on imports of industrial goods or services. We note that the increase in net exports does not necessarily imply an increase in the two-way level of world trade—merely that the imbalance between production and consumption in each region has increased (even though at this stage we have left the balance of payments for each economy unchanged).

Table 6.2 The probable route (non-systemic)*

	Economy Group		
	High	Middle	Low
Income			
Total	+N	+NL	+VL
Rich HH	+L	−LM	−L
Poor HH	−L	+L	+LL
Capital	+L	+NL	−VL
Employment			
Skilled	+VL	−L	−LL
Unskilled	−LL	+L	+LL
Production			
Agriculture	−H	+VH	+LM
Industry	+VL	−M	+VL
Services	+VL	−L	−L
Net exports			
Agriculture	−MH	+VH	+LM
Industry	+VL	−M	−N
Services	+VL	−LM	−L
Commodity prices			
Agriculture	+LL	+LL	+LL
Industry	+N	+N	+N
Services	−N	−N	−N

* Percentage change relative to base year: key to scale (percentage change), N = 0, NL = 0.5, VL = 2, LL = 4.5, L = 8, LM = 12.5, M = 18, MH = 24.5, H = 32, HH = 40.5, VH = 50.

One important point to note here is that the *indirect* effect—on the change in production structure induced by the new technology—has if anything a greater impact on employment than does the *direct* labour displacing effect of the technology. (Referring back to our formal representation of the impact in Chapter 4 we note that the terms $QARy$ and $QRAy$ appear to be greater than the term $AQRy$ in so far as can we estimate these separately.) In essence this is the rationale for our use of the general equilibrium approach to tackle the problem in hand. It makes little sense to say that 10 per cent of jobs (per unit of production) are likely to be lost when new technology is introduced into a sector where the entire sector may be wiped out through new technology or reactive changes elsewhere.

In order to explain these various changes in detail we must examine our results more closely. This we shall do for each economy in turn before returning to a discussion of the overall global impact. We consider first the high income economies, since, the very size and the relatively large technology shifts there mean that mechanisms there have the determining influence on the restructuring of the world economy.

High income countries

Production of services in the high income countries has increased by nearly 3 per cent, the same amount as the increase in industrial production which makes us begin to question our prior expectations based on production costs alone given in Table 4.5. Thus, although the additional competitiveness of the industrial sector has had a devastating effect on agriculture, and has successfully competed to draw away factors of production from that sector (changing factor prices in the process), the net effect of changes in factor prices domestically and the additional demand for exports have enabled the level of service production to be maintained.

If we look at the change in the rate of profit and levels of employment, we see how this has come about. Overall in this economy, the introduction of a (on average) labour saving technology has reduced the demand for labour relative to capital in the economy. Since the amount of capital in each economy does not change (in this experiment), the total amount of labour employed falls. Given that we have built into the model the idea that when unemployment increases, wages will fall, then total wages also fall. This enables the rate of profit locally to adjust to a level commensurate with the new world price of each commodity.

An increase in the rate of profit (which is equal to the cost of capital in a perfect market since excess profits are zero) favours an expansion of production in those sectors which use relatively less capital (per unit of output). Given that in the high income countries agriculture is especially capital intensive (see Table 5.3), this has a detrimental effect on the competitiveness of the agriculture sector *over and above* the relatively lower comparative advantage obtained from the introduction of new technology. Here we see at once the importance of the point made earlier. It is not simply the change in technology which is important, but the existing structure of factor inputs and costs and changes implied for the latter. This point is emphasised by Sodesten (1980), for example, but is nevertheless often omitted in considering questions of international competitiveness when productivity gains only are considered (see for example Kendrick, 1984). There is an implicit assumption here that equal technologies are employed internationally, a suggestion which certainly does not hold at the sectoral or national level.

Production of services in the high income countries is also more capital intensive than is industrial production, so we might expect this sector, too, to be more seriously affected. The reason why this does not happen is because total wage costs (per unit of output) are higher in services than industry—so a reduction in wage rates favours this sector more than the industry sector. Thus, for all sectors there is an initial increase in competitiveness because of the introduction of the new technology, followed by a further change brought about by adjustment in factor prices (wages and interest rates), as the world economy responds to the initial change.

Referring again to Table 5.3, we see that a shift from agriculture in the industrial countries to industry and services means, on balance, a shift to more labour intensive sectors. The industry and services sectors employ respectively between seven and nine times more workers per unit of capital than does agriculture in these economies; nevertheless, total actual employment falls. But because the relative amounts of skilled to unskilled labour differ greatly between sectors, the overall impact is very different on these two groups. Both industry and services have higher costs for skilled to unskilled labour than does agriculture (about double for industry and four times higher for services). Thus, the shift away from agriculture is accompanied by a decline in the number of unskilled jobs which is not compensated for by the expansion of the industry sector. The volume of output in the service sector changes little (up by 3 per cent), but jobs are lost through the introduction of the technology (which sheds about 6 per cent per unit of output). The total level of unskilled employment consequently falls by over 6 per cent. The total number of skilled jobs on the other hand increases by over 2 per cent. This is reflected in the wages offered, and so the wage rate of unskilled workers falls while that of skilled workers rises. Because the cost of skilled to unskilled labour is relatively higher in the service sector than the industry sector, this is, again, to the comparative advantage of the latter.

Thus, it is not evident at all that the service sector in the high income countries should maintain its level of production. Other considerations, such as the comparative advantage it gains *vis-à-vis* the service sectors in other economies, and the corresponding changes in production structures and factor costs, therefore need to be brought into account. Before doing this, we look at household income distribution in the high income countries.

We have noted that both the rate of return on capital and high income wage rates increase, but low income wages fall. Income from capital, therefore, increases by about 8 per cent with gains to both household groups and government. The total level of wages also rises but the gains are unevenly distributed between households, and as Table 6.2 shows, the total income of high income households rises by about 9 per cent and that of low income houses falls by about 5 per cent.

In the high income countries the principal effects that we see, perhaps confirming the worst fears of many commentators, is that overall unemployment increases, and that wages of the unskilled fall while investment income rises. In the short run this obviously implies a considerable worsening of income distribution (which perhaps could be ameliorated by more positive redistributive mechanisms). To preserve the income of low income households would require that the taxes on high income households be raised significantly.

We should mention here that some small change in redistributive taxation has taken place via government agencies (as described in Chapter 5) in line with the increased government spending, but as far as possible we have retained a fairly neutral policy and not, for example, looked to changes in the level of social benefits to compensate for unemployment or reduced incomes. We will explore this later but point out here that redistribution also will have rather little impact on current overall levels of demand by sector since in the industrial countries as Table 5.11 shows, the composition of consumption differs rather little between high and low income households (at least in terms of our broad categories).

We will return later to the question of how acceptable such a 'scenario' is for actors in the industrial economies, but it is worth noting that such a high level of blue-collar unemployment is probably unacceptable to either government or trade unions in these countries. So too would be the high level of dependence on agricultural imports and subsidies (such as the European Common Agricultural Policy). Following the discussion in Chapter 5 we have assumed that labour and capital are mobile between sectors, but we should at least check the implication of modifying this assumption. After all, in a period of rapid restructuring, a significant amount of capital stock is likely to be scrapped well before the end of its (originally) planned life. We have the phenomenon in several industrial economies of quite modern plant being retired, underemployed, or temporarily taken out of production. Middle income nations too may find the renewed industrial strength of the high income countries implied by the experiment difficult to accommodate. The governments of most developing nations are explicit in their desire to industrialise (such as through the

Lima Plan of Action), even though many development economists have argued that rural development is likely to offer a more rapid growth in the long run

Middle income countries

The impact of the new technology on the middle income countries is also beneficial in some respects. Total domestic consumption increases more than in the high income economies. Income distribution improves markedly with the ratio of high to low income shifting so as to reverse the trend noted by several authors for newly industrial countries (for example Ahuwalia (1979), Bigsten (1983)). However, the acceptability of these changes is in question, since it implies a large shift away from industry, little increase in the rate of profit (the motivation for intro- ducing the new technology in the first place) and a 13 per cent fall in skilled unemployment (and middle class incomes).

If we follow a similar argument to that for the high income countries in order to 'explain' the results, we immediately see that the price of capital is far less important. Its price is little changed, so only the relative increase in inputs by sector (greatest in the service sector and least in agriculture) are important. (Changes in wage costs, and relative labour and total factor cost savings are more critical.)

Comparing the production cost data given in Table 4.5, we note that the competitiveness of the middle income countries is undermined more in industry (relative to the high income countries) than services, but more in services than in agriculture. Within the economy the expected production costs of services and agricultural goods are roughly the same. Thus, changes are brought about first by international market pressures, and then by changes in factor costs domestically as restructuring begins. Capital is the expensive factor of production in the economy, and this favours the sector which requires least additional capital (per unit of output) when the new technology is introduced.

On this basis, we should expect agricultural activity to increase. On the other hand, because agriculture is a labour intensive sector (see Table 5.4) such a shift is likely to increase total employment and, hence, push up wages, offsetting an increase in the competitiveness of agricultural production. The reason this does not happen is because wage rates are comparatively low in these economies and so do not reverse the changing of capital costs. In addition, while agriculture is intensive in its overall use of labour, it requires about 30 per cent less skilled labour than in- dustry or services (see Table 5.5). This results in a decrease in the economy wide demand for skilled labour and, hence, a lowering of the wage rate which offsets the increase in the unskilled wage rate. The result is, therefore, a large shift to the sector for which, this economy has a cheap factor of production i.e. agriculture.

Similar considerations explain the performance of the service sector where labour accounts for nearly 50 per cent of production costs. However, in this sector, the greater savings in wages to skilled labour help to offset the relatively high additional capital inputs.

We have noted several reasons why the situation described by the experiment may not be 'acceptable' for the middle income countries. And of course, there are again actions which might be taken to reverse the situation, for example, protection or subsidies on industry, a redistributive tax in favour of high income households, or a reduction (or lower increase) of the wage rate for unskilled labour. We have noted that the rate of profit has remained steady, but given that it is already high, simply to see the rate maintained nevertheless may be acceptable to both domestic and foreign entrepreneurs and corporations. Alternatively, governments may simply be allowed (by the now stronger industrial nations) to run increased balance of payments deficits. We will explore some of these issues later.

Low income countries

In the low income countries the results appear, at first sight, favourable for income distribution and employment of unskilled labour. The latter increases by nearly 4 per cent and consequently the real consumption of low income households rises by nearly 6 per cent. The results for skilled labour and capital are much less favourable. Skilled employment falls by 5 per cent and the rate of profit also falls by nearly 3 per cent. This has obvious significance for future growth prospects given the rather large increase in profitability in the industrialised economies. Nevertheless, the low income countries show the highest overall increase in national income. As in the middle income countries production shifts in favour of agriculture, but also marginally in favour of industry. Thus industry does not appear to be undermined by the relatively increased competitiveness of the most industrialised nations. To some extent this is surprising but the brunt of this technological change is felt by the middle income newly industrialised economies.

In the low income countries agriculture is especially labour intensive; the ratio of labour to capital costs being nearly four times that in industry, and sixteen times that in services. Clearly, any increase in the price of capital in these economies will favour agriculture and be especially against services. As in other economies, the displacement of labour from production means that (given a fixed amount of capital stock) the economy-wide average labour/capital ratio will fall. Because world prices fall less than wage costs (for reasons given earlier) profitability rises, favouring agricultural production with its exceptionally low capital/labour ratio.

The gain to national income supports the idea discussed in Chapter 5 that trading partners rather than the home economy can gain from improvements in productivity. However, the magnitude of the increase in national income observed in our experiment comes from the induced shift in production structures as much as the opportunity to purchase goods more cheaply. Our estimates of production costs using base year prices suggest that about half the gain comes from technical change and half from changes in the composition in production. It is the latter which is most responsible for the increased employment of low skill workers and consequent real wage increase. But although the low income countries increase production of foodstuffs, and more people are engaged in agriculture, the world price of food rises by nearly 5 per cent. The importance of food in the consumption basket of poor people in the low income countries (some 30 per cent of total) means that this group gains relatively less than all other groups from the technical change we have assumed. Indeed, much of the increased production is exported rather than consumed domestically.

A rich country technology?

While grouping the countries in our model into the categories of *high, medium,* and *low* income economies is a device which enables us to simplify presentation, it also begs many questions. Obviously many countries which fit into an arbitrary income band do not match the production and distribution structures attributed to that group. In preparing data we used the more diverse categories such as 'leading' and 'lagging' industrial economies. How are the apparent gains to this group of counties as a whole distributed across them? The spectrum of 'low income' economies is yet more diverse including some sixty nations. Thus even if we can argue that the model gives a broad picture of the changes promoted in those economies as a whole, it certainly need not reflect any particular situation.

Nevertheless, from a variety of such experiments, assuming a range of base year parameters and productivity shifts to represent new technology we gain an impression of the 'robustness' of our initial result. The pattern of production and income shifts for the high income countries (as a whole) is rather stable. The key feature here is the importance of competition *within* the domestic economy for capital and labour and the relative weakness of agricultural production. The economy-wide increase in labour productivity favours less capital intensive sectors.

If we allow that our model describes the fortunes of several 'interest' groups such as nations, high and low income households, governments, skilled and unskilled workers, investors, and sectors of production—we may ask who gains and who loses. On the face of it, the answer to the question posed by Kaplinsky: 'is the new technology a rich country technology?', could be, on balance 'yes' even if we do not take the capital saving possibilities of the technology into account. Most groups in rich countries gain, although agriculture is seriously impared and low income households and unskilled labour are adversely affected.

We have suggested that redistributive taxation could restore the damaged income distribution if the political will existed (although the trend in recent years has certainly not been in this direction). The strength of farming lobbies and strategic considerations in Europe and the United States suggests that some major support would be given to agriculture— at least to retain production levels. In the developing countries it seems likely that similar support for industry would be demanded. Some attempt to compensate for changes in income distribution by holding down wage pressures (especially low income labour in the middle income countries), or to further reduce wages in the low income countries seems likely. These issues will be illustrated in the next chapter. Capital generally has gained from the introduction of new technology, even though we have not so far considered the migration of capital internationally in response to changing rates of profit. This and the possibility that capital may be written off during the process of global industrial restructuring will be considered also. We note here, however that the experiments there do not cause us to amend the above remarks, at least for the short and medium run. Rather what they point to is the possibility of spirals of economic decline or concentration of production activities. This may arise if certain kinds of protectionist behaviour is engaged in internationally or if there is an accelerating tendency to 'structural obsolesence'. Before turning to the issues we explore the implications of taking the 'systemic' capital savings potential of the new technology into account, and which may be gained in the longer term.

Systemic technical change

How different are the effects of 'capital saving' through the use of infor-mation technology? Our review of the sectoral impact of information technology in Chapter 3 showed, following Bessant (1982), Ayres and Miller (1983) and Kaplinsky (1984), that the more significant impact of information technology could come from a 'system wide reorganisation of production'. This would result in a more intensive use of existing capital and the installation of production systems with greatly improved capital productivity in the future. Even though the new technology, taken process by process, with the current organisation of production generally implies a higher input of capital, because equipment can be used more intensively (for example, on a three shift rather than a two shift basis), the overall result is a decrease in capital intensity rather than an increase. Ayres and Miller (1983) demonstrate that in a single sector (metal working) taking this capital saving phenomenon into account requires a major re-evaluation of the employment implications of the new technology. If only labour saving possibilities are taken into account then, they estimate a net loss of jobs will result in that sector, but if capital savings are hypothesised then they calculate that there will be a net gain. How significant is the parallel re-evaluation for our analysis of the world-wide impact of information technology when inter-sectoral and international feedback processes are taken into consideration? Certainly, we must expect some differences with respect to the pattern of gains from international trade, since with capital augmenting technology in the export sector the gains should go unambiguously to the exporting economy as observed in Chapter 5.

We have stressed earlier that the available data on systemic changes are less reliable than data for the more immediate labour saving effects. It is partly because of this uncertainty that we explore these new impacts in a separate experiment. But an equally important reason is that the time scale over which systemic changes would be implemented is considerably less clear. Kaplinsky (1983), for example speaks of the 'factory of the future' as arriving by the year 2000: Ayres and Miller (1983), speak of changes being introduced over the next 'half century'. Following Boon (1982) and others, we have assumed that these systemic gains are likely to be obtained in a second stage of implementation i.e. after the process and plant level operational difficulties have been ironed out. Thus the tendencies observed in the last experiment (together with those responses described in Chapter 7) may well be superseded by a new round of change as the full potential of the new technologies are realised.

Table 4.3 showed our tentative assessment of the 'systemic' component of the sector-wide impact of the technology. In broad terms the pattern of change matched changes in net labour productivity. However as we have noted a number of important differences arise because the possibilities of gains from systemic changes depend on the present characteristics of production, in particular, the length of 'production runs'. Those industries which characteristically engage in 'batch' production are likely to benefit most in terms of more intensive use of capital and savings on intermediate inputs of goods, services and raw materials.

To evaluate the impact of this we repeat the last experiment of Table 6.2 with the systemic component of sectoral technical change now accounted for. The same procedure as before is adopted: the data for each sub-sector is aggregated and weighted by major sector and economic group. Because capital savings are principally of two kinds, more intensive use of equipment and reduced servicing costs for inventories, a net capital saving is calculated. In addition, a lesser saving arising from reduced intermediate consumption (per unit output) accounts for savings arising, for example, from enhanced quality control and inventory management.

The results of the new experiment are shown in Table 6.3. Compared to Table 6.2 a number of major differences are seen. In some respects these suggest a much more hopeful outcome at least for the longer run (although we should remember the optimistic bias of general equilibrium calculations). For example, in their anticipation of increased overall economic growth, the new results are dramatically different. But, in other respects, especially those concerned with income distribution and employment for developing economies, the results promise much less. Given our elaboration of the previous experiment we shall only summarise the main features and processes underlying the results here.

The most obvious feature is that our measure of real Gross Domestic Product has risen significantly in all economies. For the high income economies the increase is nearly 14 per cent, a considerable gain over Table 6.2. Furthermore, the increase is now greater than in either the middle or low income economies. Middle income economies show a GDP increase of 9 per cent compared to less than 4 per cent for low income economies, scarcely more than when no systemic changes are assumed. A second comparative feature observed here is that the rate of profit increases most in the high income economies and least in the low income economies, although here the gap between them is less marked than in the last experiment. Overall, in terms of both short-run output gains and potential for longer-run growth, the result is far less attractive to developing than to developed nations.

Before looking in more detail at the income distribution and employment effects, we should examine how this result has come about. The most obvious explanation is that we have introduced a more efficient technology worldwide with more output per unit of labour and capital; thus worldwide output increases. But unlike the previous experiment,

Table 6.3 The probable route (systemic)*

	Economy Group		
	High	Middle	Low
Income			
Total	+LM	+L	+VL
Rich HH	+M	+M	+LM
Poor HH	+LL	−VL	−VL
Capital	+LL	+VL	+VL
Employment			
Skilled	+L	+LM	+L
Unskilled	+VL	−NL	−NL
Production			
Agriculture	+MH	−HH	−L
Industry	+LM	+L	+N
Services	+LL	+M	+LM
Net exports			
Agriculture	+LM	−HH	−L
Industry	+N	+N	−VL
Services	−VL	+LM	+L
Commodity prices			
Agriculture	+VL	+VL	+VL
Industry	+N	+N	+N
Services	+LL	+LL	+LL

* Percentage change relative to base year, key as for Table 6.2.

the major gains from the new technology are not exported. In this case the countries introducing the new technology gain the greatest short- and longer-run benefits. In the previous experiment it appeared that short-run but not long-run gains would accrue to the innovating economy. In this case, therefore, gains from capital saving are shown to be unambiguously in favour of the innovating nation. In the present experiment, technical change is both capital and labour saving, but with the data we have used the capital saving effects are dominant and determine the worldwide distribution of growth. By, contrast, the earlier experiment showed that the result depends very much on existing production structures, factor endowments and technology.

This experiment clarifies the importance of the direction of technical change. The size of the increases in output are again determined by several direct and indirect contributions as considered in Chapter 4. By comparison with the last experiment, the direct effects of increasing the productivity of a more or less fixed stock of capital and the lesser savings in the use of intermediate goods are more important.

What of employment and domestic distribution? Here, the results are again determined by the variations in technology and technical change across sectors and the resulting variations in the availability of factors across economies. The fact that the new technology is, on balance, predominantly saving of unskilled labour (for each unit of output) means that again we might typically expect any gains in employment to favour skilled labour. However we noted that changes in the structure of output (i.e. changes in the relative size of sectors) have at least as great an impact on employment prospects as does technical change alone. In the present experiment we see that the shift in production structures world-wide is significantly changed. In particular, the level of output of agricultural goods in the high income countries increases. This may be surprising, in view of the fact that the major cost reductions (with inputs costed at base year prices) are in the industry sector of the high income economies (see Table 4.5). We might therefore expect this to be the most competitive sector worldwide and hence show greatest growth, in relative as well as absolute terms. Why is this no longer the case and why does the agriculture sector in these countries shows the greatest relative expansion? Principally this is because the net effect of reducing capital intensity domestically is to increase the abundance of capital relative to labour, and consequently capital becomes a relatively cheaper factor of production. The immediate consequence of this is to favour agricultural production in the high income economies above production of industrial goods or services. This is practically the reverse of the phenomenon observed in the last experiment. Again, although the technical changes effected in the other economies are not unimportant to the worldwide restructuring, the conflict for factors of production between sectors within the industrial economies are critical to the outcome domestically and internationally.

The economy wide increase in output, leading to growth in all sectors, in spite of the restructuring of production, leads to an increase in the demand for both skilled and unskilled labour. This, in turn leads to an increase in real wages for both groups and together with the general income from investment provides for an increase in the net income of both high and low income households.

Although, there is a net increase in output and the employment effects are largely positive, the distributional effects in industrial countries are little changed from the last experiment. The increase in employment for skilled and unskilled workers are respectively 10 per cent and 2.5 per cent, and the net real income gains of rich and poor households 22 per cent and 6 per cent. What is apparent is that the gap in prospects for employment and income gains between the groups remains at about 7 per cent and 15 per cent. (Again we shall consider later whether the scope for training or redistributive taxation allows for these gaps to close.)

In both groups of developing economies the distributional implications are considerably changed. In the earlier experiment unskilled labour and low income households were on balance favoured over skilled labour and capital. The world-wide change in technology was redistributive, mainly because of the industrial restructuring induced by events in the high income economies. This is no longer the case. The strength of the agricultural sector in the high income economies, with a consequent reduction in output in both middle and low income countries, means that many unskilled jobs are lost. Even though output of industrial goods and services increases in both economies, this is insufficient to offset the combined effect of the newly introduced labour displacing technology and a shifting pattern of output. While the magnitude of restructuring is greater in the middle income economies, its effect on employment is as large in the low income economies. This is because the difference in factor inputs across sectors in these countries are relatively greater (see Tables 5.3 and 5.4).

The results overall for developing countries, therefore, are very mixed. First, the results seem to suggest a growing gap in income and growth rates between the rich and poor nations. Second, they suggest that total output, profitability and upper level incomes will increase substantially in middle income countries and, to a lesser extent, in low income countries. Third, although additional skilled labour is required there is a slight decline in total employment and the net real income of poor households declines. On balance, therefore in terms of providing for improved distribution across and within economies the result has little to offer. Nor does it confront the massive unemployment problem of developing countries. In terms of its attractiveness to some contemporary governments and business in all countries the result may be more appealing, since it affords a route to increased growth and higher profitability. For the industrial nations especially the route appears to solve many problems of unemployment and recession. In this respect the result appears to parallel the findings of Leontief *et al.* (1985) noted earlier, whose detailed analysis of the impact of 'automation' on the United States suggests that the new technology may not necessarily result in unemployment.

7 Spirals of decline: restructuring and reaction

Responses to technical change

The last chapter suggested that while uncertainties about the pace and extent of the labour and capital saving potential of information technology leave a number of unanswered questions as to the impact of this technology on overall growth prospects, the distributional consequences domestically and internationally are less uncertain. In earlier chapters we have indicated several reasons why these technologies are now being installed: clearly distributional issues are one primary consideration. By asking the question of what might be the impact of a new technology we do not, therefore, wish to imply that new technologies are being assumed in the abstract. Nor do we imply that people affected by the changes will not respond so as to take advantage of further opportunities or to defend themselves against unwelcome change.

Obviously, if we consider the earlier experiments, it is the first which is likely to provoke the strongest reaction. This is for two reasons: first, because total output worldwide does not rise greatly and so more actors are made relatively or absolutely worse off and, second, because the actors which are most adversely affected (such as agricultural producers in high income economies and the wealthier populations of developing countries) generally are able to influence public policy or effect other responses. Consequently, as these issues are explored in this chapter, we shall concentrate on modifications to the first experiment (i.e. Table 6.2).

For reasons of space, we explore only a limited number of responses. This selection serves two purposes. The first is to tell us whether particular policies are likely to have the impact intended for them. The second, equally important, is to demonstrate how robust are our earlier results. given the various simplifications and approximations that our model contains.

We shall consider below, first, a number of private sector responses by domestic or international capital to maintain or increase their profitability and then examine attempts by government to protect levels of employment or international competitiveness.

Private sector responses

In the earlier experiments it was shown that changes in technology may lead to changes in the composition of output across economies. Indeed, this finding has a major bearing on our results. But there are several other effects to account for: if restructuring is considerable so that output in particular sectors falls dramatically, unprofitable capital may simply be prematurely written off or 'junked' and the economy-wide production capability declines. But alternatively, if profitability increases then idle capital (i.e. plant which has temporarily been laid off) will be brought back into production. Furthermore, as well as reinvesting across sectors, some firms will re-invest abroad if the new technology makes this possibility attractive. To some extent these processes create competing tendencies, even though they are designed to and do, indeed, raise the worldwide level of profitability.

Domestic and international capital flows

Our model assumes that within each economy capital may be switched between sectors of production. Thus, the same capital stock (equipment, land etc.) may, under different situations, be diverted from production of one commodity to another. There are some profound objections to this—the substance of the famous 'switching' controversy between the British and American 'Cambridge' schools, for example. A concise summary of the debate is to be found in Jones (1976), giving the reasons why the British school (led by the late Joan Robinson) is correct, but nevertheless ignored by the neo-classical American school (which we also do here). Even if we may argue that some machines may be used for different but similar purposes (e.g. land may be used for production of different crops within the agricultural sector), there seem fewer opportunities for switching between the sectors we have described—i.e. agriculture, industry and services.

Perhaps the differences today lie more in the switching of output between these sectors. For example, as observed in Chapter 4 it is difficult to distinguish factory farming from other manufacturing except that somewhere along the line is a live animal or crop. As Gershuny and Miles (1983) show, many services (for example laundering) and entertainment (cinema), previously consumed in the formal sector, are now consumed in the informal household sector, using manufactured goods (washing machines and televisions manufactured in the formal industrial sector). Thus, the common assumptions made in macro-economic models of increasing consumption of formal sector services as people get richer, or that as people in low income countries reach the former income levels of the rich countries they will have similar consumption habits are increasingly questioned. This is especially relevant to our present discussion since household micro-electronics are argued by many authors to be the basis for a revolution in lifestyles as well as systems of production.

When we change technology in the model, capital relocates in order to describe the new most efficient system of production. But in view of the objections to this we should test our earlier result to discover how it is amended if no capital switching is possible. We do this as follows. For each sector in each economy which was seen to contract in the above experiment (e.g. agriculture in the high income countries), we simply 'scrap' the amount of capital stock that corresponds to the lost production (i.e. scrapped capital = decline in output × appropriate capital/ output ratio). The model experiment is then repeated. The results after one round of this procedure are instructive and adequate demonstration given the lack of consensus in the literature as to what scrapping rules should be applied. The common assumption made is that of Salter, i.e. to write off all capital for which the rate of profit falls to zero, but this requires a model in which each generation of technology is explicitly represented—a vintage capital model (see Cooper and Clark, 1982).

The level of capital in the high, medium and low income groups is reduced to 89 per cent, 70 per cent and 92 per cent respectively, in accordance with the above rule, and the last experiment is repeated. The results are shown in Table 7.1. We shall not describe in detail either the results or the explanation for them since they are quite similar to the first experiment. Instead, we note the principle new features for each economy.

Immediately it is seen that in each economy total domestic consumption has fallen, not only below the experiment shown in Table 6.2, but in the high and middle income countries also below the base period level (Table 6.1). Thus, according to this test, any gains from the new technology are more than offset by the destruction of existing capital stock. The explanation for this is broadly as before—an expansion of agriculture in the middle income countries as an indirect consequence of increased competitiveness of the global leading sector, i.e. industry in the high income economies which also expands further. In the low income countries agriculture expands at the expense of industry and services (which are handicapped by the rising cost of capital). Indeed, the most significant feature of the result is the increase in rates of return in all economies. In the high income economies, despite the reduction in capital stock and declining GDP, total profits rise by 6 per cent above the base level.

The price of capital has risen for similar reasons to those given earlier

Table 7.1 The probable (non-systemic) route with accelerated write-offs*

	Economy group		
	High	Middle	Low
Income			
Total	−NL	−VL	+VL
Rich HH	+LL	−MH	−LM
Poor HH	−L	+L	+L
Capital	+LM	+VL	−VL
Employment			
Skilled	+NL	−M	−L
Unskilled	−LL	+L	+LL
Production			
Agriculture	−VH	+VH	+M
Industry	+LL	−VH	−NL
Services	+N	−LL	−LM
Net exports			
Agriculture	−HH	+VH	+M
Industry	+LL	−H	−VL
Services	+NL	−VL	−LM
Commodity prices			
Agriculture	+LL	+LL	+LL
Industry	+N	+N	+N
Services	−NL	−NL	−NL

* Percentage change relative to base year. Key as for Table 6.2.

except that instead of reducing the world demand for labour (through the introduction of labour saving technology) we have reduced the availability of capital (by writing it off). The reduction in capital means that less production is possible and hence fewer jobs are created. Therefore, overall wages fall (and given our earlier arguments about the determinants of world prices) the average rate of profit worldwide will rise. (It is possible for the rate of profit in particular economies to fall, but this depends on the size of intersectoral production shifts and differences in capital/labour ratios.)

The amount of premature scrapping (structural obsolescence) was seen to differ among the three types of economy. For the high income economies the 11 per cent or so of total capital lost is just over one year's worth of total new investment in the economy. So unless overall investment increased above present levels no increase in output above present levels would be expected. For the middle income groups the situation is potentially even more serious since the 30 per cent of capital lost represents around four years of net investment. Thus, if these estimates are even approximately correct, they suggest little possibility of offsetting the dramatic restructuring with new investment. In the middle income group (which includes the oil exporting economies) annual investment already averages around 25 per cent of gross domestic product.

To some extent the greater shift in production structures in the two developing economy groups in the model is a direct result of the fact that these economies as represented there are small compared to the industrial group. Thus, the phenomenon may arise partly from the manner in which economies have been combined; but this difference in size of economies is a fair reflection of typical contribution of individual economies of each kind to the world economy. Thus it appears that even though many industrial economies today are faced with problems of structural obsolescence, the much more serious impact is likely to fall on the developing economies.

Increasing the size of the cake: raising capacity utilisation

In contrast, and as a counter to the last experiment we might argue that the large increase in the rate of profit seen in industrial economies will encourage entrepreneurs to bring existing unused capacity back into production and as far as possible to upgrade it using new technology. As our earlier discussion in Chapter 3 shows, in some cases this may be possible—in others not. In other economies too the utilisation of existing capital stock is likely to change in response to shifting profitability. We are making a sharp distinction here between systemic changes which increase capital productivity and simply bringing production capacity out of temporary retirement.

Again, there must be some discretion about the assumptions to make here. In every business cycle, production capacity is taken in and out of production. Thus equipment may be temporarily taken out of commission or used below full capacity, but certainly not written off. In general there may be a delay of several years before a final decision is made to discard a production unit or machine. Data for the United States, for example, suggests that in 1984 the capacity utilisation of industrial plant (as aggregated with extraction and utilities as in Table 4.3) is around

81 per cent, an increase of 11 per cent over 1970 but roughly matching the 1967 to 1982 average. For India, Allagh (1984), concludes that between 25 per cent and 35 per cent of capacity is unused. Similar estimates are available for other economies and also estimates of the supply elasticity of existing stock (as opposed to new investment). Such data are again complicated by several factors, in particular, the 'scrapping criterion' used, and require a knowledge of how much investment is in completely new state of the art technology, and how much in the upgrading of existing stock. In each sector (as defined in the model), there is a spectrum of technologies but provided these do not overlap unduly we should expect our conclusions to hold. For instance, as long as agriculture in high income countries is in general significantly more capital intensive than industry, and vice versa for low income countries, the broad pattern of results should remain.

In order not to complicate matters here, in order to illustrate the phenomenon, we therefore shall simply assume that unused capital is brought back into production, pro rata, according to the change in the rate of profit. In other words we take a unit supply elasticity for this type of capital. For the high middle income countries this means that capital stock increases by around 11 per cent and 2 per cent respectively while for low income countries over 2 per cent of capital is taken out of production. Overall, in contrast to the last experiment, the size of the world cake is increased. The capital brought back into production is roughly equal to one year's total new investment worldwide. Because this effect should help to counter the tendency, discussed above, for capital to be written off during the process of restructuring, we show in Table 7.2 the combined effect of the two processes.

Overall, we see that the broad pattern of results is similar to that in Table 6.2, but with some important differences. In particular, the growth of the high income economies shows a substantial gain (around 5 per cent) while developing economies now show a decrease, and the earlier gains to low income groups and unskilled workers there are lost. The principal reason for the result is again that, because restructuring in the high income countries is less than elsewhere and the rise in the rate of profit greater, there is a net increase in the availability of capital. With a resulting smaller change in relative capital versus labour costs in these economies (compared to Table 6.2) there is less extreme restructuring domestically and so lesser effects worldwide.

Table 7.2 Capital brought back into production*

	Economy group		
	High	Middle	Low
Income			
Total	+VL	−VL	+NL
Rich HH	+L	−LM	−L
Poor HH	−LL	+VL	+VL
Capital	+L	+N	−VL
Employment			
Skilled	+VL	−L	−VL
Unskilled	−LL	+LL	+VL
Production			
Agriculture	−MH	+VH	+LM
Industry	+L	−HH	−L
Services	+NL	+LL	−VL
Net exports			
Agriculture	−MH	+VH	+LM
Industry	+VL	−MH	−LL
Services	−NL	+L	−VL
Commodity prices			
Agriculture	+VL	+VL	+VL
Industry	+N	+N	+N
Services	+N	+N	+N

* Percentage change relative to base year. Key as for Table 6.2.

Transnational capital

Shifting rates of profit between economies implies that capital, too, will migrate between economies. In the two experiments so far it has been assumed that this does not happen. The available capital is simply re-located between sectors. But if we consider capital to be an internationally increasingly mobile factor of production (as indeed transnational capital is by definition) then some account should be taken of this. In the 1970s the primary role of multinational firms investing in developing economies, appropriating technologies and repatriating income was the focus of much attention. In the 1980s the critique has been redirected, and some authors explain the collapse of some industries on the fact that multinationals have preferred to re-invest abroad and employ 'state of the art' technologies there (for example Bluestone and Harrison, 1982). Of course, the behaviour of international firms is crucial in the present context as major carriers of information technology (see for example Ernst, 1983). The *modus operandi* of these firms is an issue of hot debate, location being variously attributed to the search for inexpensive labour (Peet 1982), maximisation of worldwide profits (Frobel *et al.* 1978), or proximity to markets (for example Kaplinsky, 1984). Although international direct investment is a growing and multi-directional phenomenon, again we should not exaggerate its importance. Data shows that typically 10 per cent of total capital stock in the larger industrial and developing countries is direct foreign investment (for example UN Centre for Transnationals, 1983).

Between economies (especially the middle income countries and the rest) rates of profit differ markedly. Some authors (for example Soete and Metcalfe, 1983) take it to be a stylised fact that this is not the case, and argue a uniform global rate of return. But the evidence of much research (for example Bhagavan, 1980) and evidence on the differential rates of profit between countries by individual multinational firms suggest this is not the case. For our groups the aggregate economy wide rates of return are 12 per cent, 38 per cent and 13 per cent respectively. Several reasons why competitive rates of return to investors are different are given (e.g. monopoly rents in the oil sectors pushing up local entrepreneurial expectations across an economy or high discount rates in the face of potential economic or political instability). In the long run again there will be a tendency to such an equilibrium. But we may assume, nevertheless, that changes in relative rates of profit will induce a tendency to relocate capital or change the pattern of new investment on an international scale.

In the spirit of the last experiments, we will relocate capital stock between economies according to the shift in profitability suggested by Table 6.2, leaving total world capital stock unchanged. This means an 11 per cent increase in levels of stock in the high income countries, a 2 per cent increase in the middle income countries, and a 3 per cent decrease for the low income. In effect, what is represented here is a withdrawal of transnational capital from the low income countries to the high income economies.

The results of this experiment are shown in Table 7.3. This is explained briefly as follows. With reduced capital in the low income countries their total real consumption decreases as does the real income of both high

Table 7.3 Production relocated internationally*

	Economy group		
	High	Middle	Low
Income			
Total	+NL	−VL	−VL
Rich HH	+L	−M	−LM
Poor HH	−LL	+VL	+NL
Capital	+L	+NL	−VL
Employment			
Skilled	+VL	−L	−N
Unskilled	−LL	+LL	+LL
Production			
Agriculture	−H	+VH	+M
Industry	+L	−VH	−HH
Services	+N	+VL	+LL
Net exports			
Agriculture	−H	+VH	+M
Industry	+LL	−H	−MH
Services	−NL	+L	+LM
Commodity prices			
Agriculture	+LL	+LL	+LL
Industry	+N	+N	+N
Services	+N	+N	+N

* Percentage change relative to base year. Key as for Table 6.2.

and low income households (although not falling to the base period level). The rate of profit rises marginally favouring an increase in agricultural output. The level of skilled employment and of unskilled labour rises. The shift in wages favours the production of services as the highest ratio of skilled to unskilled labour ratio (see Table 5.5). Consequently, there is an expansion of agriculture and service sector activity at the expense of industry.

In the middle income economies the increase in capital leads to an increase in the rate of profit and wage levels. At first sight an increase in the rate of profit in conjunction with an increase in the abundance of capital, seems surprising, but the explanation is that the change in the production structure leads to an economy wide reduction in the skill/ capital ratio. This favours sectors with a high skill/capital ratio, and consequently, production of services expands at the expense of industry.

The reduced competitiveness domestically of industrial production relative to services and agriculture in both developing economies simultaneously affects the competitiveness of this sector internationally *vis-à-vis* the industrial economies. So, this economy is not excluded from the new process of restructuring, and overall the simulated relocation of transnational capital has been to the advantage of the high income countries.

Overall these last experiments tend to reinforce the picture given earlier that the high income countries overall gain most from the introduction of the 'probable' technology. However, income distribution in those economies worsens substantially. In the middle and low income countries too the gains to low income groups seen earlier are lost. Although our assumptions about the use of capital primarily in the private sector are tentative, this general picture remains. We now turn to study the effect of possible government responses to the introduction of new technology. From these experiments we shall conclude that the impact on income distribution of some public sector responses to new technology is similar to the impact of responses from the private sector.

Public sector policy support for agriculture in high income countries

Governments faced with changing income distributions, worsening employment or decline in strategic sectors, typically will seek to find ameliorative strategies. Even though some commentators consider the state to be principally a facilitating agent for domestic and international capital, it seems inevitable that other national interests must be taken into account. Here, we consider three kinds of policy: those intended to protect individual sectors, those to defend against a decline in national competitiveness, and compensatory international financial transfers.

Our earlier result (Table 6.2) showed that while the introduction of probable technology is, in several respects, favourable to the high income countries, it may have serious implications for agriculture. Therefore some attempt to protect or subsidise this sector is implied. One possibility is to impose a quota system on agricultural imports (such as no net imports) and allow local prices to rise above the level of more competitive producers elsewhere. An alternative is simply to subsidise producers (via a negative indirect tax on output, increasing the net subsidy already displayed in Tables 5.6 to 5.8). We may, therefore, ask the question—what level of subsidy is required in order to prevent any decline in agricultural output in the high income countries? (This, at least, appears to have been the objective of the European CAP over the last decade.) The answer that the model gives to this question is that a massive subsidy of some 20 per cent of the world price is required in order to protect agriculture. This is surprising given that in none of our experiments has the price of agricultural commodities risen more than about 5 per cent above that of industrial goods. The implications of this subsidy are also startling, and the action undermines many of the gains from implementing new technology in other sectors.

First, what is the impact of the subsidy? Second, why is such a large subsidy required? Table 7.4 shows that with the subsidy, the structure of production shifts back towards that of the base period in developing as well as high income economies. The latter phenomenon, at least, is intended. What is *not* intended is that the real domestic product of the high income countries is reduced by some 3 per cent below that obtained from the first introduction of the new technology, and well below even the base period (Tables 6.1 and 6.2). The employment levels of both skilled and unskilled labour falls while the rate of profit rises significantly to 31 per cent above the base year. Thus, the subsidy has served to reduce national income, but increased the share of surplus, so worsening income distribution further.

The reasons for this phenomenon are as follows: because total capital in the economy is fixed, ensuring that the level of production in this economy is maintained at the base year level as the capital/output ratio increases (as a result of new technology), means that *less* capital is available for industry and service sector activities. Although the agriculture sector of the high income countries is small, and accounts for some 6 per cent of total output there, it employs some 17 per cent of total capital outlays.

The reduction in capital in the industry and capital sectors is doubly compounded compared to our first experiment. There, the decline of the agriculture sector released significant additional capital to other sectors. Because both the industry and service sectors are labour intensive compared to agriculture, many jobs are lost relative to the base year—first, because of the loss of capital, and second, because of the use of labour saving–capital absorbing new technology. Consequently, wages are pushed down throughout the economy, and profit margins rise. This combination favours service activity rather than industry, and so the latter declines relatively despite the superior comparative advantage originally expected from the new technology. Thus, with the reduced capital stock, industrial

Table 7.4 Subsidies on agriculture in high income countries*

	Economy group		
	High	Middle	Low
Income			
Total	−VL	−VL	−NL
Rich HH	+LL	−NL	−LL
Poor HH	−L	−VL	−NL
Capital	+MH	+L	+L
Employment			
Skilled	−VL	−LL	−L
Unskilled	−L	−LL	−VL
Production			
Agriculture	−LL	+NL	+VL
Industry	−LL	+VL	+LM
Services	−NL	−L	−LM
Net exports			
Agriculture	−NL	+NL	+NL
Industry	−NL	+VL	+L
Services	+NL	−LL	−LM
Commodity prices			
Agriculture	−VL	−VL	−VL
Industry	+N	+N	+N
Services	−VL	−VL	−VL

* Percentage change relative to base year. Key as for Table 6.2.

activity suffers more than services, although both are depleted below the base year level.

World prices are determined by average world technology and average world costs (to a first approximation), and since the high income countries are the major constituent of these particular global averages, the world price for all commodities must be expected to change. The increasing price of capital relative to labour decreases the price of services relative to industrial goods (as a more capital intensive sector). But the agricultural sector is yet more capital intensive, and so the tendency is for the price of agricultural goods to rise dramatically, and this can only be offset by a massive subsidy. Thus, the requirement for a subsidy to protect a relatively small sector reaps quite disproportionate and unsatisfactory returns. After the application of the required subsidy, the relative commodity price differences have narrowed and these new world prices now largely determine the structure of production in the two developing economies. The pattern is for the shifts in production structure induced by the new technology to be reversed roughly back to those in the base year. The structure of factor prices is also restored.

The reduced income of the industrial countries has a big impact on total world demand for all goods, and the impact of this is felt in all economies. In agriculture, because the level of production in the high income countries is maintained, total production elsewhere must fall. This releases resources to other sectors and so production expands. In the middle income economies the overall production becomes less labour intensive and more skill intensive. This pushes up the level of employment and hence wages of skilled workers. In the middle and low income countries unskilled employment (and low income households real consumption) falls below the base year level. But as a result of these shifts in wage costs against the new set of world commodity prices, rates of return in the low and middle income countries rise. Although this driving up of the rate of profit could result in new investment being attracted, overall, the application of a subsidy on agriculture has been disastrous for the industrial economies, and indirectly harmed the low income groups in developing economies. To complete the picture we now explore the attempt by middle income countries to protect their industry.

Support for industry in the middle income economies

The initial experiment of Table 6.2 showed that the efforts of the middle income countries to implement new technology were frustrated by the more rapid progress of the high income industrial economies; consequently, industrial output declined. If the 'middle income' countries seek to protect their industry by subsidising their domestic production, will this be frustrated, as were the protectionist measures of the industrial countries with respect to agriculture?

A fairly modest reduction of around 15 per cent of the existing indirect taxes on industrial production in the middle income countries is sufficient to protect against expanded imports. But as Table 7.5 shows, this leads to expanded industrial production above the base year, real GDP falls below the base year. Rates of return rise very significantly and levels of employment fall.

The protection of industry has only been achieved at the expense of

Table 7.5 Industrial subsidies in middle income countries*

	Economy group		
	High	Middle	Low
Income			
Total	+N	−NL	+VL
Rich HH	+L	−M	−L
Poor HH	−L	+VL	+LL
Capital	+L	+LM	−VL
Employment			
Skilled	+VL	−M	−VL
Unskilled	−LL	−N	+VL
Production			
Agriculture	−H	+VH	+LM
Industry	+N	+VL	+NL
Services	+LL	−H	−LL
Net exports			
Agriculture	−MH	+VH	+L
Industry	+N	+N	−NL
Services	+VL	−H	−L
Commodity prices			
Agriculture	+VL	+VL	+VL
Industry	+N	+N	+N
Services	+N	+N	+N

* Percentage change relative to base year. Key as for Table 6.2.

the services sector. Generally, there has been less attention paid to the support of this sector against international competition, since much of its output is non-tradable. But as international finance, insurance and consultancy services expand, this is becoming increasingly less true. Any attempt to protect the service sector, while stabilising industrial imports, cannot be effected. Although subsidising services may, in the first instance, raise the output of services, it adversely affects industrial output, and if further protection is given to industry this in turn weakens services. This cycle of support for first one sector and then the next, could lead to a situation in which overall real national income falls even further below the base period. The larger the shift in the production structure, the more likely will be the amount of capital that will be written off prematurely. Even if new investment was very rapid, it is unlikely that no such scrapping would occur. While subsidising particular sectors to prevent the decline of individual sectors would reduce this, it could lead to a deleterious cycle of protection.

Devaluation and wage controls

An alternative response by governments to the predicament of the middle and low income countries would be to devalue the currency. The principle aim of this obviously would be to make the export sector, in particular, the threatened industrial sector, more competitive. The success of such a policy depends on the supply elasticity for exports and imports (see for example Sodersten, 1980). If the demand for exports increases faster than a fall in export price from a devaluation the policy may be successful, all else being equal. But if the demand for exports is rather price inelastic then dropping the export price will have marginal impact on demand—it will simply reduce income pro-rata with the devaluation. Similarly, if demand for imports is rather insensitive to price, the economy may simply end up paying more for a fixed quantity of goods.

We must distinguish here between short- and long-run effects of devaluation. In practice, in the short run local prices (in domestic currency terms) fall relative to imports, so domestic consumers prefer local products. In the longer run domestic and world prices fall into line as production and factor markets adjust. Thus our model reflects only the long-run situation. In both economies real national consumption falls as a result of the devaluation, and in the middle income economies, if the purpose of the devaluation is to protect the industry sector, it fails, although the results are less adverse than when industrial subsidies are attempted.

Since currency devaluation is often seen as a device to reduce real wages and so increase competitiveness, we might examine this more directly by simulating such a policy directly in the model (i.e. adjusting labour supply conditions so that a given number of workers are 'available' for lower wages). The practical measures to achieve this are varied, keeping nominal wage increases below the rate of inflation through an agreed wages policy or deliberate repression. Here the results are more varied, as shown in Table 7.6. In the middle income countries, national real income increases as does employment of skilled and unskilled labour. Industry is little helped, however, and the real income of rich and poor households falls. In the low income countries neither production structures nor levels of employment are greatly affected.

Table 7.6 Wage controls in middle income countries*

	Economy group		
	High	Middle	Low
Income			
Total	+NL	+LL	+L
Rich HH	+L	−LM	−LL
Poor HH	−LL	+LM	+LM
Capital	+L	+NL	−VL
Employment			
Skilled	+VL	−VL	+VL
Unskilled	−LL	+M	+LM
Production			
Agriculture	−HH	+VH	+H
Industry	+L	−VH	−M
Services	−N	+LM	+LL
Net exports			
Agriculture	−HH	+VH	+MH
Industry	+LL	−HH	−M
Services	−NL	+L	+NL
Commodity prices			
Agriculture	+LL	+LL	+LL
Industry	+N	+N	+N
Serivces	−N	−N	−N

* Percentage change relative to base year. Key as for Table 6.2.

On balance in these experiments the high income countries gain more from the devaluation or reduction in real wages than do the developing countries. When wages are controlled, unskilled employment and both low and high income consumption in the industrial economies all rise. Thus the richest economies gain from a worsening of real incomes in the poorest.

Nevertheless, the simulated incomes policy can have a positive impact on the developing economies. Why is this? The principal reason is that, in the model, there is a relatively high demand elasticity for exports, especially for goods from the middle income countries. Because these economies are exporting mainly in to the much larger market of the high income countries, reducing wage rates (or more precisely, reducing wage rate increases) and so increasing competitiveness leads to a situation in which output and employment gains more than compensate for the initial wage control. By contrast, wage controls in the industrial economies are seen to have a negative effect since cutting wage rates leads to a reduction in demand and, because their markets in developing countries are small, exports to poorer countries cannot compensate for a reduction in domestic demand.

Redistribution in industrial countries?

The implication of all experiments for unskilled labour and low income households in the industrial countries are that the number of jobs and real incomes will fall. But since with the new technology, total incomes will increase, the problem, in principle, could be viewed largely as one of income redistribution or the need for retraining and job sharing.

Table 7.7 shows the result of raising the *rate* of net taxes (direct taxes net of household subsidies) of high income households to a level required to maintain the poor household incomes at the base year level. The effect of this is to reduce rich household incomes below the base year level. Unless considerable unused capital is brought back into production, or new investment rapidly increased, there is simply very little additional real income to be distributed. Redistribution alone in the industrial economies would have rather little impact on the results we have given for production and employment levels. So long as the overall level of investment in the economy was maintained the change in the overall composition of demand and hence employment would be little changed (since within our broad categories consumption propensities differ little between high and low income households).

Obviously, any redistribution could be arranged in a variety of ways, for example, higher wage rates for low skilled workers or changes in the structure of direct and indirect taxes. The problem is not whether the option is economically possible but whether it is politically acceptable. Since one major reason for introducing new technologies is to raise rates of return it is unlikely that entrepreneurs would want to see this income eroded by any direct or indirect means. Further, if governments see the need for new technology in order to confront increased competition from low wage developing economies, they are unlikely to push for increased real incomes for low income households when the 'market' indicates that real wages should fall. Many studies (for example Peet, 1983) contend that with the present wave of rationalisation in industry,

Table 7.7 Redistribution in rich countries*

	Economy group		
	High	Middle	Low
Income			
Total	+N	+NL	+VL
Rich HH	−NL	−LM	−L
Poor HH	+N	+L	+LL
Capital	+L	+NL	−VL
Employment			
Skilled	+VL	−L	−LL
Unskilled	−LL	+LL	+LL
Production			
Agriculture	−H	+VH	+LM
Industry	+VL	−M	+VL
Services	+VL	−L	−LL
Net exports			
Agriculture	−MH	+VH	+LM
Industry	+VL	−M	−N
Services	+NL	−LM	−L
Commodity prices			
Agriculture	+LL	+LL	+LL
Industry	+N	+N	+N
Services	−N	−N	−N

* Percentage change relative to base year. Key as for Table 6.2.

transnational firms are seeking low cost production sites and especially those where labour costs are low and tax and other public commitments (such as environmental controls) are at a minimum.

However household real incomes are increased they ultimately represent an increased 'cost' on production, and any country increasing its 'welfare' programme will be handicapped in the international market place. Only if governments collectively agreed to maintain some pattern of subsidies or income would this not be so; unfortunately, this is far from the case.

The same rationale speaks against the idea of job sharing, so that all workers are employed but not necessarily full time. From the employers' side there is the complaint that ultimately this entails higher supplementary labour costs, while workers with jobs protect them against those without. Similar questions arise with the concept of a dualistic welfare society such as those reviewed by Gershuny and Miles (1983) and others. In this economy, a highly productive 'formal' sector would cater for the substantive material needs of a population—most of whom would not be employed in this sector, but would instead take part in informal production of non-essential crafts and social services. Again from the view point of our model, there are no real objections to this idealised image, only the political willingness seems in question.

As Freeman *et al.* (1982) point out, there is scope for considerable social conflict, and, whether some kind of incomes policy, for example, can be made to stick depends on the social learning process. Of the three 'solutions' indicated, only 'retraining' of low skilled employees seems more generally acceptable, and this is likely to be slow (since the available evidence suggests that low skilled employees do not in general move from old industries into the new 'high tech' industries). What then is the impact of increasing the proportion of skilled workers in the labour force of each economy? Does increasing skills through greater education and vocational training provide the panacea? In several senses the answer appears to be yes, especially if we take account of the capital saving possibilities of the technology as in Table 6.2. Table 7.8 shows the results of assuming that the size of the skilled workforce in the two developing economies increases by 50 per cent (to about 14 per cent and 6 per cent respectively) and that in the industrial economies increases by one quarter (to around 25 per cent). At first sight, at least, the result suggests a relatively great improvement in national income and the growth potential of all economic groups. (The gains in the middle income countries especially are at the expense of the agricultural sector and attempts to block this, lead to an overall decline in output for these economies as considered earlier in Table 7.4.)

Income distribution across economies has worsened, with the high income economies showing a GDP increase of nearly 20 per cent, but only 11 per cent for the two developing groups. Nevertheless, the amount of growth is considerable and, in addition, the income distribution between high and low income households has improved. This is largely because the number of skilled workers employed has increased and a significant share of this wage income now goes to low income households. The number of unskilled jobs has risen much less (and indeed has fallen in the middle income economies), although the unskilled labour force (i.e. those who could be employed) has been reduced. Profit income in all economies has risen faster than household income while the real wage rate for skilled

Table 7.8 A more highly skilled labour force*

| | Economy group | | |
	High	Middle	Low
Income			
Total	+M	+L	+L
Rich HH	+LL	+LL	+LL
Poor HH	+M	+L	+LM
Capital	+LM	+H	+MH
Employment			
Skilled	+LM	+LM	+LM
Unskilled	+LL	−LL	+NL
Production			
Agriculture	+HH	−VH	−LM
Industry	+L	+HH	+H
Services	+M	+LL	+LM
Net exports			
Agriculture	+MH	−VH	−M
Industry	−VL	+M	+L
Services	+NL	−LL	−VL
Commodity prices			
Agriculture	+L	+L	+L
Industry	+N	+N	+N
Services	+NL	+NL	+NL

* Percentage change relative to base year. Key as for Table 6.2.

labour has fallen very considerably in all economies—by some 18 per cent in the high income group, 44 per cent in the middle income countries and 63 per cent in the low income countries. This is because as the number of skilled workers increases supply exceeds demand—at least in relative terms—and their wage bargaining strength declines. Thus, while newly skilled workers receive substantially improved wage rates, the existing skilled labour force suffers an almost as great decline. (Hence the tendency by some unions to exclude even workers with requisite skills from admission to certain 'skilled' jobs.) Indeed, examining the results more closely reveals that as the number of skilled workers increases, their wage level has fallen to such an extent that the total wage paid to labour has not risen. There is greater equality between wage labour but *not* between capital and labour. Thus, the result clearly suggests that while information technology has the potential for raising aggregate living standards, its effect on the distribution of income either between economies or within could indeed lead to a reduction in the living standards of many people.

8 Playing the wild cards: imitative versus integrative technologies

In Chapters 6 and 7 we have explored how information technology could impact on employment and distribution in the world economy, if most rapid progress in its adoption is in the high income economies. Although present trends, reviewed in Chapters 2 and 3, suggest this to be the most likely event, other possibilities must not be discounted.

In this chapter we look at two main alternatives. First, what happens if the pace of introduction of new technologies proceeded much faster than we have anticipated? In particular, we must ask whether yet more rapid progress by developing economies along a route which imitates that already mapped out by the industrial nations is likely to contribute very much to the alleviation of poverty and unemployment? Again, how important in this respect will be capital saving systemic changes? Second, we ask whether alternative arrangements for using the technology would not lead to better results (in industrial as well as developing economies), and whether, the new technology should not be used to directly confront these twin problems? In particular we are interested to begin not simply to explore the impact of new technologies on the world economy, but to help to clarify in operational terms some key characteristics of a relevant research and development policy, and to show how policies towards domestic and international markets can either reinforce or undermine this strategy.

Route two: plausible technologies

Rapid catching up by the developing economies

The 'technology gap' between rich and poor countries may well continue to widen but what happens if the technology gap should instead close, or begin to close after some time? The argument of several authors, cited earlier, has led us to speculate about this possibility. First, authors such as Soete (1982) and Jacobsson (1982) consider that the technology systems of some newly industrial nations are already sufficiently strong to permit them to compete successfully in the production of new technology. Second, the idea that the pace of technical change in the new long wave may slow down. This would be felt first in the high income industrial countries and only subsequently in the developing economies after they had narrowed the technology gap. (This situation was illustrated in Figure 4.1.)

Under what circumstances can we envisage the 'plausible' route materialising? Obviously the self-reinforcing dynamic for growth in the high income countries anticipated in the last experiments must fail. Either firms in industrial countries must experience new difficulties in implementation and domestic and international policies fail to prevent an intensifying round of recession, or international firms discover that the historic argument for locating production in peripheral regions (i.e. low labour costs) still applies and the requisite skills and other resources are available, or that developing countries make progress of their own accord.

We might expect the impact of new technology in the developing countries to be potentially much greater than in the industrial countries, if only because existing technology is so much more labour intensive. Reducing the number of jobs per unit of output by an average of 20 per cent in the industrial economies would (with no change in total output) increase unemployment from roughly 10 per cent to 30 per cent. But to assume the same new technology throughout the least developed economies where labour/output ratios on average are from 15 to 700 times higher than in the industrial economies, would (with no change in output) mean that less than 5 per cent of the population would be fully employed. The rate of implementation is of course constrained by availability of necessary skills and finance, therefore, the assumptions we make about this second route are much more modest than just implied. Table 8.1 shows the corresponding assumptions of Table 4.3 for the 'probable' technology route. The rate of change in productivity in the three groups of industrial economies has generally slowed down (although not in extraction and advanced services), while in all three developing country groups, the pace of productivity change has increased. For reasons just indicated, in agriculture and the 'basic' major sub-sectors of industry and services, the impact is greatest in the least industrialised low income economies. As before, we aggregate both sectors and economy types into three groups, and calculate the aggregate impact for each sector in each economy.

The table also shows the extent of 'systemic' changes. These estimates are obviously more tenuous, but certainly some speculation is in order on the basis of our review. Principally we have argued that the opportunities for systemic changes are less in developing countries. Kaplinsky (1983), for example, has argued that this is a primary reason for believing that the 'factory of the future' is a first world technology.

Table 8.1 Impact of plausible micro-processor related techniques on factor productivity*

	Group 1	Group 2	Group 3	Group 4	Group 5	Group 6
Agriculture						
Systemic	−NL	−NL	−VL	−LL	−LL	−L
Skilled	+NL	+NL	+VL	+VL	+VL	+L
Unskilled	−VL	−VL	−LL	−L	−L	−L
Capital	+N	+N	+LL	+L	+L	+M
Extraction						
Systemic	−LM	−LM	−LM	−L	−L	−L
Skilled	+VL	+VL	+VL	+VL	+VL	+VL
Unskilled	−L	−L	−L	−LM	−LM	−LM
Capital	+VL	+VL	+VL	+VL	+VL	+VL
Basic industry						
Systemic	−LL	−LL	−L	−L	−L	−LM
Skilled	+NL	+NL	+VL	+VL	+VL	+VL
Unskilled	−NL	−NL	−LM	−MH	−MH	−H
Capital	+NL	+NL	+VL	+VL	+VL	+VL
Intermediate industry						
Systemic	−L	−L	−L	−LM	−LM	−LM
Skilled	+NL	+NL	+NL	+VL	+VL	+VL
Unskilled	−LL	−LL	−L	−MH	−MH	−MH
Capital	+NL	+NL	+NL	+VL	+VL	+VL

Advanced industry						
Systemic	−LL	−LL	−LL	−VL	−VL	−VL
Skilled	+VL	+VL	+VL	+NL	+NL	+NL
Unskilled	−M	−M	−M	−LL	−VL	−VL
Capital	+VL	+VL	+VL	+NL	+NL	+NL
Utilities						
Systemic	−L	−L	−L	−VL	−VL	−VL
Skilled	+VL	+VL	+VL	+NL	+NL	+NL
Unskilled	−NL	−NL	−NL	−NL	−NL	−NL
Capital	+VL	+VL	+VL	+NL	+NL	+NL
Basic services						
Systemic	−L	−L	−L	−LL	−LL	−LL
Skilled	−L	−LL	−LL	−NL	−NL	−NL
Unskilled	−L	−LL	−LL	−NL	−NL	−NL
Capital	+L	+LL	+LL	+NL	+NL	+NL
Advanced services						
Systemic	−L	−L	−L	−L	−L	−L
Skilled	−NL	−VL	−VL	−VL	−VL	−VL
Unskilled	−LM	−LM	−LM	−LM	−LM	−LM
Capital	+LM	+LM	+LM	+L	+L	+L

* Percentage change relative to base year. Key as for Table 6.2.

To explore the impact of our plausible technology we shall again take a two stage approach. Generally, with this new data, we must expect a parallel set of results to emerge, but with differences arising because of the relative size of the economies and different production structures. Changes in the industrial countries, for example, imposed rather dramatic restructuring on the developing economies. As noted earlier, the world price system is largely determined by the average technology used in world production, and this is heavily weighted by the contribution of the industrial economies. As long as the developing economies remain small, even very substantial changes in technology there will have relatively little overall impact on the industrial nations. This does not mean, however, that major types of activities within our classification such as shipbuilding, footwear, or textiles will not be seriously affected, but in terms of our broad categories the industrial economies should exhibit greater stability to externally induced changes. Of course, if we consider interactions between economies in our industrial country group then a more detailed mosaic would emerge, with, for example, the extension of new centre-periphery arrangements within the group.

With this observation we now describe the impact of introducing 'plausible' new technology into the world economy. As Table 8.1 shows the greatest productivity advances are now in the medium and low income countries. Since these advances are substantial, we might expect the pattern of industrial specialisation worldwide also to be dramatically changed, and the situation of developing countries reversed. To what extent is this the case? Table 8.2 gives changes from base period while a comparison with Table 6.2 provides a comparison with the 'probable' technology experiment.

Perhaps the most striking feature is the similarity between the two tables: certainly the new result does rather little to improve income distribution or raise employment. The combined national real income of the developing economies does not rise as much as the rich economies' suggesting that cost reducing productivity increases are again to the benefit of importers rather than exporters, in the first instance. Profitability increases in developing economies are now comparable to those in the high income economies. But apart from these two differences the pattern of change in production structures and income distribution is remarkably like that described in our 'probable' technology experiment.

This result is certainly surprising given the magnitude of the changes contemplated but we have indicated the reason for it above. Competition between agriculture and industry in the high income countries as the economy wide productivity changes dominates the behaviour in the rest

Table 8.2 The plausible route (non-systemic)*

	Economy group		
	High	Middle	Low
Income			
Total	+NL	+N	+NL
Rich HH	+LL	−LL	−VL
Poor HH	−VL	+VL	+NL
Capital	+LL	+L	+L
Employment			
Skilled	+VL	−L	−LL
Unskilled	−VL	−NL	+N
Production			
Agriculture	−H	+VH	+M
Industry	+LL	−MH	−MH
Services	+NL	−VL	+NL
Net exports			
Agriculture	−MH	+VH	+M
Industry	+VL	−M	−M
Services	−N	−NL	+VL
Commodity prices			
Agriculture	+VL	+VL	+VL
Industry	+N	+N	+N
Services	−N	−N	−N

* Percentage change relative to base year. Key as for Table 6.2.

of the world economy. Although slower technical change now is assumed for the high income economies, it is still sufficient to promote structural shifts domestically and abroad.

As we might expect, in the high income economies the situation of low income households and unskilled labour is now less adversely affected. What is more surprising is that industrial production increases more in this experiment even though productivity changes in the industrial sector are least in the high income economies. Calculating the production costs of industrial goods at base year factor and intermediate input prices suggests that the middle income countries are most competitive in this sector, followed by the low income countries. The smaller increase in the price of capital and skilled labour, and the less substantial fall in the wage rate for unskilled labour promote a smaller shift to agriculture, but tend to favour industrial production rather than services.

This pivot between agricultural and industrial technology is not the only determining factor, so we cannot take the changes in individual developing countries to be merely a result of changing world prices and net demand for imports of the high income economies. For example, although net exports from the industrial countries are little changed, relative world prices and differences in the sectoral and national pattern of technical change lead to a different pattern of specialisation in the developing economies. Agriculture in the low income countries is now more competitive (at base year input prices) than either industry domestically or agriculture in the middle income countries. Thus agricultural exports from these economies tend to replace those previously predicted for the middle income economies.

Overall, plausible technology in the middle income economies appears to have a deleterious effect. National real income is not increased above the base period and the employment of both types of labour falls. A single positive result is the predicted rise in the rate of profit, but even this is almost matched by corresponding increases in other economies. In the low income countries a similar conclusion might be drawn. In particular the unskilled employment creating and redistributive effects of technical change in the high income countries are largely offset by the introduction of massively labour displacing technologies at home.

How robust are these conclusions in the face of uncertainties in the base year data and estimates of plausible technical change? On balance we are perhaps slightly less confident than for our possible technology route. For example, some experiments suggest a weakening rather than a strengthening of industry in the high income economies (relative to the probable technology experiment) and even an overall decline in real income in those countries. On the other hand the broad sectoral, employment and profitability shifts seem fairly secure.

As far as possible we want to avoid tedious replication here of earlier experiments. We might accept, for example, that attempts to protect agriculture in high income or industry in middle income countries through subsidies repeats our earlier findings. But with a greatly increased rate of profit in developing economies the response of internationally mobile capital or domestically unused capital should be more considerable. Consequently we have re-examined in turn the effects of discarding capital, bringing capital back into production and redistributing capital worldwide. In particular, the relative importance and offsetting consequences of these processes are changed. A second question is whether there are significant differences in the private and public sector response to this new technology. Finally, we must explore the effects of taking the systemic 'capital saving' component of the new technology into account.

Restructuring and systemic change

The last chapter illustrated the competing consequences of underutilised capital being reinstated while other capital is discarded as a result of changing composition of output. As before we take the amount of capital prematurely scrapped in each economy to depend on the degree of restructuring—if a sector declines rather than switching capital to new production it is written-off. In this new experiment therefore the overall decline in output income in the developing economies is rather high.

Considering first only the effects of restructuring, in the low income economies national real income is reduced by some 4 per cent below the base period. The general picture obtained in Table 8.2 becomes more exaggerated and income differences and restructuring is more acute. In the middle income economies national income also falls by some 10 per cent below the base period. Despite a reduction of about 3 per cent in capital in the high income countries, national real income remains more or less unchanged. Given the lesser restructuring in the high income economies, the major changes there come from the writing-off of capital in the middle and low income countries. Overall the tendency for capital worldwide to become more expensive favours growth in the high income economies. The changes observed here are larger than for the equivalent 'probable' technology experiment, and certainly greater than those resulting from a redistribution of capital worldwide. This too tends to be at least useful to the middle income countries despite their showing the greatest increase in the rate of profit when 'plausible' technology is introduced.

To take account of laid-off plant being brought back into production the experiment is repeated with capital stock in each economy again adjusted in line with their new rates of profit. The combined results show that the industrial economies again show the greatest increase in national income. But while all economies receive a share from the increased size of the 'world cake', the bulk of this gain goes to capital and skilled labour in the two developing regions and to skilled labour in the high income economies. In the low income economies the tendency towards agricultural production is greatly reduced and consequently the level of unskilled labour falls. In the middle income countries a similar pattern is seen. Here the industry sector expands in response to the worldwide increase in demand (rather than from improved competitiveness as a result of new technology).

Finally we examine the impact of the systemic capital savings shown in Table 8.1. In this experiment, shown in Table 8.3, we include the combined effect of capital saving technical change and reinvestment. Taking account of systemic changes is seen to again have a dramatic impact on overall growth but much less on distribution or employment. The increase in GDP of the middle income economies is greatest at over 12 per cent with the other economies showing an increase of over 10 per cent. The change in the pattern of output corresponds to that seen in Chapter 6. The decline in agricultural output in the high income countries

Table 8.3 The plausible route (systemic)*

	Economy group		
	High	Middle	Low
Income			
Total	+LL	+LL	+LM
Rich HH	+LM	+L	+VL
Poor HH	−NL	+VL	+LM
Capital	+VL	+H	+H
Employment			
Skilled	+LL	−LL	−LM
Unskilled	+N	−L	+NL
Production			
Agriculture	−VL	+LM	+MH
Industry	−N	+HH	+VH
Services	+L	−MH	−MH
Net exports			
Agriculture	−VL	+VL	+LM
Industry	−LL	+MH	+MH
Services	+LL	−H	−HH
Commodity prices			
Agriculture	+NL	+NL	+NL
Industry	+N	+N	+N
Services	+VL	+VL	+VL

* Percentage change relative to base year. Key as for Table 6.2.

is reversed because of capital-saving technology which reduces the relative scarcity of capital in these economies. Although the large increases in national income are uniformly distributed, the substantial increases in profitability in the two developing country groups suggest that subsequent growth in these countries would be especially rapid. Whether this growth would have a great impact on either employment or the incomes of poorer households is to be questioned since in these typical experiments total employment in middle and low income economies show a net decline and the observed increases in real income are due to the assumed redistributive taxation and the increased investment income of poorer households. In high income economies there is an increase in both skilled and unskilled employment, although there is no change in income distribution.

A comparison of this experiment with the corresponding result for 'probable' technology shows that on balance the developing economies gain more via the plausible technology route, provided that the capital saving changes can be implemented. The significance of these last experiments is that even with greatly increased productivity (relative to industrial economies) and significant injection of new capital unskilled and total employment in both developing economy groups falls. This suggests that the plausible technology route is hardly likely to solve the massive unemployment problem in developing countries or help to improve the distribution of national income. (In the experiment shown the income of low income households rises but this is mainly the result of mechanistic increases in domestic transfers built into the model— whether these are realistic is considered later.) Nevertheless, this kind of approach to technology underpins the export oriented industrialisation policies of many developing economies. As we saw in Chapters 2 and 3 the desire to jump onto the new technology bandwagon is manifest in developing economies as well as industrial economies. This technology route also has built in dynamic reinforcing elements since as Table 8.3 shows, the rate of profit in development countries remains high relative to that in the industrial countries. Thus there is every incentive for international firms as carriers of new technology and market forces to systematically transfer investment to middle and low income economies.

This last result is emphasised by simply asking the question of what happens when the capital stock in developing countries is significantly increased (say by some 50 per cent)? In this case the strengthening of the industry sector in developing countries is at the expense of agriculture and services. This leads to a systematic decline in the situation of unskilled labour and low income households in industrial economies and national income falls below that of the base period. We emphasise here that in this experiment (as in the last), the shift in production structure in industrial economies as a result of domestic technical change and market forces is no longer the most significant determining factor in the result. Expansion of production in the developing countries alone appears insufficient to offset the labour displacing effects of new technology.

What happens if also we assume, as in Table 7.8, that there is a significant increase in the availability of skilled workers for the labour force? The results show that now national output increases more in the developing than in the industrial economies, and profitability too remains high with the possibility of higher long run growth. On the other hand there is little change in the domestic situation discussed at the end of Chapter 6 whereby skilled wage rates fall so that the ratio of total wages to profits in all economies is reduced.

Route three: possible technologies

Taken together, the above results for 'probable' or 'plausible' technologies provide a rather bleak outlook for, especially, unskilled employment and low income households in all economies.

The initial experiment with 'probable' technology (Table 6.2) appears favourable to these groups in developing countries, but only because of a restructuring induced by external market forces. But beyond this experiment our results suggest even this gain would not materialise. First, the growth of production capacity through new investment or the revitalisation of old capital favours the high income economies, and tends to reverse the initial shifts in income distribution. Second, even if this does not happen (assuming a much lower supply elasticity for capital), then government action in high income economies to protect domestic agriculture will have the same effect. Both ways, the low income groups are adversely affected.

These 'probable' technology experiments assume that the already industrialised nations have the edge in the introduction of new technology. But even when this assumption was reversed and we made the, at least plausible, assumption, following Soete (1983) and others that developing countries, through either their own endeavours or transfer of technology and investment by international firms, have it, the problems of unemployment and poverty in the developing nations are not alleviated. Further, as Ernst (1982) and Freeman (1984) have emphasised, if developing countries simply react passively to the strategic decisions of international firms and the more industrial economies, they will remain in a dependent and very vulnerable position, whether or not some of the most advanced techniques are employed in the export oriented enclaves within their territories.

This leads us back to the question of whether there is any conceivable strategy which will ensure that the undoubted potential benefits of new technology are shared more equally and without excessive stress? Most of the public and private sector responses reviewed above, are reactionary, defensive and reflexive. Obviously in the case where real national income or total world income increases it is, in principle, always possible to re-distribute through international and domestic transfers so that all parties benefit. This idea underpins the rationale of the free market—since free trade and liberal policies in general lead to greater output, they should be followed and any casualties of the process afforded limited assistance. Even if the current trend in international and domestic economic policy was not for redistributive and welfare oriented transfers to become mini-mal, such assistance by itself is seen not to be sufficient. It is only con-structive in the longer term if it helps to bring about a more fundamental restructuring of economic relationships which relieves the economic dependency of the recipients.

The present trends in social redistribution do not suggest that workers who become structurally unemployed because of new technologies (or for any other reason) will be adequately supported, even should the total wealth of society increase. For the foreseeable future it seems reasonable to maintain then that the jobless will lose economic power—hence the emphasis on employment as well as income in this volume. Unless people are involved both as producers as well as consumers with a mutual de-pendence on each other, the consequent mutual responsibility towards each other is less likely to be maintained.

Appropriate, alternative, or adaptive technology in developing economies

When we seek to identify technology routes other than those examined above we too are beset by several problems. Not least is the lack of empiri-cal evidence: even our data for other routes is extremely tentative. Many studies in the 1970s promoted the variants on the concepts of 'appro-priate' and 'intermediate' technology, such as those of Schumacher (1973), Stewart (1976), Singer (1977), Singh (1979) and Bhalla (1979). The data from these studies suggests that in terms of production costs 'appropriate' techniques can often compete favourably with modern sector techniques.

Indeed, as the extensive review by Vitelli (1980) showed most comparative studies set out to test this point. But to demonstrate the potential for improved profitability is not enough. According to Bhagavan (1980) the reason why such technologies are not adopted is that entrepreneurs are 'making enormous profits anyway' using inappropriate technology. Shifting to generally smaller scale more labour intensive appropriate technology would reduce their ability to control their production system and stretch specialised and scarce management resources.

The earlier results and discussion have demonstrated that technology is a powerful determinant in the growth and distribution of income and employment, and it follows that technology 'policy' can be an equally effective instrument in achieving and maintaining equitable objectives. Governments dedicated to primarily market oriented economic policies are not likely to place distribution at a premium, and if they rely on 'trickle down' to ensure the relief of social hardship, are not likely to encourage entrepreneurs to adopt redistributive production techniques, or to promote researchers to develop them. Perhaps quite the reverse. On the other hand, governments which are concerned to relieve unemployment and the waste of human resources and potential, but recognise also the power of international and domestic markets, can use technology choice as one instrument of policy to achieve a broader set of economic and social goals. Domestic and international markets can both reinforce and undermine the objectives of technology and other policy. In particular, use of labour intensive 'appropriate' techniques, increases employment and, through the market, pushes up wages and demand, and hence creates additional employment. But this reinforcing mechanism in the domestic market can be undermined by the behaviour of international markets. Conversely, because international markets create a 'discipline' which encourages entrepreneurs and governments to manage their resources in an optimally 'efficient' manner, so ideally both sets of mechanisms should be used to reinforce the broad objectives of social and economic policy.

There are, however, other objections to 'appropriate' technology. Bhagavan (1980) also argues that adoption of appropriate technology (especially when viewed as slightly modified 'traditional' technology) is to condemn developing countries forever to an outmoded system of production. But this does not account for the probability, emphasised by our experiments here and those of other authors (for example Royer, 1984) who have studied the impact of different kinds of technology on employment in developing countries in a long-term macro-economic context, that modern technology, with the anticipated rates of accumulation in developing economies, will not begin to resolve the unemployment problem for several generations. Some authors have even calculated (for example Parker, 1984) or argued (for example Felix, 1977) that the unemployment problem may never be solved through use of such technology. Consequently authors such as Royer (1984) have proposed that the traditional sector in dualistic systems of production should be deliberately maintained in order that low income groups are supported economically until they can be assimilated into the modern sector. For Royer this amounts to an internal protection of the traditional economy through a quota system analagous to those adopted in the international arena.

It is however necessary to explore possibilities even beyond this strategy, since it still accepts the idea that the eventual technology in the modern sector low income countries will mimic the direction set by the industrial economies. This obviously is not the only route to follow and certainly is unlikely to be the most appropriate. There are other 'possible' technologies which are implicit in the broader conceptual studies of Herrera (1976), Rahman (1976) and others. Had Mexico or India, for example, become the imperial global power, then the technological problems prioritised and the manner in which they were solved, would be different from those tackled in Europe and North America. Technology today would be more relevant to the needs of South America or Asia and less so for the subdued nations of Europe and North America, as should be the technologies they would develop for the future.

Obviously today's technology and knowhow, wherever it is drawn from, forms the starting point of future technological routes, and in today's conditions must confront a range of objectives. UNCSTD (the United Nations Committee on Science and Technology for Development) has suggested there is similtaneously a need for 'defensive', 'strategic' and 'long-term capacity building' technology policies by developing countries. The first would counteract the initial impact of changing technology elsewhere, the second would prepare these countries to exploit new technologies, while the third would enable these countries to become more innovative in their own right (see Sagasti 1985).

Many of the characteristics of such technology policy are subtle and well beyond the limited parameterisation in our model. Also we have to recognise some evident short term limitations: as Wad (1984) and our review in Chapters 3 and 4 suggest, opportunities to 'leap-frog' ahead of the industrial countries to the frontiers of technology are limited. Nevertheless, there are opportunities to sidestep into a new and more socially desirable direction. Consequently, we shall now explore some alternatives for future science and technology policy in developing countries, by demonstrating how, and under what conditions, alternative technologies introduced into the model lead to acceptable levels of growth and equitable distribution of output and employment.

Autarky is not enough

One obvious 'defensive' measure to eliminate the pressures from international markets felt by these nations would be for developing countries to 'delink' from the world economy or at least from the dominant industrial economies. Different arrangements for delinking have been the subject of several studies (UNIDO (1979), Contreras (1978)). Since international trade policy is one component of the alternatives we consider below, we will demonstrate, at the outset, the consequences of the complete elimination of international trade between the three groups of economies in our model. Conventional theory would suggest that developing countries would lose in terms of real national income from such 'autarkic' arrangements. Since encouraging free trade is of benefit to all participating nations, frustrating it is generally to the detriment of all parties.

The result of simply delinking the medium and low income economies from the high income economies without any change in technology or other policy (shown in Table 8.4) largely supports this proposition, although for the middle income countries a small increase in real value added is observed after delinking (the observed fall in household income arises because international income transfers are eliminated together with international trade). For the low income countries the result demonstrates that they gain roughly twice as much (in terms of increases to real national income), from North–South trade as do industrial economies. Furthermore, it suggests that cutting off trade can damage unskilled rather than skilled employment in developing economies, if their export sectors are, in aggregate, more unskilled labour intensive than the economy as a whole. This apart, the result shows that the net contribution of international trade to total employment is rather small. This is because, when trade is balanced, every job gained through additional exports can be offset by jobs lost through corresponding imports. Furthermore, as was shown in Chapter 7, even these small benefits could be lost, when the extensive restructuring of developing economies as a result of the introduction of new technology anywhere in the world is taken into account.

The results show that autarky alone may be a short term defensive measure, but is certainly not costless, and can even exacerbate the situation

Table 8.4 Regional autarky with the base year technology*

| | Economy group | | |
	High	Middle	Low
Income			
Total	−N	+N	−NL
Rich HH	+NL	−LL	−LM
Poor HH	−N	−VL	−LL
Capital	+NL	−NL	+VL
Employment			
Skilled	−N	+NL	+N
Unskilled	−N	+N	−VL
Production			
Agriculture	+NL	−LL	−LL
Industry	−N	−NL	+NL
Services	−N	+VL	+N
Net exports			
Agriculture	+NL	−VL	−VL
Industry	−NL	+LL	+LM
Services	−N	+VL	+NL
Commodity prices			
Agriculture	+NL	−N	−VL
Industry	+N	+N	+N
Services	−N	+N	−N

* Percentage change relative to base year. Key as for Table 6.2.

for domestic employment and distribution in developing countries. On the other hand, from our earlier results, it is evident that much technology policy in poor economies may be ineffective in the face of the very great pressures which changes in rich economies impose on them via market forces. In part this is a result of the very large relative size of the industrial economies. Even conventional trade theory acknowledges that the accepted wisdom concerning the benefits of trade breaks down under these conditions. Our own investigations (reported in Cole (1983) and Cole and Miles (1984)) using the results of empirical studies of 'appropriate technology' cited above, suggest these technologies are only likely to be effective in conjunction with active trade and social policies. Otherwise they may be worse than useless. Such findings reinforce the fundamental point made in this book, that when developing economies are obliged to comply with world market prices set by the very different technology of other economies their own development options are severely constrained. Important development alternatives are foregone unless a technology policy can be designed which takes account international forces, as well as domestic social and economic goals.

An extended invention possibility function for blended and integrated techniques

What technologies might then be adopted, and how would other policies affect their impact on employment and distribution? To explore this question we use the concept of an invention possibility function described in Chapter 4. Although we have enumerated a number of difficulties with this concept, it remains intriguing, especially if it clarifies questions about technical change, which are then susceptible to empirical research. One question to be answered by researchers looking for applications of the new technology in developing countries should be, 'What is the innovation possibility function for these societies?'

If several inputs are considered then the innovation possibility function becomes a multi-dimensional surface from which the induced direction of technical change can be hypothesised. This is shown in Figure 8.1 for three dimensions: capital, skilled and unskilled labour. For simplicity, in this diagram, we omit the three types of intermediate good, taxes and subsidies included in the model, which also determine an entrepreneur's choice of technique. The surface of Figure 8.1 represents the constraints on innovation in the face, for example, of limited research and development funds. These resources may be used to explore cost reducing innovations or, as we assume, to discover technologies that will help to foster a wider set of objectives. As the choice of technique moves over the multi-dimensional surface so implementation of that technology in the model will induce changes in the predicted levels of employment, income and its distribution, as finally determined by shifts in commodity and factor markets, locally and internationally, as well as technology *per se*. Turning the problem on its head then, we may simply set ourselves acceptable targets for the social and economic variables and ask what technology is consistent with them and whether it lies inside the innovation possibility surface.

In the experiments below we aim to ensure that all labour, both skilled and unskilled is fully employed. Table 5.10 showed that in the low income

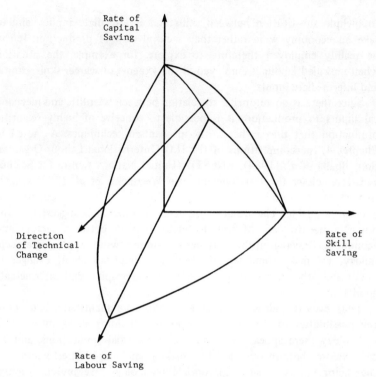

Figure 8.1 Invention possibilities for low income economies

economies as much as 17 per cent of skilled labour and 56 per cent of unskilled labour was underutilised. Beyond this we are aiming for an increase in national output, household income and the potential for sustained economic growth, in such a way that a reasonable balance is maintained between the level of production and consumption in each major sector. Thus these economies should not become overly dependent on imports of any commodity.

In characterising technologies it is useful also to make a distinction between the scientific knowhow involved in production and mere mechanisation. For example, Barscht (1977), on the basis of empirical studies in India and the Philippines demonstrates the potential of increasing agricultural yields through the use of greater scientific inputs to production, rather than increased mechanisation. 'Mechanisation' in the guise of increasing capital/labour ratios has been the principle dimension of most theoretical and empirical studies of choice of technique (for example Vitelli 1980). In our model, the concept of mechanisation is extended to include substitution between skills and intermediate inputs, and to take an economy wide rather than sectoral view of production. It can be readily employed therefore to explore, for example, the situation when unskilled labour is employed at the expense of scarcer skills, capital and intermediate inputs.

Since there is no automatic correlation between scientific and mechanical inputs to production, it is possible to conceive of highly scientific production that uses rather lowly mechanised techniques. As noted in Chapter 4, the compilations of the ILO (International Labour Organisation, Bhalla *et al.* (1984), UNCSTD (United Nations Centre for Science and Technology for Development, von Weizsäcker *et al.* 1984) suggest that there is considerable potential, although little firm quantitative data are available. The studies considered in Chapter 3 suggest that the opportunities for use of new technologies vary between sectors and economies. Drawing on these studies and on reviews of 'appropriate' technology, we make some tentative initial assumptions about changes in factor and other inputs to production (labour, capital and intermediate goods).

Thus, even though we have rather little precise quantitative data about the possibilities for upgrading traditional techniques using information technology there appear to be numerous potential applications, and we can explore these in our model by making semi-empirical estimations of the factor inputs to such appropriate technology. We prefer to adopt some rather conservative figures here so that there can be no dispute that the technology we are assuming is technically feasible, even though there may be institutional difficulties in its actual innovation. We assume that in all sectors the number of unskilled and skilled workers (per unit of production) *increase* while inputs of capital and intermediate inputs decrease. (This assumption is rather different from the assumption to be made if 'traditional' rather than 'integrated' or 'blended' techniques were to be considered, since in that case the use of unskilled labour would *decrease,* see Cole 1983.) The changes in factor and other inputs are chosen in such a way that production costs (at base year prices) remain *unchanged.* This last assumption means that we shall be examining the impact of substitution effects between factors rather than changes in competitiveness arising from shifts in productivity, and also that we are not claiming impossible feats for developing country research and development institutions. In some respects our assumptions may be overly cautious since many of the empirical studies show that production costs are *reduced* even when traditional 'appropriate technologies' are adopted.

In the experiments that follow, in each sector, capital and intermediate inputs have been reduced in all sectors by 10 per cent, while skilled labour inputs increase by 5 per cent. Unskilled labour inputs then increase so as to leave total production costs unchanged, at base year factor and commodity prices. The changes are shown in Table 8.5. The greatest increases in total labour intensity are in activities which currently have the lowest labour to capital ratios and the greatest increases in skill intensity are in activities which currently employ least skilled labour. Obviously these figures are debatable but they certainly reflect the spirit of what appears to be possible by combining traditional and emerging technologies. We turn now to the question of what happens when this technology is adopted on an economy wide scale and show that its impact depends greatly on how international trade and domestic social and economic policy are managed.

Possible technology with autarky and open markets

What happens when the existing technology of the low income economies is replaced by this new technology?

We examine again the consequences in a situation of autarky, i.e. international trade across the economy groups remains blocked. The results given in Table 8.6(a) show that many of the objectives with respect to income, employment and distribution are met even with these cautious assumptions about a possible technology.

The Table shows that real national income has increased by about 19 per cent. Levels of skilled and unskilled employment too have risen sharply by 18 per cent and 35 per cent respectively. From Table 5.10 we see that this exhausts the supply of skilled labour but some unskilled labour is still underemployed. The income of poor households has risen

Table 8.5 Adaptive technology for low income economies—changes in inputs by sector*

Sector	Agriculture	Industry	Services
Intermediate inputs	−L	−L	−L
Skilled labour	+L	+L	+L
Unskilled labour	+L	+VH	+LM
Capital	−L	−L	−L

* Percentage changes relative to base year. Key as for Table 6.2.

Table 8.6 Blended technology with autarky and open markets*

	Economy group		
	(a) Low	(b) Low	(c) Low
Income			
Total	+M	+VL	+M
Rich HH	−L	−VL	−L
Poor HH	+M	+LL	+H
Capital	−L	−NL	−L
Employment			
Skilled	+M	−VL	−L
Unskilled	+H	+VL	+HH
Production			
Agriculture	+LL	−VH	+H
Industry	+L	+VH	+HH
Services	+LM	−M	−MH
Net exports			
Agriculture	−LL	−VH	+LM
Industry	+LM	+VH	+MH
Services	+NL	−MH	−HH
Commodity prices			
Agriculture	+VL	+N	+VL
Industry	+N	+N	+N
Services	+NL	−N	+N

* Percentage change relative to base year. Key as for Table 6.2.
(a) No international trade or transfers.
(b) Base year technology in high and middle income economies.
(c) Probable technology in high and middle income economies.

by 20 per cent, while the income of rich household incomes has fallen by 19 per cent. Because of the great increase in employment, the wage income of all households has risen dramatically even though wage rate increases have been constrained to around 10 per cent (in order to maintain profitability at a level which should sustain the existing rate of growth). Although the investment income of rich households has fallen, this is countered by increased wage income—the fall in household incomes is therefore primarily due to the removal of income transfers from abroad in the autarkic economy. (As the social accounting matrix in

Table 5.8 shows, foreign transfers contribute about 16 per cent of income to these households.)

Although the rate of profit has fallen by 10 per cent, an increased total income enables the rate of saving to be maintained so that the rate of overall economic growth need not be adversely affected. Indeed, because capital intensity has been reduced by 10 per cent, the present rate of growth should be more than maintained. We should contrast this with those earlier experiments where the capital intensity increased, demanding that an increasing share of output must be devoted to new investment if even current growth rates are to be maintained. The introduction of the 'possible' technology, then, appears to meet many of the macro-economic objectives we have specified, at least with autarkic trade policies. Obviously such a 'scenario' begs many other questions of policy, but what is demonstrated clearly is that as unutilised human resources are brought into production, real household and national income can rise dramatically.

If the same set of technology and other policies were to be adopted in an *open* trading economy, what then is the effect? The results of this, given in Table 8.6(b) and 8.6(c) show that the gains by low income countries may be more or less undermined, depending upon the kind of technology employed in other competing economies.

First, if the technologies of the high and middle income economies are the same as in the base period then virtually all the gains are lost (see Table 8.6(b)). The increase in total real income is reduced to 3 per cent, the employment gains are eliminated and in addition the composition of production is seriously changed. Although industrial output increases greatly, the low income economies become increasingly dependent on imports of agricultural products. If other processes considered in Chapter 7 are taken into account also, it is clear that the net impact of combining open trade policies and labour intensive production techniques (whether upgraded through the integration of emerging technologies (or not) can lead to a potentially disastrous situation.

The magnitude of the change from Table 8.6(a) might be surprising given that production costs for the new technology are taken to be competitive at base year world prices. However, it has to be remembered that since the purpose of adopting labour intensive techniques is to increase employment, and so push up wage rates, this immediately forces up production costs, making the goods non-competitive in world markets. If the system of production is protected from world markets, then prices still rise but wages rise even faster so enabling multiplier processes in the domestic economy to thrive. If not, the gains will be simply 'competed' away.

The constraints imposed by world markets on the low income economies need not always be so severe. Such effects depend critically on the technology employed by foreign producers. Table 8.6(c) shows the situation when 'probable' technology is assumed for the high and middle income countries. The local situation is determined still by relative world prices and demand for commodities, but because of the relative weakening of the agricultural sector in the high income economies (discussed in conjunction with Table 6.2), agriculture in the poorest countries can expand, and with this so many of the positive effects of the labour intensive 'possible' technology remain. Indeed Table 8.6(c) shows that total income has risen by some 22 per cent, the number of unskilled jobs has increased by 44 per cent, and the income of poor households has risen by 34 per cent above the base period. Despite these gains, there are also some losses, in particular, the service sector declines and, in consequence of this, many skilled jobs are lost.

Adaptive technology and the direction of technical change

The last result suggests that even though the choice of technique is a response to domestic needs it must take account of changes in technology elsewhere. Further, this is not simply a matter of matching sector by sector the advances of other countries. For example, as discussed in Chapter 4, the greatest reductions in production costs as a consequence of using probable technology, in either the high or middle income economies, are in the industry sector followed by services and lastly agriculture. But in the experiment shown in Table 8.6(c), the service sector rather than agriculture or industry sectors in the low income economies, is most adversely affected. This is because the combination of domestic and international market forces represented in the model is such as to make services in the low income economies relatively uncompetitive, either in its ability to compete for labour and capital or to sell goods internationally. Consequently, the service sector must be made more competitive if the imbalance between domestic production is to be restored, and if the number of skilled jobs is to be increased, and if the economy is to survive the world free trade environment.

To illustrate this we assume that the cost reductions in the service sector of the low income economies match those in the high income economies. In this case the increase in unskilled jobs (per unit of output) shown in Table 8.5 falls to around 14 per cent. The result is shown in Table 8.7. Total output has risen now by nearly 26 per cent and unskilled

Table 8.7 Technology adapted to international markets*

	Economy group		
	High	Middle	Low
Income			
Total	+NL	+NL	+MH
Rich HH	+LM	−LM	−NL
Poor HH	−L	+L	+H
Capital	+L	+NL	−L
Employment			
Skilled	+VL	−L	+LM
Unskilled	−LL	+LL	+HH
Production			
Agriculture	−H	+VH	+HH
Industry	+NL	−M	+LL
Services	+LL	−L	+LL
Net exports			
Agriculture	−MH	+VH	+M
Industry	+VL	−M	−LL
Services	+NL	−L	−L
Commodity prices			
Agriculture	+LL	+LL	+LL
Industry	+N	+N	+N
Services	+N	+N	+N

* Percentage change relative to base year. Key as for Table 6.2.

employment by nearly 50 per cent while output in all sectors has increased well above the base period.

In the spirit of achieving a deliberate set of social and economic objectives, therefore, we have asked what direction of technical change is required to maintain an acceptable balance? As we have seen, there may be rather little that developing economies can do to change world prices, but by adapting technology so as to balance factor and commodity prices, it may be possible to maintain a stable and internationally competitive economy. Indeed, if this is not done, then the whole strategy of attempting to bring unused human resources into play is undermined. A strategy of modifying technology therefore should not be aimed only at specific low income sectors, but rather should be an economy wide approach.

This obviously has implications for strategies which propose that development should proceed with traditional and modern technologies existing side by side. What is needed is an integrated, rather than a dualistic, technology system, in which the appropriate features of traditional and new technology are combined in a way which can systematically adapt to the changing world economic environment. For this to happen, rapid technical change in the less industrialised countries takes place in response to changes in the industrial countries, but the direction of change is qualitatively different. First, the composition of production and products are geared towards domestic markets; second, the improvements in productivity are concentrated on non-labour inputs as far as possible; and third, the concentration of effort takes account of economy-wide changes.

It may be argued that what is suggested here is more or less what a free market, left to itself, would do anyway. In particular, entrepreneurs will respond to both world commodity prices and factor costs before deciding to innovate or employ a new technology. But in this decision they are motivated primarily by questions of profitability, with employment at best a secondary consideration. The argument that if, left to itself, the market will ensure the 'correct' choice of technology in order to maximise output, means little when the observed result is that large numbers of people are socially and economically marginalised through unemployment. In public corporations a wider range of social criteria are addressed. Clearly also, the way governments set about encouraging new investment can determine the direction of technical change. Giving tax breaks on new capital spending rather than providing subsidies for the creation of new jobs will obviously push investors towards a capital intensive rather than a labour intensive choice of technique. Furthermore, when the capital intensive technologies are more readily available through transfer from richer economies, and only modest research and development undertaken in the developing economies, firms and governments, however well motivated are left with little effective choice.

These lead us beyond the scope of the present book. The question of how to stimulate the research and development effort in developing countries has been discussed in many of the references cited in this chapter, especially for the promotion of integrated and blended techniques. What we have tried to do here is to define the concepts in operational terms and to clarify their strategic and practical implications and the relevance of other instruments of policy. In the next chapter, after reviewing the overall findings of our study, we shall attempt to fit our conclusions in a broader and longer term context.

9 Income distribution, employment and growth: fortune's wheel

The agenda revisited

The question of whether information technology will destroy or create jobs, in what sectors, in what countries and over what time frame is immensely complicated. Such questions cannot be answered unambiguously and we have not attempted to do so here. In Chapter 1 we suggested the agenda which must be addressed for better understanding of the issues to be obtained. The point of studying the phenomenon is not to predict what will happen, but to anticipate what could happen and so to change course and escape unintended consequences.

The first set of questions we addressed related to the characteristics of information technology—what sectors and what countries are in a position to implement the technology, and on what timescale, and whether there are generalisations to be made about its impact on labour and capital productivity, and hence its capacity to create or destroy jobs?

The second set of questions concerned the relative importance of indirect versus direct effects of the technology, in particular the importance of intersectoral and international market forces, and how these could affect the pattern of specialisation, trade structures and commodity dependence of different types of economy?

The third set of questions concerns the economic ranking of nations. Will information technology serve to close or widen the growing gap between rich and poor countries? If countries engage in a trade war, will short-run tactics undermine potential long-term gains? Indeed, can all countries gain in a 'devil take the hindmost race' to implement new technology?

Next are questions of employment and income distribution within different economies: whether the new technology will create wealth but destroy jobs or radically change the distribution of income between capital and labour, or even between different kinds of labour? Included here is the question of to what extent domestic policy can help to foster the potential gains or alleviate the potential inequities and social hardship arising from the new technology?

Finally there is the question of whether and how the technology might be used to confront the development needs of low income countries. If so, what new directions should be explored?

What technology, when and where?

What countries are in a position to innovate information technology, and in what sectors? Our review of the available literature in Chapters 2 to 4 shows that, despite the increasing number of sectoral and sub-sectoral studies in industrial and developing countries, there is not yet a concensus although a number of clear alternatives are hypothesised. From the more empirical of these studies we have made a systematic cross country and cross sectoral estimation of the productivity impact of information technology which enables some of the alternatives to be explored and compared.

The weight of opinion tends to support the idea that in the medium term the most significant use of the technology will be in the high income industrial economies. The differences between the industrial economies seem to be less than those between these countries as a group and the rest of the world. For the developing economies the evidence points to considerable barriers to implementation, including the lack of supporting infrastructure, knowhow and capital. These difficulties are less severe in the so-called 'newly industrialised' economies and capital rich oil exporting economies, which comprise our 'middle income' group, than in the remainder of the developing low income economies. Obviously these are gross generalisations—within each group there are exceptions, which suggest that distinct alternatives must be examined.

Across sectors, another general pattern emerges; in each economic group the industry sector (comprising also extraction and utilities) appears to be taking the lead with information technology, followed by services and lastly agriculture. But here too the picture is very uneven and we have subdivided these sectors according to their degree of technological 'sophistication' and their propensity for new technology. These characteristics to some extent run counter to each other, since the gains from new technology are most favourable to industries where 'batch' production is the norm.

As yet, the most widely asserted characteristic of information technology is that it displaces labour, especially unskilled labour, at the cost of increased capital inputs. It is this characteristic which has led to widespread fears that unemployment will increase if the technology is used extensively, even though particular industries become more competitive as a result. In the medium term 'systemic' applications of the technology may increase capital productivity (and reduce intermediate and raw material inputs) significantly also, changing dramatically any assumptions about its employment impact. In the empirical studies reviewed, this uncertainty leaves the greatest unanswered questions.

Although there is some indication that the technology gap is growing between a select group of 'first division' dynamic economies and the lagging mixed and centrally planned industrial economies, taking account of their somewhat different needs and applications, these countries do not appear to be dramatically less successful in implementing information technology. For this reason these economies have been treated as a single group for this exploratory analysis.

While the pattern observed is not surprising and is, in our opinion, the most probable outcome (i.e. effective appropriation of the technology by the industrial economies) is by no means a certainty, and at least one alternative seems plausible. If the technology matures, so that the pace of innovation in the high income economies slows, then foreign direct investment, transfer to technology and indigenous enterprise could together substantially reverse this assumption of 'business as usual'. This would fit with some theories of the 'long wave' in economic development. To explore this further, from our empirical review we made a revised assessment of how the use of the technology would vary between sectors and economies.

Several distinctive technological 'routes' for the future of technical change therefore emerge. In order to confront this uncertainty and also to take account of the time scale for realising the full potential of new technology, the alternatives are examined in turn. With the 'probable' route new technology has greatest impact on productivity in the high income economies and least in the low income economies. With the 'plausible' route the greatest impact is in the developing countries. For both routes two types of change are examined: non-systemic technical change (mainly labour saving) and systemic change (both capital and labour saving). Generally we expect that capital saving effects will take longer to realise.

Tables 9.1(a) and 9.1(b) summarise the changes in comparative advantage across sectors and economy groupings for the 'probable' and 'plausible' technology routes for both non-systemic and systemic technical change. These calculations were made assuming no change in wages and other input prices. In other words, no indirect downstream or upstream effects of the change in technology are accounted for. Thus they reflect changes in the competitive position of sectors and countries coming from a comparative micro-economic analysis.

Table 9.1a Sectoral impact of comparative advantage: probable route*

Economy group	Non-systemic			Systemic		
	High	Middle	Low	High	Middle	Low
Agriculture	+VL	+NL	+N	+H	+L	+N
Industry	+M	+LL	+VL	+VH	+HH	+H
Services	+L	+VL	+NL	+MH	+H	+L

Table 9.1b Sectoral impact of comparative advantage: plausible route*

Economy group	Non-systemic			Systemic		
	High	Middle	Low	High	Middle	Low
Agriculture	+NL	+LL	+LM	+LM	+M	+M
Industry	+L	+M	+M	+H	+VH	+VH
Services	+L	+LL	+VL	+H	+H	+MH

* Key to scale: N = 0, NL = 0.5, VL = 2, LL = 4.5, L = 8, LM = 12.5, M = 18, MH = 24.5, H = 32, HH = 40.5, VH = 50.

Is there a third possibility for information technology? One school of thought considers that for the developing economies simply to parrot the industrial economies in their use of information technology, would not address the enormous problems of unemployment and underemployment that they face, nor would it relieve the technological dependence of the poor world on the rich. Although, here especially, the data are sparse, we have used our empirical review and other studies of appropriate technology to clarify some of the characteristics of this possible technology route for the least industrialised economies. The direction of technical change here is designed to ensure that the entire workforce is employed. Even though we consider this third technological route to be much less probable (for institutional rather than engineering or scientific reasons), we can, nevertheless, speculate about it. In this case we have used our economic model to provide estimates of the technology needed to maintain full employment and other goals and then consider whether this is inconsistent with what we believe to be the possibilities for the new technologies.

Direct verus indirect effects

Most studies of changes in comparative advantage due to technical change calculate first order production cost savings only (as above) and make similar assumptions about demand. But this micro-economic approach is begged by a macro-economic question. If technical change is very widespread and it is anticipated that relative factor prices and income distributions change, then anticipated cost savings must change also. If all countries in the world more or less simultanteously jump onto the bandwagon of new technology, from a fear that they will otherwise be left behind, will the status quo simply be maintained, or worse? The expansion of one country's output may be at the expense of another, but if this means lost production capacity, jobs, wages and demand, what then sustains the expanded output of the first country? What happens if governments intervene to slow down the process of restructuring or to increase the availability of scarce resources (such as specialised skills)? This is the crux of much of the agenda we have enumerated. To go beyond the simplest attempt to take account of such effects has required the use of a model in which factor and commodity price changes are calculated explicitly and their ramifications observed.

We have used a model of the world economy (described in Chapter 5) which is relatively simple yet reflects the very great differences between countries, their technology, income distribution and markets. Because the empirical data on this new technology is ambiguous, and several alternatives appear for its future use, we have left out detail to preserve flexibility. However, we have retained sufficient detail and precision to identify paradoxes in some of the 'conventional wisdoms' which surround the global race to new technology and the increasing reliance placed on the 'magic of the market'.

A number of distinctive experiments allowed us to examine the different technology routes and policies, and to unravel some of the complexity and ambiguity which surround the new technology. Rather than dispute the fine details of individual parameters we have assumed quite large variations so that we can be somewhat more confident in our broad conclusions. Our calculations show clearly that existing production structures and market conditions are at least as important in determining the consequences of technical change, as is the technical change itself. Key results

Table 9.2 Employment, distribution and growth by technology route
and economy type*

	Economy group		
	High	Middle	Low
	9.2a *Probable (non-systemic)*		
Growth	+N	+NL	+N
Distribution	−L	+LM	+L
Employment	−LL	+LL	+LL
Structure	−M	−M	−L
	9.2b *Probable (systemic)*		
Growth	+L	+LL	+VL
Distribution	−LM	−MH	−MH
Employment	+LL	+VL	+VL
Structure	+M	−HH	−L
	9.2c *Probable (write-offs)*		
Growth	−NL	−VL	+VL
Distribution	−L	+LM	+LM
Employment	−LL	+NL	+VL
Structure	−VH	−H	−LM
	9.2d *Plausible (with other policy)*		
Growth	+LM	+MH	+M
Distribution	−LL	−LM	−LM
Employment	+LL	+NL	+LL
Structure	+M	−HH	−L

Table 9.2 (*cont.*)

	Economy group		
	High	Middle	Low

9.2e *Possible (adaptive)*			
Growth	+N	+NL	+MH
Distribution	−L	+LM	+H
Employment	−L	+LL	+H
Structure	−M	−M	−N

* Key to scale (percentage change): N = 0, NL = 0.5, VL = 2, LL = 4.5, L = 8, LM = 12.5, M = 18, MH = 24.5, H = 32, HH = 40.5, VH = 50.

Note: Entries are averages of data appearing in earlier chapters. A plus sign indicates an improvement in, e.g. income distribution or employment. The entries for structure indicate the change in output of the most affected sector.

from our analysis in Chapters 6 to 8 showing changes in economic structure and growth, employment and income distribution are summarised in Table 9.2. Included here are results corresponding to the 'probable' route alternatives of Tables 9.1(a) and 9.1(b), as well as two other experiments for the 'plausible' and 'possible' technologies. Despite some ambiguities, certain patterns again emerge from the calculations as a whole. The implications of these for the questions of our agenda are now reviewed.

International distribution and growth

How might information technology affect income distribution and growth across countries? Our calculations demonstrate that the technology has the potential to raise living standards world-wide, but whether this will happen is by no means a foregone conclusion.

If the anticipated improvements in labour and, more especially, capital productivity are realised, then all economies should see a significant overall improvement in national income. If the 'probable' trend materialises, so that the technology is innovated in the industrial economies, and the developing countries lag behind, then the international income gap will widen. But the reverse does not necessarily hold: if the developing economies eventually set the pace in implementing the technology—the apparently optimistic assumption of our 'plausible' trend—the gains wᴜ be more evenly spread. This is shown by the first three results in Table 9.2.

Thus with technology induced expansion, 'trickle up' from poor to rich countries seems to be stronger than the vaunted 'trickle down'. The gap may close, but only slowly unless government action (considered below) reinforces the growth potential. In this sense, as a stimulus to greater national prosperity, the technology, as presently implemented appears to be a 'first world' technology. We would not claim that this makes discussion about where the technology will be located irrelevant but it certainly makes discussion about 'what kind of technology?' and 'what other economic and social policy?' at least as relevant. This is especially the case when temporal and distributional questions are addressed.

What can we say about economic growth? Our model does not directly 'predict' economic growth since the contribution of investment to subsequent capital formation is not treated fully. But if we take shifts in the rates of profit across economies, together with changes in total output as indicators of growth prospects, then some clear growth tendencies are seen. Generally profitability increases most in the economy introducing the new technology, whether or not it is capital saving, and whether or not GDP also rises. When technical change is predominately labour saving, capital becomes scarcer; but even when technical change is capital saving profits still increase. (This is in part because price reductions for intermediate goods contribute to equipment and inventory savings and so help to offset increased labour costs.) In addition, strong multiplier effects are again crucial as increased employment stimulates increased demand and so on.

The tendency for profitability to follow successful innovation suggests a strong reinforcing dynamic as internationally mobile capital (through international firms, in particular) relocates to take advantage of the new mosaic of opportunity. Although we have only treated the international finance sector exogenously, it is evident that such processes can increase further the gaps in GDP and other changes in the world economy, even though they generally help to increase world output further. Thus growth prospects are generally good if the technology is successfully implemented (i.e. *both* capital and labour saving potential is realised) and even point to a possible catching up by some developing economies.

Restructuring into decline?

Despite the optimistic growth prospect above, there are also mechanisms which could lead to slower or even negative growth in the low income economies, or even the world economy at large as a result of failure to achieve innovation promises, overly competitive and reactive public policies and the accelerated junking of productive capacity.

In the first place, if information technology remains primarily labour displacing, then the results indicate that the initial benefits of new technology, wherever it is introduced, will be exported. Worse, if the expected capital savings are not achieved (or are only achieved after an extended time) then it is less likely that all countries will gain. In this case important multiplier effects in the domestic and international economy will contribute little and, also, there will be less additional output to 'trickle down' or distribute to adversely affected sectors, workers or countries.

Changes in technology, through their effect on commodity and factor prices, induce changes in the composition of production. The latter have at least as great an impact on employment and income distribution as do changes in technology alone. For example, if production shifts from labour intensive agriculture to capital intensive industry in developing countries, and to capital intensive agriculture from less capital intensive industry in developed countries, jobs may be lost even though the value of output has increased.

The results show structural effects to be of great significance for developing economies. While all the results stem from changing technology and induced shifts in the domestic and international composition of output, it is changes in international markets which determine the situation of developing economies, especially the export oriented middle income economies. A decrease of only a few percent in the demand for industrial imports by the high income countries has a tremendous impact on the size of the industrial sector in export oriented developing economies, but not vice versa. As a result, the structural shifts induced by changes in world technology are much greater in developing economies than in the industrial economies.

Combining the first two results of Table 9.2 shows that a systematic but potentially disruptive process of economic restructuring may arise if the labour saving characteristics of the new technology are felt before the capital saving effects come into play. In this case successive and opposite pressures to restructure national economies would follow. Initially, the agriculture sector of the industrial economies would suffer from decreasing investment, but then, as capital saving technologies are introduced in other sectors, the sector would again expand. The relative size of the high income countries in the world means that changes in the structure of their economies force complementary changes elsewhere in the world and so middle and low income economies face first an expansion and then a collapse of agriculture. Developing economies are then pushed into a situation of dependence for this good, to add to their substantial technological dependence.

These results suggest that low income economies could be trapped in a cycle of poverty by international forces. The rapid restructuring of economies implies that much existing capital may simply be 'junked' as changes in market conditions make it unprofitable. Thus the total production capacity will decline unless new investment more than replaces the accelerated depreciation. (see Table 9.2(c).) Because structural shifts are more in evidence in the developing economies, they are especially susceptible to this effect. In high income economies the direct effects of this process are less but the possibility of 'knock on' effects arises. As developing economies experience a decline, so the demand for industrial country exports falls, and hence their output also.

In the short run, therefore, it is not difficult to construct a scenario in which all economies could become worse off. The defensive policies which high income nations typically would adopt (such as subsidies to weakened sectors), have a deleterious effect on the developing economies and backfire domestically, while comparable domestic or international efforts to support developing economies are relatively ineffective. Thus any optimism about the long-run possibilities for growth in developing countries must be strongly tempered by the spectre of an extended crisis, and also the likelihood that the technology will do little for growth or income distribution.

Employment and income distribution

Can the new technology create jobs as well as wealth? For the industrial economies the answer is 'yes' but again this depends on whether capital saving gains are realised, and this appears to be more important than whether the technology is introduced faster in the industrial than in the developing world. Providing, and when, capital savings are achieved employment could be maintained or even increased. If these capital saving innovations are not achieved then increases in demand at home or abroad will not compensate for increases in labour productivity. However the new jobs are mainly skilled and so the skill composition of the workforce must change also. Thus our conclusion here matches those detailed studies for the United States and other industrial OECD economies (referred to earlier) that the new technology does not necessarily lead to job destruction in the long term, but we believe that shorter term structural problems are evident (both in our calculations and in fact!).

For the developing countries the answer to our question about employment is probably 'no'. Certainly the successful innovation or transfer of a capital saving technology can create additional skilled jobs, but given the reported difficulties of making the facilitating 'systemic' gains, the net effect on employment is small and unlikely to impact greatly on the massive overall level of unemployment. Ironically, the otherwise least favourable route, in which the low income economies lag behind the higher income countries in introducing labour saving technology, offers as many unskilled jobs, entirely because of the induced expansion of the very labour intensive agriculture sector. However, even this possibility would be easily undermined by protectionist policy in the industrial economies or other kinds of new technology in that sector. Generally the situation in the middle income countries is worse, as the agricultural sector is less labour intensive and represents a smaller share of national output.

What of income distribution within countries? The calculations show that these are diverse and changes in national income can have a very heterogeneous impact on the different workers and households or the division between capital and labour. Because of the complementarity in production we have noted above, there is a pattern whereby a worsening in income distribution in the high income economies often means an improvement in distribution in the developing economies, but this effect is complicated by the very different technologies of the various economies. In the high income economies there is a strong tendency for income distribution to worsen: typically the new technologies reduce the unskilled labour wage bill, increase skilled wages somewhat and increase profitability (and total profits substantially). In the middle and low income economies, household income distribution generally improves until the effect of capital saving technology is felt, and then worsens following the pattern set by employment.

Typically, the rate of profit increases most sharply in the economy which is most successful in introducing new technology, and usually increases throughout the world economy. Thus a major worldwide shift in the distribution between capital and labour would accompany both the probable and plausible technologies. In most cases this is reflected in the distribution between rich and poor households, and sometimes disguises the shift in income distribution between categories of labour.

In many cases, therefore, a clear conflict between growth, income distribution and employment arises.

Public sector policy

The calculations just reviewed suggest that market processes alone lead
to significant changes in national income and its distribution, employment
and the pattern of specialisation. How effective can public sector policy
be in stabilising these changes or assisting nations as they jockey for
position in the global technology race? The answer depends on the particular economy and sector in question and the nature of the stress induc-
ing change. Subsidies on strategic sectors such as agriculture (in industrial
economies) are at the expense of overall output: so long as entrepreneurs
can redirect investments between sectors rather massive subsidies are
needed and this has the tendency to push down overall growth and to
transfer the problem of sectoral decline to other sectors. Currency revalua-
tion and international transfers are not well represented but show little
effectiveness, either as a way of improving international competitiveness
on a sustained basis or of compensating for differences in economic
performance. On the other hand, wage controls and more especially
changes in the composition of the labour force appear as critical. Wage
controls in developing economies in particular can increase competitiveness of these economies and lead to increases in the income of rich and
poor households provided exports into high income economies are not
impeded through short run protectionist policies. But the reverse does
not hold for the high income economies because the necessary increased
demand for exports cannot come from the much smaller markets of the
Third World.

Typically, the calculations suggest that without adequate public sector
policy the consequences of restructuring may be harsh, but that with the
wrong policies the situation is even worse. Provided an appropriate combination of public sector policies can be imposed, then the considerable
potential increase in output that results from the capital saving aspects
of the probable or the plausible technology can be exploited to enhance
income for all economies and household types—leaving the appearance
of improved growth rates and improved distribution. Indeed, many of the
redistributive processes between skilled and unskilled labour can be
offset through adequate education and retraining programmes, but while
this reduces wage differentials, it widens the gap between capital and labour
as a group. This is seen from the third result in Table 9.2.

But two unwelcome features emerge here. First, while income equality between labour categories and households improves, income inequality between capital and labour increases and the wage income of skilled labour declines systematically as their numbers increase. Second, while this can lead to increased employment in the industrial economies, it has no significant impact on the unemployment crisis in developing economies. Clearly, given a relatively great increase in output and growth prospects some redistributive policies could create a more desirable picture, and 'job sharing' could provide a semblance of equal and universal employment. But to achieve this assumes the successful worldwide adoption of information technology and carefully co-ordinated domestic and international policy.

Alternatives for low income economies

What happens to the least developed economies if these conditions are not fulfilled? The conclusion must be that the weakest nations and the weakest populations would lose—even the most 'optimistic' scenario leaves developing economies with a massive unemployment problem.

The experiments suggest that it is very difficult for developing economies to design an independent strategy which makes use of new technology, so long as their economies are exposed to the full force of world markets. This is first because the relative economic weight of the high income countries in the world means that with existing technology they dominate the operation of international markets. Thus while changes in these economies have very real impact on the rest of the world, the reverse is not the case, so that domestic structures there face much greater adjustment problems. Second, even when the new 'plausible' technology is introduced in the developing economies, the extent to which they ultimately gain financially depends on whether the technology is transferred (but still appropriated) by international firms, and whether these firms repatriate income or reinvest locally. Certainly new investments in new technology in the low income countries are likely to result from international firms seeking cheaper labour markets, while in the middle income economies, even though local innovation may be more important, foreign loans and ownership are prevalent.

Can developing countries avoid this trap of unemployment, and of technological and commodity dependence, by using the new knowhow (rather than the new technology) in another fashion? We have explored the possibility that technologies which are tailored to the needs of different types of economies and policies could be evolved. These would not represent straightforward transfer or marginal adaptation, but deliberate and continuous integration of knowhow into a locally based technological system. Although an increasing number of illustrations of possible applications are given in the literature, we can only speculate here about the quantitative properties of this technology on the basis of the new empirical researches available: many more are needed.

One particular direction has been explored which would increase the number of jobs up to the full complement of the workforce and also maintain a rather independent production system (i.e. one in which net imports of major commodities are small). In order that such innovation may be reasonably argued as being within the capability of a limited research and development system, it is assumed that production costs with the 'blended' technology are the same as with the techniques currently employed. Even with these rather conservative assumptions about technology, our calculations show that it is possible to raise incomes by a significant amount and still maintain an acceptable rate of growth. Table 9.2(e) gives this result.

Obviously there is no magic involved here: with the new technology all human resources are employed more productively and some capital and material savings are made. While incomes and more especially the rate of economic growth would be somewhat less than the most optimistic calculations described above, they are considerably better than other possibilities we have reviewed. From the point of view of achieving a more balanced, equitable and indigenously derived path of development, the postulated alternative may have much to recommend it, at least as a way of 'bypassing' some of the massive structural changes.

An agenda for the future

We have presented a rather large and potentially bewildering array of empirical evidence and calculations. Sometimes these appear to be conflicting and ambiguous. We would be the first to recognise the limitations and flaws in our analysis—but we believe it has confirmed that the agenda for research should not ignore the questions we have sought to answer, simply because they are complex. Certainly the results do not hold out much hope for anyone who would seek simple answers to the questions raised. But the results also fall into a pattern which demonstrates clearly some of the dominant tendencies of a market oriented world economy as it begins to employ radically new technology.

Many of the results described, for example the gross impact of capital saving or the need to upgrade labour force skills, follow from sectoral studies and simple theorising. But, in addition, we have shown that structural, price, multiplier and inter-economy effects are also likely to contribute to the net outcome. Further, the direction of technical change is as important a variable for many employment and income distribution issues as is where the technology is to be located. We emphasise also that intersectoral commodity and factor market effects are as important as direct effects, and, finally that in a world of free trade, the technology and trade choices made by industrial economies substantially determine the outcome for the developing economies. Thus, whatever the outcome for the industrial economies, the problems faced by the less industrialised economies are worse and far more difficult to resolve.

What are the implications of the calculations? What do they tell us about the future? If we accept the results at face value, then we can begin to build up a picture of how information technology might help to shape the world economy, and the situation of rich and poor people and nations, over the next decades. Suppose we try to piece together the findings as a sequence of events, can we place the alternatives in some kind of context? It is quite likely that actual development will comprise a mixture of the separate paths we have examined, but emphasising the 'probable' route. One possible composite 'scenario' is indicated by Figure 9.1 which follows through the logic of our calculations as successive stages based on the options for technical change. Even if we cannot accept this image of the future it may nevertheless help us to clarify the agenda for future research.

The first stage in the sequence sees the increasing use of information technology, especially in the high technology industrial sectors of the richest countries, but increasingly in the middle income economies and some suitably located low income economies. The technology is primarily labour saving at this stage, and this is also true of the expanding applications in the services sector.

The first stage sees a state of near crisis in the world economy. New investment is increasingly capital intensive and economic growth is slow until returns in the high income countries begin to rise. While there is both a capital and skill shortage, many unskilled jobs are lost as the older capital intensive sectors, especially agriculture, decline and labour saving equipment is introduced. Loss of jobs, and protectionism, serve to reduce demand and create a pattern which means that investment picks up only slowly, and capital stock is unused or depreciated. The demands of the unemployed and reduced revenues oblige governments systematically to cut back on education and retraining programmes, risking their future participation in the technological race. But this financial constraint also means that rich countries are unable to maintain their stranglehold

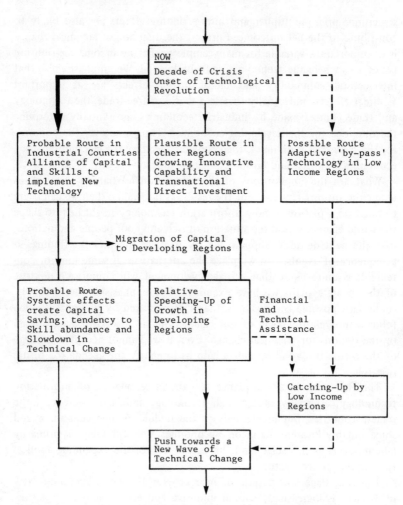

Figure 9.1 A schematic scenario for information technology (*Note*: Strength of vertical lines indicates likelihood of route and direction of change.)

on agricultural markets and the decline of this sector in developing countries reverses. Unfortunately this does rather little to improve incomes of the rural population. This is because the national situation in developing economies is typically worse than in rich countries and growth rates are generally less. Consequently most increased agricultural income is needed to prevent the collapse of the more critically affected urban sector.

After some time, the situation of skilled workers and firms in the high income economies begins to improve and this coalition of knowhow and capital slowly pushes the new technology in two directions: as reliability of the basic components improves the rate of transfer into developing economies increases, and, relocation of functions in industrial economies facilitates systemic gains. This in turn pushes the world economy into its next phase of structural change.

With capital savings achieved through systemic reorganisation of production, greater growth follows. This is accompanied by an increasing demand for skills, which now governments can belatedly begin to fill through increased expenditure on education. But as experience is gained with the new technologies, the momentum of transfer to developing economies has increased, and much more rapid growth is seen there also. Generally these countries show an extremely high rate of growth, which typically exceeds that of even the stronger industrial economies. However, the benefits of growth remain largely with the entrepreneurial and skilled elite and a substantial segment of the population is left in relative poverty. Despite the rapid growth, little is done to improve their condition as welfare oriented policies would reduce national comparative advantage in an increasingly competitive world. In industrial economies, the coalition between skilled labour and capital begins now to fail; as the skilled labour force increases, and their premium wage levels fall, profits rise to an unprecedented high level worldwide.

Eventually the need to take risks in the use of new technology falls away, and in addition, the full potential of the technology is realised, productivity gains are now incremental and the momentum of technical change shifts to developing countries. The technological 'revolution' is over, at least in the high income economies. Nevertheless, within the withering of this revolution are the seeds of the next. The high rate of capital growth as technical change slows leads once again to a situation of labour scarcity in industrial economies and eventually to declining rates of return. This accelerates the shift in the locus of production, and also stimulates a new wave of technical change.

What, within this short and partial account are the lessons? One obvious answer if global unemployment and poverty are to be confronted is the need to shift the emphasis of technological development from the probable to the possible route. Is a more directed path of technical change possible, when much evidence suggests innovation to be a complex process of serendipity and cross fertilisation between dispirate activities? Long-wave theories suggest technical change is also an almost mechanistic response to economic and social forces (and vice versa). But if this is true and the 'innovation cycle' is indeed the result of mechanistic responses by institutions (especially firms) to changes in market conditions or to the inability of institutions to adapt to change, it may be possible to redirect and smooth its path.

Until the post-war era, the (so-called) business cycle was a phenomenon to be feared. In the post war era government policy did much to reduce the severity of these cycles. Eventually, greater understanding may dampen the effects of the innovation cycle also. For Schumpeter, each long-wave cycle was unique, deriving from events such as wars or climate and fortuitous discovery and innovation, but nevertheless sharing common features. Clearly war, and the preparation for war, and climatic uncertainty are still major factors in economic life, but scientific discovery and innovation is arguably far more determined by conscious and directed social effort than in the past. Thus innovation cycles eventually should be viewed as 'acts of God' no more than business cycles, and social decisions about innovation should be made in the light of that knowledge. The requisite level of understanding may be something for the future, surely before the new wave of innovation speculated above. Until then we may at least continue to comprehend from detailed empirical sectoral and economy wide studies both the potential and the dangers of the present wave of new technology, and respond using presently understood policy measures.

This argument emphasises that technology should become a central and explicit variable of long-term global social policy, and not just the instrument of short-run national and commercial gain witnessed as many governments and firms today jump headlong on to the high technology bandwagon. In terms of the very urgent needs of the poorest developing countries, the suggestions that new science and traditional technology can offer an alternative policy for the present must be further examined. For example, if, as our scenario sketches, the first stage of innovation does indeed prove beneficial to Third World agriculture (and is not cancelled by other kinds of innovation or protection), then this could prove a launching pad for such a strategy. Although, ultimately to achieve sustained long run growth, these countries must have steady improvements in labour productivity, in the short run many resources are wasted for want of adequate technology. Our calculations show that it may, in principle, be possible to design a technology which is adaptive to the external economic environment. This may be more than simply a 'defensive' approach suggested by some authors since it should permit developing countries to take advantage of the opportunities within international markets and also provide decent levels of employment and income domestically. To a considerable degree the success of such an approach will depend on the co-operation of richer countries—providing markets, finance and technical knowhow. The time scale for this kind of co-operation to emerge may rival that for other wishful proposals, but without it the outlook for many people, a third of the world population, is unacceptably bleak.

Bibliography

Abernathy, W., *et al.* (1983), *Industrial Renaissance: Producing a Competitive Future for America,* Basic Books, New York.

Acero, L., Cole, S., and Rush, H. (1981), *Methods for Development Planning: Scenarios, Models and Micro-Studies,* UNESCO, Paris.

Ahuwalia, A., *et al.* (1979), 'Growth and Poverty in Developing Countries' *Journal of Development Studies,* Vol. 16.

Allagh, Y. *et al.* (1984), 'Policy Modelling for Planning in India', in Cohen *et al.* (1984).

Arnold, E. and Senker, P. (1982), 'Designing our Future; the Implications of CAD Interactive Graphics for Employment and Skills in the British Engineering Industry', Occasional Paper 9, Engineering Industry Training Board, Watford.

Amin, S. (1974), *Accumulation on a World Scale: A Critique of the Theory of Underdevelopment,* Monthly Review Press, London.

Arrow, F. (1974), 'Limited Knowledge and Economic Analysis', *American Economic Review,* Vol. 184, pp. 1–10.

Ayres, R. and Miller, S. (1983), *Robotics: Applications and Social Implications,* Ballinger, Cambridge, Mass.

Barron, I. and Curnow, R. (1979), *The Future with Micro-Electronics: Forecasting the Effects of Information Technology,* Frances Pinter, London.

Bartsch, W. (1977), *Employment and Technology Choice in Asian Agriculture,* Praeger, New York.

Bessant, J. (1980), 'The Influence of Micro-Electronics Technology', in Cole, ed. (1981), *Technological Alternatives for Development,* Vol. 1, UNITAR, New York.

Bessant, J. (1983), 'Technology and Market Trends in the Production and Application of Information Technology', *Micro-Electronics Monitor,* No. 8, UNIDO, Vienna.

Bessant, J. (1983), 'The Diffusion of Microelectronics', in J. Sigurdson and S. Jacobsson (eds), *Technological Trends and Challenges in Electronics,* RPI, Lund, Sweden.

Bessant, J. (1984), 'Competition, Technical Change and the UK Foundry Industry', *Steel Castings Trade and Research Journal,* Autumn.

Bessant, J. (1985), *An Overview of Flexible Manufacturing Systems,* UNIDO, Vienna.

Bessant, J. (1985), 'The Integration Barrier', *Robotica* (forthcoming).

Bessant, J. and Dickson, K. (1982), *Computers and Employment: an Annotated Bibliography,* Heyden, London.

Bessant, J. and Lamming, R. (1983), 'The Socioeconomic Impact of Technological Change in the Food and Drink Processing Industry', Working Paper, ILO, Geneva.

Bessant, J. and Verstoep, N. (1984), 'Making the Future: Developing the Individual and the Organisation' in J. Rijnsdorp (ed.), *Training for Tomorrow*, Pergamon, Oxford.

Bessant, J., Lamming, R., and Arnold, E. (1984), 'Human Factors in Systems Design for Computer-integrated Manufacturing', in T. Lupton (ed.), *Human Factors in Manufacturing*, IFS Publications, Kempston, Beds.

Bessant, J., Guy, K., Miles, I., and Rush, H. (1985), *IT Futures; A Review of the Literature on the Social Implications of Information Technology*, National Economic Development Office, London.

Bhagavan, M. (1980), 'A Critique of "Appropriate" Technology for Underdeveloped Countries'; UNITAR Conference on Alternative Development Strategies and the Future of Asia, New Delhi.

Bhagwati, J. (1958), 'Immiserizing Growth: A Geometrical Note', *Review of Economic Studies*, Vol. 25, pp. 201–5.

Bhagwati, J., Brechter, R., and Hatta, T. (1982), 'Generalized Theory of Transfers and Welfare', mimeo, Colombia University, New York.

Bhalla, A. (1979), *Towards Global Action for Appropriate Technology*, Pergamon, Oxford.

Bhalla, A., James, D., and Stevens, Y. (1984), *Blending of New and Traditional Technologies*, Tycooly, Dublin.

Bhargava, P. (1981), 'Microprocessors for the Indian Environment', paper presented to the FLACSO Seminar on Microelectronics, Buenos Aires, December.

Bigsten, A. (1983), *Income Distribution and Development: Theory, Evidence and Policy*, Heinemann, London.

Blauner, P. (1984), *Alienation and Freedom: the Factory Worker and his Industry*, University of Chicago Press, Chicago.

Bluestone, B. and Harrison, B. (1982), *The Deindustrialization of America*, Basic Books, New York.

Boon, G. (1982a), *The Interrelated Impact of Microelectronics Technology on the First, Second and Third Worlds*, Technology Scientific Foundation, Noordwijk, The Netherlands.

Boon, G. (1982b), 'Changing Comparative Advantage', *IDS Bulletin*, March.

Bourden, C. (1983), 'Labour Productivity and Technological Innovation: From Automation Scare to Productivity Decline', in Hull and Utterback, eds (1983).

Braun, E. and Macdonald, S. (1978, 1st edn: 1982, 2nd edn), *Revolution in Miniature*, Cambridge University Press, Cambridge.

Braun, E. and Senker, P. (1981), *New Technology and Employment*, Manpower Services Commission, London.

Braverman, H. (1974), *Labour and Monopoly Capital,* Monthly Review Press, New York.

Bright, J. (1958), *Automation and Management,* Harvard University Press, Boston.

Burns, J., *et al.* (1983), *The Food Industry,* Heinemann, London.

Caves, R. and Jones, R. (1981), *World Trade and Payments,* Little, Brown, Boston.

Chapman, D. (1980), 'Why Telling Fortunes is Better than Telling Fairy Tales', *Search,* Vol. 11, No. 6, pp. 179–82.

Chichilnisky, G. (1980), 'Basic Goods, the Effects of Commodity Transfers and the International Economic Order', *Journal of Development Economics,* pp. 505–19.

Chichilnisky, G. and Cole, S. (1978a), 'Growth of the North and Growth of the South: Some Results on Export Led Growth with Abundant Labour Supply', Harvard Institute for International Development, Discussion Paper No. 42, Boston.

Chichilnisky, G. and Cole, S. (1978b), 'A Model of Technology, Distribution and North–South Relations', *Technological Forecasting and Social Change.*

Chichilnisky, G. and McLeod, D. (1984), 'Agricultural Productivity and Trade, World Bank Global Analysis and Projections', Division Working Paper, No. 1984–4, Washington, DC.

Child, J. (1977), *Organisation: A Guide to Theory and Practise,* Harper and Row, London.

Clarke, J., *et al.* (1982), 'The Asian Electronics Industry Looks to the Future', *IDS Bulletin,* March.

Cline, W. (1982), 'Can the East Asian Model of Development be Generalised?' *World Development,* Vol. 10, No. 2, pp. 81–90.

Clower, R. (1965), 'The Keynesian Counter-revolution: A Theoretical Appraisal', in Hahn, F. and Brechling, F., eds, *The Theory of Interest Rates,* Macmillan, London.

Cohen, S., *et al.* (1984), *The Modelling of Socio-Economic Planning Processes,* Gower, Aldershot.

Cole, S. (1978), 'Income and Employment Effects in a Model of Innovation and Transfer of Technology', Science Policy Research Unit, also in Acero *et al.* (1981), *Methods for Development Planning,* UNESCO, Paris.

Cole, S., ed. (1980), *The UNITAR Macro-Model—National Models in the World Economy: Model Structure and Estimation,* Vol. 1; Sussex, June 1980.

Cole, S. (1982a), 'After Cancun: The Magic of the Market', *Futures,* reprinted in Tandon *et al.* (1984), *The New World Order,* Harvester (forthcoming).

Cole, S. (1982b), 'A Micro-Processor Revolution and the World Distribution of Income', *International Political Science Review,* Special Issue.

Cole, S. (1983), 'The Constraints of World Agriculture on Basic Food Production', in M. Levy and J. Robinson, *Energy and Agriculture: Their Interesting Futures*, Harwood, London.

Cole, S. (1984), 'Issues of Industrial Policy and Regional Development in an International Context', North–Eastern Region Science Association, State University of New York, Buffalo.

Cole, S. and Metcalf, J. (1970), 'Model Dependent Scaling for Attitude Questionnaire Item', *Socio-Economic Planning Sciences*, Vol. 5.

Cole, S. and Miles, I. (1980), 'Labour Supply in the Major World Regions', UNITAR Working Paper, Science Policy Research Unit, University of Sussex (mimeo).

Cole, S. and Miles, I. (1984), *Worlds Apart: Technology and North–South Relations in the Global Economy*, Harvester/Rowman & Allanheld, Brighton.

Cole, S. and Nunez-Barigga, A. (1981), 'Basic Needs Technology: A Starting Point for a Macro-Economic Evaluation', UNITAR Working Paper, Science Policy Research Unit, University of Sussex (mimeo).

Contreras, C., *et al.* (1978), 'Technological Transformation of Developing Countries: Preliminary Ideas for Action at the National and International Level', Research Policy Programme, University of Lund (mimeo).

Cooper, C. and Clark, J. (1982), *Employment, Economics and Technology*, Harvester, Brighton.

Cortes, C. (1984), 'Informatics Policy in Colombia', unpublished doctoral dissertation, Manchester University.

Cross, M. (1983), 'Technological Change and Changing Skills Requirements', Technical Change Centre, London (mimeo).

De Meza, D. (1983), 'The Transfer Problem in a Many Country World: Is it Better to Give than to Receive', London School of Economics (mimeo).

Dell'Mour, R., *et al.* (1982), 'Micro-Electronics and Unemployment in Austria', International Institute for Applied Systems Analysis, Laxenberg.

Diwan, D. and Livingstone, D. (1979), *Alternative Development Strategies and Appropriate Technology*, Pergamon, Oxford.

Dixit, A. (1983), 'The Multi-Country Transfer Problem', Princeton, (mimeo).

Dixon, P. and Vincent, D. (1979), 'The Implications of Technical Change in Australia to 1990', Eighth Conference of Economists, Melbourne.

Ernst, D. (1982), *The Global Race in Micro-Electronics: Innovation and Corporate Strategy in a Period of Crisis,* Campus, Frankfurt.

Felix, D. (1977), *The Technological Factor in Socio-Economic Dualism: Toward an Economy of Scale Paradigm for Development Theory*, Washington University.

Findlay, R. and Grubert, H. (1959), 'Factor Intensities, Technological

Progress and Terms of Trade', *Oxford Economic Papers,* No. 11, pp. 111–21.

Fleck, J. (1984), 'The Employment Effects of Robots', in T. Lupton, ed. *Human Factors in Manufacturing,* IFS Publications, Kempston, Beds.

Foxley, A. (1976), 'Redistribution of Consumption: Effects on Production and Employment', *Journal of Development Studies,* Vol. 12, No. 3.

Freeman, C. (1977), *The Kondratief Long Waves, Technical Change and Employment,* OECD, Paris.

Freeman, C. (1984), 'Myth and Reality in Electronics', *Futures,* Vol. 16, No. 1.

Freeman, C. and Guy, K. eds (1984/5), *Technological Trends and Employment,* Gower, Aldershot.

Freeman, C., Clark, J., and Soete, L. (1982), *Unemployment and Technical Innovation: A Study of Long Waves in Economic Development,* Frances Pinter, London.

Frobel, F., Heinreichs, J., and Krey, O. (1980), *The Tendency Towards a New International Division of Labour,* Cambridge University Press, Cambridge.

Gale, D. (1974), 'Exchange Equilibrium and Coalitions', *Journal of Mathematical Economics,* Vol. 1, pp. 63–6.

Gershuny, J. (1979), 'The Informal Economy', *Futures,* February.

Gershuny, J. and Miles, I. (1983), *The New Service Economy,* Frances Pinter, London.

Gordon, D. (1983), *Long Swings and the Non-Reproductive Cycle,* AEA.

Graham, E. (1982), 'Technological Innovation and the Dynamics of the US Comparative Advantage in International Trade', in *Technological Innovation for a Dynamic Economy,* C. Hill and S. Utterback, eds, Pergamon Policy Studies on Science and Technology, Oxford.

Halevi, G. (1980), *The Role of Computers in Manufacturing Processes,* John Wiley, Chichester.

Hatvany, J., *et al.* (1983), *World Survey of CAM,* Butterworths, Guildford.

Herrera, A. (1973), *Technological Innovation as an Expression of Culture,* Ildis, Quito.

Hines, C. and Searle, G. (1980), *Automatic Unemployment,* Earth Resources Research Ltd, London.

Hoffman, K. and Rush, H. (1980), 'Micro-Electronics, Industry and the Third World', *Futures,* August.

Hoffman, K. and Rush, H. (1982), 'Micro-Electronics and the Garment Industry', *IDS Bulletin,* March.

Hoffman, K. and Rush, H. (1983), *Microelectronics and Clothing; the Impact of Technical Change on a Global Industry,* ILO, Geneva.

Hufbauer, G. (1970), 'The Impact of National Characteristics and Technology in the Commodity Composition of Trade in Manufactured Goods', in Vernon, R., ed. (1970).

IBRD (World Bank) (1983), *Development Reports 1980-1983*, IBRD, Washington.

Jackson, R. (1984), *Food-Energy Technology*, Technical Change Centre, London.

Jacobs, J. (1984), *Cities and the Wealth of Nations: Principles of Economic Life*, Random House, New York.

Jacobsson, S. (1982), 'Electronics and the Technology Gap', *IDS Bulletin*, March.

Jacobsson, S. and Edquist, C. (1984), *Trends in the Diffusion of Advanced Manufacturing Technology*, Research Policy Institute, Lund, Sweden.

Johnson, H. (1955), 'Economic Expansion and International Trade', *Manchester School of Economic and Social Studies*, No. 23, pp. 95-112.

Jones, H. (1976), *An Introduction to Modern Theories of Economic Growth*, McGraw-Hill, New York.

Jones, R. (1970), 'The Role of Technology in the Theory of International Trade' in Vernon, ed. (1970).

Jones, R. (1982), 'Income Effects and Paradoxes in the Theory of International Trade', Rochester University (mimeo).

Kaplinsky, R. (1982), 'Comparative Advantage in an Automating World', *IDS Bulletin*, March.

Kaplinsky, R. (1983), 'International Context for Industrialisation in the Coming Decades', *Journal of Development Studies*.

Kaplinsky, R. (1984a), *Automation: Technology and Society*, Longmans, London.

Kaplinsky, R. (1984b), 'Changing Patterns of Industrial Location and International Competition; the Role of TNCs and the Impact of Microelectronics', UNCSTD, New York.

Kaplinsky, R. (1985), *Microelectronics and Employment Revisited*, ILO, Geneva (forthcoming).

Katz, J. (1978), *Technological Change, Economic Development and Intra and Extra Regional Relations in Latin America*, UNDP/ECLA, Buenos Aires.

Kendrick, J. (1984), 'Productivity Trends and the Recent Slowdown: Historical Factors and Causal Factors', *Contemporary Economic Problems*, Washington, DC.

Kennedy, C. (1964), 'Induced Bias in Innovation and the Theory of Distribution', *Economic Journal*, Vol. 74, pp. 541-7.

Kravis, I., Heston, A., and Sommers, R. (1982), *World Product and Income: International Comparisons of Real Product*, John Hopkins University Press, Baltimore.

Krugman, P. (1979), 'A Model of Innovation, Technology Transfer and the World Distribution of Income', *Journal of Political Economy*, Vol. 87, No. 21.

Leach, B. and Shutt, J. (1985), 'Chips and Crisps; Labour Faces a Crunch' in T. Forester, ed., *The IT Revolution*, Basil Blackwell, Oxford.

Leontief, W. (1936), 'A Note on the Pure Theory of Transfers', *Explorations in Economics,* New York.

Leontief, W. and Duchin, F. (1985), *The Impact of Technology on Employment, 1963-2000,* Oxford University Press (forthcoming).

Lerner, A. (1936), 'The Symmetry Between Export and Import Taxes', *Economica,* Vol. 3, pp. 306-13.

Lewis, W. A. (1954), 'Economic Development with Unlimited Supplies of Labour', *The Manchester School,* May.

Lluch, C., Powell, A., and Williams, R. (1977), *Patterns in Household Demand and Saving,* Oxford University Press, World Bank, Washington.

Locksley, G. (1981), *A Study of the Evolution of Concentration in the UK DP Industry with Some International Comparisons,* EEC, Brussels.

Lysy, F. (1981), 'An Expository Note on Chichilnisky's Model of North-South Trade', Johns Hopkins University.

Machlup, F. (1962), *The Production and Distribution of Knowledge in the USA,* Princeton University Press, Princeton, N.J.

Malinvaud, E. (1977), *The Theory of Unemployment Reconsidered,* Blackwell, Oxford.

Mandel, E. (1980), *Long Waves of Capitalist Development,* Cambridge University Press, Cambridge.

Mandeville, T., *et al.* (1980), 'The Fortune Teller's New Clothes: A Critical Appraisal of IMPACT's Technological Change Projections', *Search,* Vol. 11, pp. 14-17.

Mandeville, T. and Macdonald, S. (1983), 'Information Technology and Employment Levels', in S. Macdonald *et al.,* eds, *The Trouble with Technology,* Frances Pinter, London.

Mansfield, E. (1968), *The Economics of Technical Change,* Norton, New York.

Maxwell, P. (1983), 'Specialisation Decisions in Electronic Production: Lessons from the Experience of Two Argentine Firms', in J. Sigurdson and S. Jacobsson, eds, *Technological Trends and Challenges in Electronics,* RPI, Lund, Sweden.

Meagher, A. (1980), 'Empirical Estimation and Aggregation for a Computable Global General Equilibrium Model', in Cole, S., ed., 'National Economics in the World Economy', UNITAR, New York.

Meagher, A. and Cole, S. (1984), 'Growth and Distribution in India: A General Equilibrium Analysis', in Cohen *et al.* (1984).

Mensch, G. (1st edn 1976; 2nd edn 1984), *A New Push of Basic Innovations,* Institute of Management, Berlin.

Mensch, G. (1977), *Stalemate in International Technology 1925-1935: The Interplay of Stagnation and Innovation,* Institute of Management, Berlin.

Metcalfe, J. and Soete, L. (1983), 'Notes of the Evolution of Technology and International Competition', Workshop on Technology Policy in the 1980s, University of Manchester.

Metzler, L. (1949), 'Tariffs, the Terms of Trade, and the Distribution of National Income', *Journal of Political Economy*, Vol. 57, pp. 1–29.

Morehouse, W. (1981), 'Technological Intelligence and Other Strategies for Enlarging Developing Country Access to Microelectronics Technology', paper presented at FLACSO Seminar on Microelectronics, Buenos Aires.

Moseley, R. (1979), 'Technical Change and Employment in the Post-war Gas Industry', *Omega*, Vol. 7, pp. 105–12.

Mozak, A. (1978), 'Introduction to ACC Technical Working Group of the UN Committee for Development Planning', New York, January 1978.

Murray, R. (1972), *Underdevelopment, International Firms, and the International Division of Labour*, Institute for Development Studies, Sussex.

Nordhaus, W. (1969), *Invention, Growth and Welfare: A Theoretical Treatment of Technical Change*, MIT Press, Cambridge, Mass.

Nordhaus, W. (1973), 'World Dynamics: Measurement without Data', *Economic Journal*, Vol. 83, pp. 1156–83.

Northcott, J., et al. (1985), *Microelectronics in Industry*, Policy Studies Institute, London.

OECD (1982), *Microelectronics, Productivity and Employment*, Organisation for Economic Co-operation and Development, Paris.

OIW/OAW (1981), *Mikroelektronik; Anwendungen, Verbreitung und Auswirkung an Beispiel Osterreichs*, Springer Verlag, Vienna.

Olson, M. (1982), *The Rise and Decline of Nations*, Yale University Press, New Haven.

Parker, K. (1984), *Scenario Based Experiments using SARUM*, Technical Change Centre, London.

Parkinson, S. (1984), *New Product Development in Engineering*, Cambridge University Press, Cambridge.

Pavitt, K. (1980), 'Technical Innovation and Industrial Development: The Dangers of Divergence', *Futures*, February.

Peet, R. (1983), 'Relations of Production and the Relocation of United States Manufacturing Industry Since 1960', *Economic Geography*, Vol. 59, No. 2.

Perez-Perez, C. (1983), 'Structural Change and Assimilation of New Technologies in the Economic and Social Systems', *Futures*, October.

Perez-Perez, C. (1985), 'Microelectronics, Long Waves and World Structural Change', *World Development*, forthcoming.

Perry, D. and Watkins. A. (1977), 'The Rise of the Sunbelt Cities', *Urban Affairs Annual Review*, Vol. 14.

Porat, M. (1977), *The Information Economy*, US Dept. of Commerce, Washington, DC.

Pyatt, G. and Roe, A. (1979), *Social Accounting for Development Planning with Special Reference to Sri Lanka*, IBRD, Washington.

Rada, J. (1980), *The Impact of Microelectronics*, ILO, Geneva.

Rada, J. (1982), 'Technology and the North–South Division of Labour', *IDS Bulletin,* March.

Rahman, A. (1979), 'Alternative Technology: Some Basic Questions', Indian Institute of Advanced Study, Delhi.

Rosenberg, N. (1983), *Inside the Black Box: Technology and Economics,* Cambridge University Press, Cambridge.

Rothwell, R. (1984), 'The Role of Small Firms in the Emergence of Technology', *Omega,* Vol. 12, No. 1.

Rothwell, R. and Soete, L. (1983), 'Technology and Economic Change', *Physics and Technology,* Vol. 14.

Rothwell, R. and Zegveld, W. (1980), *Technical Change and Employment,* Frances Pinter, London.

Royer, J. (1984), *The Impact of International Policies and Development Styles,* Department of Economics, University of Geneva.

Sachs, I. (1966), 'Levels of Satiety', in *Collected Papers,* Centre for the Study of Humanity, Paris.

Sadler, P. (1980), 'Welcome Back to the Automation Debate', in Forester, T., ed., *The Microelectronics Revolution',* Basil Blackwell, Oxford.

Sadulet, E. (1983), *Croissance inégalitaire dans une économie sous-development,* Libraire Droz, Geneva.

Sagasti, F. (1985), *Crisis, Knowledge and Development: A Review of Long Term Perspectives on Science and Technology for Development,* GRADE, Lima, Peru.

Salter, W. (1966), *Productivity and Technical Change,* Cambridge University Press, Cambridge.

Samuelson, P. (1971), 'On the Trail of Conventional Beliefs about the Transfer Problem', in Bhagwati, J. *et al.,* eds, *Trade, Balance of Payments and Growth,* North Holland, Amsterdam.

Schonberger, R. (1982), *Japanese Manufacturing Techniques,* Free Press/Macmillan, London.

Schumacher, E. (1973), *Small is Beautiful: A Study of Economics as if People Mattered,* Blond and Briggs, London.

Scrimgeour, J. (1981), 'CAD/CAM: a Challenge and Opportunity for Canadian Industry', *Engineering Journal,* Vol. 4, No. 4.

Senker, P., *et al.* (1980), *Microelectronics and the Engineering Industry; the Need for Skills,* Frances Pinter, London.

Sharma, K. and Qureshi, M. (1979), *Alternative Technology,* Institute of Advanced Study, Simla.

Sigurdson, J. and Grandstrand, O. (1984), unpublished notes on field trip, presented at Third Conference on 'Technological and Industrial Policy in China and Europe', Beijing.

Sigurdson, J. and Jacobsson, S. (1983), *Technical Trends and Challenges in Electronics,* RPI, Lund, Sweden.

Singh, A. (1979). 'The Basic Needs Approach to the New International

Economic Order: The Significance of Third World Industrialisation', *World Development,* Vol. 7.

Singer, H. (1977), *Technologies for Basic Needs,* International Labour Organisation, Geneva.

Sodersten, B. (2nd edn 1980), *International Economics,* Macmillan, London.

Soete, L. (1982a), *International Diffusion of Technology and Economic Growth: A Historical Perspective*; Science Policy Research Unit, Sussex.

Soete, L. (1982b), 'Technical Change, Catching Up and the Productivity Slowdown', in J. Sigurdson and O. Grandstrand, eds, *Technological and Industrial Policy in China and Europe,* RPI, Lund, Sweden.

Solow, R. (1957), Technical Change and the Aggregate Production Function, *Review of Economics and Statistics,* August.

Sorge, A., *et al.* (1982), *Microelectronics and Manpower,* Gower Press, Aldershot.

Steffens, J. (1983), *Office Automation,* Policy Studies Institute, London.

Stewart, F. (1976), 'Technology and Underdevelopment', Macmillan, London.

Stewart, F. and James, J. eds (1983), *The Economics of New Technology in Developing Countries,* Frances Pinter, London/Westview, Boulder, Colorado.

Taylor, L. (1979). *Macro Models for Developing Countries,* McGraw Hill, New York.

Thirsk, W. (1980), 'Aggregation Bias and the Sensitivity of Income Distribution to Changes in the Composition of Demand: The Case of Colombia', *Journal of Development Studies,* Vol. 18.

Tigre, P. (1983), *The Brazilian Computer Industry,* Frances Pinter, London.

UNCSTD (1983), *Transnationals in World Development: A Survey,* UN Centre on Transnational Corporations, UN, New York.

UNCTAD (1983), *Trade and Development Report,* Geneva.

UNCTN (1983), *Salient Features of Investment by Transnationals,* UN, New York.

UNIDO (1979), *The Technological Self-Reliance of Developing Countries: Towards Operational Strategies,* UNIDO International Centre for Industrial Studies, Vienna.

United Nations (1975–77), *Yearbook of National Account Statistics:* Vols I & II, *Individual Country Data,* and Vol. III, *International Accounts Statistics,* New York.

Urquidi, V. and Nadal, A. (1980), *Some Observations on Economic Theory and Technical Change,* El Colegio de Mexico, Mexico.

Van Duijn, J. (1981), 'Fluctuations in Innovations Over Time', in C. Freeman (1984), *Long Waves in the World Economy,* Frances Pinter, London.

Van Duijn, J. (1983), 'Theories of the Long Wave', in Bianchi, *et al.*, *Long Waves, Depression and Innovation*, IIASA, Laxenburg.

Vernon, R. (1966), 'International Investment and International Trade in the Product Cycle', *Quarterly Journal of Economics*, No. 80, pp. 190–207.

Vernon, R., ed. (1970), *The Technology Factor in International Trade*, Columbia University Press, New York.

Vernon, R. and Davidson, W. (1978), 'The International Spread of US Based Technology Intensive Firms 1945-1975', Harvard School of Business Administration, Working Paper No. 40.

Vitelli, G. (1980), 'The Chaotic Economics of Technical Change: A Survey Throughout the Choice of Technique', Institute for Development Studies, University of Sussex (mimeo).

Voss, C. (1984), 'The Management of New Manufacturing Technology', Australian Graduate School of Managment, Working Paper.

Wad, A. (1984), 'Limitations and Opportunities for Developing Countries Of Emerging Micro-electronic Technologies', in von Weizsäcker, *et al.* (1984).

von Weizsäcker, C. (1966), 'Tentative Notes on a Two Sector Model with Induced Technical Progress', *Review of Economic Studies*, Vol. 33, pp. 245–51.

von Weizsäcker, E., Swaminathan, M., and Lemma, A. (1984), *New Frontiers in Technology Application*, Tycooly, Dublin.

Wilkinson, B. (1983), *The Shopfloor Politics of New Technology*, Heinemann, London.

Winch, G., ed. (1983), *Information Technology in Manufacturing Processes*, Rossendale, London.

Yago, G. and McGahey, R. (1984), 'Can the Empire State Strike Back? The Limits of Cyclical Recovery in New York', *New York Affairs*, Vol. 8, No. 3.

Zisman, M. (1978), 'Office Automation; Revolution or Evolution?', *Sloan Management Review*, June.

Index